DEAD MEN WALKING

DEAD MEN WALKING

BILL WALLACE

Piatkus,
An imprint of
Little, Brown Book Group
100 Victoria Embankment
London EC4Y 0DY

An Hachette UK Company
www.hachette.co.uk

www.littlebrown.co.uk

Photo credits: Getty Images

Futura

FUTURA

First published in Great Britain in 2010 by Futura

Copyright © Omnipress 2010

The moral right of the author has been asserted.

A CIP catalogue record for this book
is available from the British Library.

ISBN 978-0-7088-6402-9

Typeset in Great Britain by Omnipress Limited
Printed and bound in Great Britain by CPI Mackays, Chatham ME5 8TD

The views expressed in this publication are those of the author.
The information and the interpretation of that information are
presented in good faith. Readers are advised that where ethical
issues are involved, and often highly controversial ethical issues
at that, they have a personal responsibility for making their own
assessments and their own ethical judgements.

CONTENTS

PART THREE: DEATH ROW USA

PART FOUR: WOMEN ON DEATH ROW

INTRODUCTION

To take the life of another human being is the ultimate act of betrayal of the very principles that separate us from the animal kingdom, a step into a place where dignity, humanity, compassion and reason are absent and can never again be found. The murderer gives up all right to be a part of the world and he or she is rightly punished with great severity, sometimes with the ultimate sanction of death, but more often by having his or her liberty removed for the remainder of his or her natural life.

Punishment for murder is, of course, a vexed and complicated issue. The urge to execute killers has waxed and waned over the years, particularly in the United States where they still anguish over methods and ethics. California has not executed anyone for a number of years as judges argue about it and medical personnel refuse to participate in anything that might be in breach of their ethical code. Meanwhile, hundreds of people join the queue for death on death row. In fact, of the fully developed countries, only Singapore, Japan and the United States have retained the death penalty.

Murder, nonetheless, continues to flourish.

In Britain, capital punishment was ended in 1964 and finally banned in 1969, but many wonder if to spend the rest of your life in a prison cell might not be a worse punishment. Feeble-minded child killer, John Straffen was British legal history's longest serving prisoner, spending fifty-six years in prison; although he also spent a considerable part of his life in other institutions. There are other prisoners for whom, as they say, life means life. Men such as the Soham murderer, Ian Huntley and the Suffolk Ripper, Steve Wright, the killer of five prostitutes in the east of England, are unlikely ever to be released. Nor will Peter Sutcliffe, the Yorkshire Ripper, a vicious and merciless murderer, ever be freed. These men are just too dangerous. Denis Nilsen, killer of fifteen young men in Cricklewood and Muswell Hill between 1978 and 1983 has acknowledged that he should not be freed and one shudders to think what an individual who kept bodies in his small flat for months to assuage his terrible loneliness, might do if released. For some, of course, life meant a very brief life. The Boston Strangler, Albert DeSalvo, was stabbed to death at the age of forty-two by persons unknown only five years into his life sentence. American cannibal/killer, Jeffrey Dahmer, served only two years of his 957-year sentence before being bludgeoned to death by a deranged fellow inmate while Fred West, the evil serial killer of young girls and women at 25 Cromwell Street, Gloucester, hanged himself before his case even came to court. Few mourned.

Many, of course, have paid the ultimate penalty over the years, some of them at the end of high-profile cases where the justice of the verdict has been called into question. The Italian anarchists, Nicolo Sacco and Bartolomeo Vanzetti, may just have been the scapegoats the American public was looking for at a time when it was frightened out of its wits by the global upsurge of communism. Their fates were sealed from the moment they were arrested on a trolley car in Massachusetts and they were duly electrocuted in 1927 on very little evidence. Ruben Cantu was executed in 1993, but almost certainly did not commit the murder for which he died. The police were unable to pin anything else on him but they made this one stick. Was Bruno Hauptmann really the kidnapper and murderer of Charles Lindbergh's baby in 1932? The jury thought so, but many people did not agree and they argue about it to this day. Timothy Evans, hanged in 1950 for the murder of his wife and daughter was in fact victim to the cunning of English serial killer, John Reginald Christie, and it took decades to eventually clear

Evans' name. Other cases such as those of Derek Bentley and James Hanratty add uncertainty to the unbending process of the law. Perhaps we should listen carefully to the words of exonerated American death row inmate, Ray Krone, released after ten years of hell: 'There is a serious problem with the death penalty and there are serious mistakes made. The punishment is irreversible, irrevocable. We can't bring back someone when we execute them…'

Others, however, have gone to the gallows, or the electric chair or have lain down on the gurney for the lethal injection, accepting their guilt and, sometimes, glad to finally be making their exit from a world that has been a struggle from the beginning. In 1977, Gary Gilmore, the first man executed in America following the US Supreme Court's 1972 declaration that capital punishment was cruel and unusual, had to argue his way to the firing squad that dispatched him in Utah. He wanted to end the unequal struggle that had been his miserable existence since birth and finally got his wish. Men such as Ted Bundy, killer of thirty young women and John Wayne Gacy, murderer of thirty-two young men, however, went to the electric chair fully aware of what they had done. Their depraved urges had meant that the consquences of their actions became less important to them than the actions themselves.

The last man to hang in Australia, Eric Edgar Cook, declared himself to be a cold-blooded killer who just wanted to hurt people. His one-man crime spree in Perth, during which he randomly murdered eight people and terrorised the population of an entire city, is an example of just how far a person can stray from normal, acceptable behaviour.

Of course, the living hell of death row could be looked upon as worse than anything. The appeals process drags on for many years in America, and people sit in their prison cells counting down the days until the last appeal has been exhausted, the appeal to the governor for clemency is denied, and the warden and the priest turn up at the cell door. At that moment, after long years of struggle against the system, the short walk to death will begin. Of course, before that, the rituals of execution will have been carried out. The last meal request, endlessly fascinating, will have been released to the press. None, of course, will ever be as extensive as that ordered by Karl Chamberlain, murderer of thirty-year-old Felecia Prechtl in 1991. His order ran for pages and was a veritable banquet. It is not reported how much he actually ate. Chamberlain had waited seventeen years for death. Michael Morales committed murder when he was twenty-one years old. He is now fifty-one and still waiting to take that last walk. In 2006, he was just hours from being executed by lethal injection when California started a year-long argument about capital punishment. He still sits in his cell at San Quentin, waiting. Kenny Richey, a Scottish-born man convicted in Ohio in 1987 of killing a little girl in a fire it was alleged he started, also came close, but eventually, after a worldwide series of protests, was released a few years ago when forensic evidence came under close scrutiny. He had sat on death row for twenty-one years. Another British man, Krishna Maharaj hopes the same thing might happen to him. He spent fifteen years on death row before his sentence was commuted to life imprisonment. A millionaire when he was convicted in 1987 at the age of forty-eight, Maharaj has spent his entire fortune on legal costs and now languishes in prison in Florida, aged seventy-one, for a crime he insists he did not commit. And many agree with him.

Again, however, there are those killers for whom death is almost too good. Richard Ramirez, the 'Night Stalker', a power-freak for whom age, gender and sex seem to have been irrelevant, killed thirteen men, women and children on America's west coast between June 1984 and August 1985. The terror he inflicted on his victims was unimaginable and he still waits for execution on death row all these years later. Richard Allen Davis, killer of innocent twelve-year-old Polly Klaas and serial attacker of women, is similarly beyond the pale, existing in a world outside the normal. Many will cheer when Davis is finally wheeled out of the execution chamber, his life gone in a haze of drugs from the lethal injection that will kill him.

These days, women are of course the equal of men in many areas. Murder is no different, although sometimes it is for different, more practical reasons. Insurance, for instance. Husband killers, Betty Lou Beets, Judi Buoenano and Velma Barfield, were serial insurance claimants as well as serial killers, although it took the authorities some time to put two and two together. Barfield killed other family members too, and finally paid for it with a lethal injection. Of course, there are also women killers who were just plain bad, although it could be argued that their evil deeds were the result of dreadful childhoods, violent and abusive parents and bad decisions. Prostitute Aileen 'Lee' Wuornos killed 7 men between 1989 and 1990 in Florida. When the brutality of her childhood is taken into account, however, there is an inevitability about the way she turned out. Her family story contains incest and terrible violence, and her father was a child rapist who hanged himself in prison.

As you read this, there are countless men and women shuffling in handcuffs and shackles from one part of a prison to another, some into a room where their lives will finally end. They are paying the ultimate penalty or are waiting to make that payment. They are Dead Men Walking.

PART ONE

LIFERS

GEORGE 'MACHINE GUN' KELLY

His name sits comfortably with some of the most notorious characters of the epoch that was host to the phenomenon known as the Mid-West Crime Wave – names such as 'Baby Face' Nelson, 'Pretty Boy' Floyd and John Dillinger. But he was one of the lucky few of those cold-blooded killers to survive that era. While most of the most infamous gangsters of the time died in a hail of bullets fired either by the police or by other gangsters, George 'Machine Gun' Kelly lived until 1954, his last twenty-one years spent behind bars, seventeen of them in the notorious Alcatraz.

He was also unlike other gangsters of the era, in that he went to college. Born George Barnes in 1895, into a fairly well-to-do family living in Memphis, he grew up in Chicago after his family moved there when he was two years old. He never got on with his father and was even able to make his hatred for him pay, foreshadowing the gangster he was growing up to be. Once when he was a teenager, he saw his father go into the house of a woman with whom he was having an affair. Rather than run home and tell his mother, the young George brazenly walked into his father's office the next day and blackmailed him into increasing his allowance and giving him the use of the family car.

He made good use of the car too, in the bootlegging activities he had first got into while still attending high school. He was arrested at one point but was released after a judicious phone call from his father who still had influence in the city.

When his mother died, however, George Barnes was devastated, blaming his father's infidelity for her poor health.

Graduating from high school, he enrolled at college in Mississippi to study agriculture – but it was to be a brief stay in academia. His college career was a disaster, with a poor academic performance and a catalogue of rule-breaking. He returned to Memphis where he met the woman who would become his wife, Geneva Ramsey, daughter of a wealthy local businessman, George F. Ramsey. Geneva's father was understandably concerned about the reputation of the young man who was pursuing his daughter and forbade her from seeing him. Barnes was nothing if not persistent, however, and one night persuaded Geneva to elope with him. They went to Mississippi to return a few days later as man and wife.

George Ramsey had little option but to offer his new son-in-law a job in his business building levees and railroads in the Mississippi River Valley and soon it looked like Barnes was at last turning his life around. He and Ramsey began to treat each other with mutual respect, the older man becoming the father Barnes never really had. Disaster struck in the mid-1920s, however, when George Ramsey was killed in an accidental explosion.

From then on, everything started to go wrong. Geneva's mother sold her husband's business, but tried to help her daughter and son-in-law make a new start. Everything they touched failed, however, forcing Barnes to return in desperation to bootlegging. Geneva was furious, especially when he was arrested and she had to bail him out with $200,000 borrowed from her mother. She threatened to divorce him.

When his first son, George Jr – known to them as Sonny – was born, Barnes showed that he had learnt nothing from his experience of his own father by being a poor parent, once actually throwing the infant across the room during a heated argument with Geneva. His drinking was making it impossible to hold down a legitimate job and he took his frustration out on his wife and his son. Thankfully, when his second child arrived, a boy named Bruce, he was entirely different towards him.

Eventually, when the marriage finally fell apart, Barnes left for Kansas City where he found work in a grocery store. Soon, however, he was pleading with Geneva for another chance and before long she and the boys joined him. When she discovered he was stealing from the store, she threatened to leave him again. They argued and he beat her. She left him for good.

In Kansas City, under the name George R. Kelly, he developed a small bootlegging business which grew until he was operating in Texas, Oklahoma, Tennessee and Mississippi. But the law caught up with him in Santa Fe in 1927, when he was arrested and sent to prison for a few months. Released, he moved to Tulsa, Oklahoma where he was arrested for vagrancy and then for selling alcohol on an Indian reservation, a serious federal crime which earned him three years in Leavenworth Penitentiary.

He was out again in 1930, making for St. Paul in the company of Kathryn Kelly, a woman he had met and fallen in love with while working as a bootlegger in Oklahoma City. A three-times married thief and prostitute, she is credited with buying him his first tommy gun and creating the 'Machine Gun' Kelly image, handing out spent cartridges to friends and relatives as souvenirs. In September 1930 they were married in Minneapolis.

Before that, however, George R. Kelly had launched a new career, as a bank robber. A couple of former inmates at Leavenworth, Francis 'Jimmy' Keating and Thomas Holden, whom Kelly had helped to escape, showed their gratitude by inviting him to be part of a gang planning to rob the Bank Of Willmar in Minnesota. Amongst other gang members were the notable hoods, Verne Miller, Sammy Silverman and Harvey Bailey. They escaped with $70,000, but it was a heist notable for the level of violence used; a cashier was viciously pistol-whipped and one of the gang callously fired his machine gun into a crowd of onlookers, wounding two women.

Other bank robberies followed. In September 1930, he helped divest a bank in Ottumwa, Iowa of a substantial sum of cash and with Fred Barker, Holding, Keating and Larry DeVol grabbed $40,000 from the Central State Bank of Sherman, Texas.

Albert L. Bates was a career criminal with whom Kelly hooked up in 1932. Together, they earned a huge payday when they robbed a bank in Colfax,

Washington State, of $77,000. The police were onto them, however, and Kelly and Kathryn narrowly escaped when their home in Fort Worth, Texas, was raided.

Machine Gun Kelly's last bank robbery took place on 30 November 1932. With Bates and Eddie Doll, a gangster from Chicago, they hit the Citizen's State Bank of Tupelo, Mississippi, netting $38,000. Following the robbery, the bank's chief teller said of Kelly, who had disappointingly only brought along a .38 calibre revolver, 'He was the kind of guy that, if you looked at him, you would never have thought he was a bank robber.'

Kidnapping was another of his specialities. By 22 July 1933, he and his associates had kidnapped several people and won substantial ransoms. Their next target was Charles F. Urschel, a wealthy oil man who lived in a mansion in Oklahoma City. Kelly and Bates simply strode onto the front porch of the Urschel mansion where the oil magnate was playing bridge with his wife and another man. Kelly, machine gun in hand, and unsure which of the men was the target of their kidnapping, ordered the two men into his car. When they had left the city, they looked in the men's wallets and threw out the one who was not their prey.

Urschel was taken to a 500-acre ranch in Paradise,

Texas, owned by the gangster Boss Shannon, Kathryn Kelly's stepfather. He was chained to a bed and next morning, over breakfast, the kidnappers read to him the newspaper articles about the kidnapping.

Kathryn had, meanwhile, driven off to attempt to establish an alibi for herself, meeting a friend who was a detective. The astute policeman noticed red dirt on the wheels of her car and Oklahoma newspapers lying on the back seat. He put two and two together and on his return to his office phoned the FBI. When Mrs Urschel was shown a photograph of Kelly, she immediately identified him as one of the kidnappers.

Charles Urschel, meanwhile, was using every opportunity to find evidence that might help the FBI if and when he was released. He would listen for planes flying overhead and five minutes later would ask the time. He estimated the times of these flights to be 9.45 a.m. and 5.45 p.m. He tried to memorise the mineral taste of the water and anything else that might pinpoint the location.

Urschel was ordered to write several ransom notes, one to his wife and one to a friend, John G. Catlett. A third was sent to another family friend, E. E. Kirkpatrick, asking for $200,000 in used notes. He was to place an advert in the *Daily Oklahoman* reading, 'FOR SALE – 160 acres land, good five-room house, deep well. Also cows, tools, tractors, corn and hay. $3,750.00 for quick sales TERMS'. Kirkpatrick was then instructed to take the train to Kansas City on the night of 29 July, travelling alone. He was to keep watch for two bonfires burning, one after the other on the right hand side of the train. When he saw the second, he should throw the bag containing the cash from the train's observation platform. Once that was done, Urschel would be released.

Kirkpatrick got the money – all of it in marked notes – and boarded the train, but he was accompanied by John Catlett. One story says that Kelly had car trouble and was unable to get to the spot where the bonfires were to be set. Another says that Catlett was spotted boarding the train and the operation was aborted. There was another plan, however, in the event of anything going wrong with the first one. Kirkpatrick had to check into the Muehlenbach Hotel in Kansas City, under the name E. E. Kincaid and await further information. At 5.45 p.m. that afternoon, he was telephoned and told to take a taxi to the La Salle Hotel and walk west, carrying the bag containing the money in his right hand.

As he walked along Linwood Boulevard, a large man wearing a turned-down Panama hat, approached. It was none other than Machine Gun Kelly. 'I'll take that grip,' he said tersely. Kirkpatrick asked him when Urschel would be freed and Kelly hissed back that he would be home in twelve hours.

On 31 July, Charles Urschel did, indeed, arrive home after being dropped twenty miles outside Oklahoma City. The following morning, he was telling the FBI everything he knew about his kidnappers and the place where he was held. The search began and they quickly located the Shannon Ranch as the place where Urschel had been held. On 12 August it was raided and Harvey Bailey, Boss and Ora Shannon were arrested. On the same day, Alfred Bates was picked up in a Denver hotel. Five other men were arrested to whom Kelly and the gang had sold a portion of the marked cash.

Hearing of her mother's arrest, a distraught Kathryn wrote a threatening letter to the Oklahoma Assistant Attorney General, Joseph B. Keating, 'The entire Urschel family and friends, and all of you will be exterminated soon. There is no way I can prevent it. I will gladly put George Kelly on the spot for you if you will save my mother, who is innocent of any wrongdoing. If you do not comply with this request, there is no way in which I can prevent the most awful tragedy. If you refuse my offer I shall commit some minor offense and be placed in jail so that you will know that I have no connection with the terrible slaughter that will take place in Oklahoma within the next few days.'

Meanwhile, one day Kathryn picked up a family of hitchhikers, Luther Arnold and his wife and their daughter Geraldine. She immediately saw an opportunity to use the Arnolds to help her and George get away. They paid the Arnolds to let them borrow Geraldine who would provide perfect cover for their true identities while they travelled. No one would be looking for a couple with a child in tow. They set out for Chicago, stopping in Texas to bury $73,000 of the ransom money at the ranch of an associate called Cass Coleman. George, meanwhile, had written to Charles Urschel threatening death for his family if the Shannons were convicted.

From Chicago, they made their way to Memphis where they hid in the home of Machine Gun's long-time friend, John Tichenor. They then went down into Mexico, having sent Geraldine back to her parents, but returned to Memphis as everything began to unravel.

The Arnolds were soon picked up and twelve-year-old Geraldine was, of course, a wealth of information, information that led the FBI straight to Memphis and the home of John Tichenor. On 26 September 1933, two police officers knocked on the door of Tichenor's house. It was opened by George 'Machine Gun' Kelly pointing a .45 automatic at them. One of the officers pushed his shotgun against Kelly's stomach and the two eyed each other for a moment in a tense standoff. Kelly realised the game was up, however. He threw down his gun and put his hands in the air. He was at last in custody. On 1 October, he and Kathryn were flown to Oklahoma City to face trial in an extraordinary convoy of nine planes.

Their letters did nothing to help Ora and Boss Shannon. The couple were each sentenced to life imprisonment. On the day that sentence was passed, as Kelly was being escorted out of court in handcuffs, he walked past Charles Urschel. He put his finger across his throat in a cutting motion, and snarled, 'You'll get yours yet, you_____'.

Their own trial ended as expected. On the morning of 12 October, it took the jury less than an hour to find George 'Machine Gun' Kelly and Kathryn Kelly guilty of kidnapping. They, too, were sentenced to life imprisonment.

Kathryn and her mother were paroled in June 1958 and after Ora's death in 1980, Kathryn became a recluse until her own death in 1985, at the age of eighty-one.

As he was being led to the train to go to

Leavenworth after his trial, Kelly had joked with reporters that he would not be there long, that he was going to break out. He never did, however. In 1934, he was transferred to the new escape-proof Alcatraz located on a rock in the middle of San Francisco Bay, where he would remain until 1951 when he was sent back to Leavenworth. He died there of a heart attack in 1954, aged fifty-four.

Kelly undoubtedly harboured regrets about some of the decisions he had made in his youth. In a letter to his kidnap victim, Charles Urschel, written towards the end of his life, he observed plaintively, 'These five words seem written in fire on the walls of my cell: Nothing can be worth this!'

JOHN STRAFFEN

In 1951, when John Straffen entered Broadmoor Institution in Berkshire, George VI was on the throne, Clement Atlee was prime minister of Britain, and food was still being rationed in Britain following World War Two. Straffen, aged twenty-one at the time, had already spent half his life in institutions. He would spend the remainder of it locked up, apart from four fateful hours in 1952, when he escaped and murdered again. By the date of his death, on 19 November 2007, he had become British legal history's longest-serving prisoner, having spent fifty-six years behind bars.

John Thomas Straffen was born in Bordon in Hampshire in 1930, the son of a soldier who was posted to India when John was two years old. The family would remain there for six years, during which time, sometime before he was six years old, John was struck by an attack of encephalitis which caused severe damage to his cerebral cortex, leaving him with a low IQ and mental age for the rest of his life.

Returning to Britain, the family settled in Bath in

Somerset, but very soon afterwards, eight-year-old John was getting into trouble for truancy and theft. He was referred to a Child Guidance Clinic and appeared before a juvenile court in June 1939 for stealing a purse from a girl. He was sentenced to two years' probation and his probation officer, noting that John did not seem to know the difference between right and wrong, referred him to a psychiatrist. He was certified under the Mental Deficiency Act. In 1940, aged ten, he was reported to have an IQ of fifty-eight and a mental age of six.

At Bedford Court residential school which he attended from the age of twelve, he was disruptive and found it difficult to make friends. An increasingly violent tendency emerged when he strangled two geese belonging to a member of staff. By sixteen, his IQ was sixty-four and his mental age had risen, but only to nine years and six months. He was discharged and returned to Bath where he worked as a machinist in a clothing factory. Meanwhile, however, he was breaking into houses and stealing small items which he hid, never trying to sell them or take them home with him.

He was arrested in summer 1947 for strangling five chickens and was also a suspect in a burglary. When interviewed, he happily confessed to the burglary, also admitting to a number of crimes in which he was not even a suspect. His mental capability was taken into consideration and he was committed to Hortham Colony in Bristol, an institution that prepared offenders such as Straffen for release back into the community. In 1949, he was transferred to a lower security facility at Winchester, but after stealing a bag of walnuts in February 1950 he was sent back to Hortham. Later that year, he left the institution without permission and made his way home. When police arrived to take him back, he struggled with them and had to be subdued.

By 1951, he was considered to have responded well enough to treatment to be allowed home leave and found employment during this at a market garden. Nonetheless, aged twenty-one his certification under the Mental Health Act was renewed for another five years. When his family appealed against this ruling, he was reassessed and his certificate was revised to only six months with a discharge at the end of that time.

On 15 July 1951, Straffen killed for the first time.

He was on his way to the cinema when he saw five-year-old Brenda Goddard picking flowers in the garden of her foster parents' house in Bath. When he told her that he knew a better place to pick flowers, Brenda agreed to go with him. Shortly afterwards, he lifted her over a fence into a wooded area and strangled her, before banging her head against a rock. Without concealing the body, he continued on to the cinema.

He had no real record of violence but police, considering him a suspect in Brenda's murder, interviewed him on 3 August. When they checked with his employer to work out his movements on the day of the murder, Straffen was sacked from his job.

Five days later, he met nine-year-old Cicely Batstone and invited her to go to see a film with him. When they left the cinema, he took her by bus to a meadow on the outskirts of Bath where he strangled her. This time, however, a number of people had seen him with Cicely. The bus conductor had once worked with him and knew him well, a courting couple who had been near the scene of the murder recognised him and a policeman's wife also came forward, having seen them together. The next day, he was arrested.

He immediately confessed to the murders of both Cicely Batstone and Brenda Goddard and was charged with murder. At the end of the month, he was committed to trial for Brenda's murder.

At Taunton Assizes in October 1951, Straffen was found unfit to plead, the judge, Justice Oliver, memorably commenting, 'In this country we do not try people who are insane. You might as well try a baby in arms. If a man cannot understand what is going on, he cannot be tried.' Straffen was sent to Broadmoor, originally an asylum for the criminally insane, but now a hospital whose inmates were described as patients.

Astonishingly, despite a ten-foot-high wall, John Straffen succeeded in escaping from Broadmoor on 29 April 1952, when he climbed up onto the roof of a shed and scrambled over the wall. He had put his ordinary clothes on under his work clothes that morning. Walking into the nearby village of Crowthorne, he chatted with a woman in her garden, joking about the possibility of escapes from the nearby hospital. Ninety minutes later, he saw five-year-old Linda Bower riding on her bicycle. He strangled her.

Moving on, he asked a woman in her garden for a cup of tea and she generously offered to drive him to the nearest bus stop. As they drove off, Straffen noticed some men in uniforms and learning that they were police officers, leapt from the car and fled. The woman told the policemen about her passenger's strange behaviour and Straffen was pursued, recaptured and taken back to Broadmoor.

When the little girl's body was discovered at dawn the following day, police immediately went to Broadmoor to interview Straffen. Without telling him why they were there, they questioned him about what he had done while he had been free. He became defensive, blurting out, 'I did not kill her… I know what you policemen are, I know I killed two little children but I did not kill the little girl…I did not kill the little girl on the bicycle.' On 1 May he was charged with Linda Bower's murder and, Broadmoor having failed to keep him locked up, was remanded to Brixton prison.

At his trial on 21 July, he pleaded not guilty but, controversially, evidence was introduced about his previous murders. A medical expert testified that Straffen had admitted that he knew murder was wrong, saying that it was one of the Ten Commandments. This persuaded the jury that he was, indeed, sane and they found him guilty of murder in just under an hour. John Straffen was sentenced to death.

On 29 August, however, after his appeal failed, the Home Secretary at the time, David Maxwell Fyfe recommended that he be reprieved. No reason was given at the time, but it later emerged that he believed Straffen to be insane.

And so began John Straffen's fifty-six-year-long tour of England's prisons.

It began with Wandsworth Prison where he remained for four years before being transferred to Horfield Prison in Bristol. Prisoners planning an escape included Straffen in their plans because they felt he would be a huge distraction for the police. The escape was foiled, but it caused outrage amongst local residents. A 12,000-signature petition demanded that Straffen be moved away from their area.

Two years later, he was moved, to Cardiff Prison, returning to Horfield in 1960. When the new high security wing was opened at Parkhurst Prison on the Isle of Wight, Straffen was its first occupant on 31 January 1966, arriving there just before six of the Great Train robbers.

His neighbour in the top security E Wing at Durham Prison, to which he was transferred in May 1968, was the Moors murderer, Ian Brady. During this time, Straffen was described as 'a shambling lunatic' who was only in prison because no mental hospital could hold him. He would circle the exercise yard relentlessly, banging the fence every few minutes. As ever, he remained a solitary, friendless figure who talked to no one. In 1984, he was still there when Kenneth Barlow, who had killed using insulin, was released from prison after serving twenty-six years. Straffen now had the dubious honour of being Britain's longest-serving prison inmate.

It seemed obvious that Straffen would never be released and his name was high on a list of twenty such prisoners compiled by then Home Secretary, Michael Howard in 1994. His life of working as a cleaner in the prison craft shop and tea-making for warders looked set to continue indefinitely. He was, by this time, getting on well with prison staff and was known to them by his first name. Other inmates, however, still avoided him.

The old claims that he had been unfit to stand trial resurfaced in 2001 on the fiftieth anniversary of his arrest. Doubt was also introduced into whether he killed Linda Bower, a crime Straffen had always insisted he did not commit. Some have even claimed that the little girl was killed after Straffen had been taken back into custody. Nonetheless, the Criminal Cases Review Board turned down his request for an enquiry in December 2002.

In May 2002, the authority of the Home Secretary over the release of lifers was challenged in the European Court of Human Rights. The success of this case implied that Straffen might eventually be released but before that could happen, John Straffen died, aged seventy-seven, at Frankland Prison in November 2007.

His old Durham Prison neighbour, Ian Brady, took on the mantle of Britain's longest-serving prisoner, but at 44 years he still has a few more to do before he overtakes John Straffen's long stretch.

ALBERT DESALVO
THE BOSTON STRANGLER

'Me? I wouldn't kill no broads. I love broads.'
Albert DeSalvo

He was never charged with the murders that made him one of the most infamous individuals of the twentieth century and the Boston Strangler case, the reign of terror between June 1962 and January 1964 that left thirteen women dead in the Boston area, has never been closed. Many, however, believe he was not responsible for all of the murders. There are inconsistencies – in one case, he remembered killing his victim with his bare hands, but she was in fact strangled with scarves and a stocking. Recent DNA testing has also come up with surprising new evidence. Did his attorney, the famous F. Lee Bailey persuade him that, given his catalogue of sexual offences, if he pled guilty to the Boston Strangler killings, he would be sent to the more lenient regime of a psychiatric hospital rather than the harsh environment of the federal prison system? Was there more than one Boston Strangler, as some suggest, operating in the area at that time, each copying and building on the other's acts? We may never know the answers to these questions, but one thing is for certain, whether he was or was not the Boston Strangler, or whether he was the only one, Albert DeSalvo's criminal career was extraordinary and extensive.

The first victim of the killer they came to call the Boston Strangler was fifty-five-year-old divorcee, Anna Slesers, murdered on 14 June 1962. Found by her son, she was naked and had been hit on the head with a blunt instrument before being strangled with the belt of her housecoat. Her legs had been left spread grotesquely wide apart and she had been sexually assaulted with an unknown object. Her apartment had been ransacked, the contents of her handbag scattered across the floor, but her jewellery and gold watch had not been taken, leading investigators to grimly conclude that robbery was not the motive.

With this first killing, the killer established his method and his signature – the trademark left behind to perversely stamp his identity on the act, a feature of many serial killings. He would gain entry posing as a workman. His victims were exclusively women. They were sexually assaulted and strangled, using items of their own clothing –

stockings, undergarments or belts – or a pillow and these were then tied in an elaborate bow around the dead woman's neck. Variations included biting, bludgeoning or stabbing.

Sixteen days after he had killed for the first time, he struck again, his victim a sixty-eight-year-old woman, Nina Nicholls who was on the phone when the doorbell rang. She hung up, telling the friend to whom she had been speaking that she would call back. She never did, however, and her worried friend called the building's janitor and asked him to check that she was alright. She was found in the same position as his first victim. He had used a wine bottle to sexually assault her and two nylon stockings were tied around her neck in a neat bow. Although they found semen on her thighs, there was none inside her vagina. Once again, he had left valuables behind.

Three hours later that same night, he killed again.

Nina Nicholls had been attacked at around five that evening. At around eight, he was in the Boston suburb of Lynn, strangling another divorcee, sixty-five-year-old Helen Blake. Her body was only discovered a couple of days later when friends became worried that they had not heard from her. A brassiere was tied around her neck in a bow and she had been sexually assaulted with an object. He seemed more interested in her valuables this time as he had stolen a couple of diamond rings from her fingers and had tried to break into a metal strongbox.

The city of Boston was in shock and women were warned not to open their doors to strangers; it was evident from the lack of signs of forced entry that the killer had been allowed to enter the apartments of his victims. All police leave was cancelled and every detective in Boston was put onto the Strangler case. They brought in forensic psychiatrists who created a profile of the killer, describing him as a man aged between eighteen and forty who was suffering from delusions of persecution and who felt antipathy towards his mother, as the victims had so far all been older women. They tried to find a match in their files and some men were brought in for questioning, but none of them seemed to be the Strangler. It all seemed irrelevant when seventy-five-year-old Ida Irga was found strangled on 21 August. He had strangled her with his bare hands, using a pillow case to tie in a bow around her throat. Her legs had been spread apart on two chairs, exposing her private parts.

For three months nothing happened, but on 5 December he struck again, destroying the profile of the mother-hater by killing a younger woman, twenty-one-year-old Sophie Clark who was the only African-American woman he murdered. She had been raped – the first instance where rape could definitely be established – and a semen stain on a carpet nearby indicated that he had also masturbated over her body.

One of Sophie Clark's neighbours had earlier that day opened her door to a man claiming to have been sent to do some repairs in her apartment. When he started to make comments about her figure, she became afraid and, thinking fast, told him that her husband was asleep in the bedroom. He fled, saying it was the wrong apartment. It was a lucky escape but she was able to provide investigators with their first description of the assailant. He was twenty-five to thirty years old, of average height, with honey-coloured hair.

He continued to smash the psychological profile by next attacking two young women, one of whom fought him off. When twenty-three-year-old Patricia Bisquette failed to turn up for work on the last day of January 1962, her boss became concerned. Her apartment was checked and she was found dead in bed with the covers pulled up to her chin. She wore the customary bow around her neck.

A fortnight later a German girl, Gertrude Gruen

showed enormous pluck by biting the Strangler's hand when he threw his arm around her neck in her apartment. She began to scream and he fled.

Mary Brown died on 9 March in Lawrence, an industrial town twenty-five miles north of Boston. Her skull having been smashed with a piece of lead piping, this murder was not initially attributed to the Strangler, or the 'Phantom' as the press were calling him at the time. He had exposed her breasts and a fork he'd viciously stuck into one had been left there.

His next victim also showed a deviation from his customary method. Twenty-three-year-old Beverley Sams had been stabbed repeatedly. Everything else was as usual, however.

He took a break through the summer of 1963, but on 8 September, fifty-eight-year-old Evelyn Corbin was found with semen in her mouth as well as in her vagina.

On 23 November, Joanne Graff was murdered and on 4 January 1964, nineteen-year-old Mary Sullivan was found seated on her bed with a broom handle horrifically inserted in her vagina. There was semen in her mouth. The Strangler had a sense of humour; at her feet was a greetings card wishing investigators a happy new year.

It was his last murder.

Albert DeSalvo was arrested after he had entered the apartment of a young woman on 27 October 1964, pretending to be a detective. He tied her to her bed, sexually assaulted her and then left, saying 'I'm sorry' over his shoulder as he walked out the door. Her description of him was recognised by detectives and led to his arrest. Then, when his photograph was released, scores of women came forward to identify him as the man who had attacked them.

He was identified as the Green Man who, following the end of the Boston Strangler murders, terrorised women in a wide area that extended to Massachusetts, New Hampshire, Connecticut and Rhode Island. He was a rapist who dressed entirely in green, like some kind of super-antihero and he was prolific, on one occasion raping four women in one day, gaining entrance to their apartments and threatening them with a knife, although he was never physically violent.

The identification of DeSalvo came from another identity that he had been given several years previously – the Measuring Man who had been the perpetrator of a series of bizarre attacks in the early 1960s. He would knock on an apartment door and when it was opened by an attractive young woman, he would introduce himself as an employee of a modelling agency on the lookout for prospective models. He would tell the young woman she could earn $40 an hour, reassuring her that it was all above board and would involve no nudity. All he needed to do, he said, was take her measurements. He would take out a tape measure and take down her vital statistics. If she had not thrown him out by then, he would tell her that someone from the agency would call if she was suitable. He would then leave.

DeSalvo, born in 1931, had endured a troubled upbringing, often suffering beatings by his abusive father. By the time he was a teenager he had already embarked on a criminal career but to get away from his increasing troubles, enlisted in the US Army. He was posted to Germany where he met his future wife, Imgard. The couple returned to the United States when he received an honourable discharge in 1956.

He was viewed by others as a hardworking, devoted family man but he was still getting into trouble, usually for breaking and entering. Nonetheless, he still managed to hold down a job. At home, however, there were also problems. Imgard had given birth to a daughter with disabilities and she was fearful of becoming pregnant again in case another child might be similarly afflicted. DeSalvo, however, had a voracious sexual appetite, requiring sex sometimes five or six times a day. When Imgard refused to comply with this exhausting regime, he called her frigid and became increasingly sexually frustrated.

In 1961, he was sentenced to eighteen months in jail when he was arrested for the Measuring Man attacks, admitting to assaulting three hundred women and breaking into an astonishing four hundred apartments. The Boston Strangler murders began just two months after his release from prison.

In 1964, when he was first held on the Green Man rapes, DeSalvo was incarcerated in Bridgewater State Hospital. One day, he suddenly confessed to another inmate, George Nassar, that he was the Boston Strangler. It sounded tue, because he demonstrated an intimate knowledge of the murders. However, as has been pointed out, DeSalvo possessed a photographic memory and much of the information could have been gleaned from the detailed accounts of the killings that had appeared in newspapers and magazines. It was even suggested that, knowing he was going to spend the rest of his life in prison, he confessed so that his wife and disabled daughter might make some money from movie deals and book rights.

An astonishing piece of plea-bargaining ensued by which it was agreed that DeSalvo should only stand trial for the Green Man rapes. Thus, he was convicted only of rape and robbery and in 1967 was sentenced to spend the rest of his life in prison, which was what the authorities wanted.

In February 1967, DeSalvo and two other inmates escaped from Bridgewater State Hospital and a massive manhunt was launched. He left a note on his bunk addressed to the superintendent of the hospital, claiming that he escaped in order to focus attention on conditions at the hospital. He was on the run for only a day and was recaptured at Lynn, Massachusetts. Following the escape, he was transferred to Walpole maximum security prison. Six years later, he was found stabbed to death in the prison's infirmary. His killer or killers have never been identified, but some speculate that he was dispatched to prevent him from revealing the identity of the real Boston Strangler.

The files on the Boston Strangler killings remain open.

CHARLES MANSON

Charles Milles Maddox was born in 1934 in Cincinnati, Ohio, to sixteen-year-old unmarried teenage prostitute, Kathleen Maddox. His name was changed to Manson when Kathleen was briefly married to a labourer, William Manson, but Kathleen filed a paternity suit against a Colonel Scott who is said to have been a worker on a nearby dam project. He may have been the father of one of the twentieth century's most evil killers.

Manson's childhood was unrelentingly harsh and at one time his mother, reputedly an alcoholic, is said to have tried to sell her son to a childless waitress for a pitcher of beer. Kathleen went to prison in 1939 for robbing a petrol station, leaving Manson in the care of her parents in West Virginia and following her release she lived with him in a series of cheap motel rooms. Tragically, Manson recalls her embrace of him on the day she was released from prison as his sole happy childhood memory.

Unable to look after her increasingly unmanagable son, Kathleen succeeded in getting him sent to the

Gibault School for Boys at Terre Haute, Indiana. Needless to say, he hated its discipline and endless rules and made no fewer than eighteen attempts to escape. On one occasion when he made it back to his mother, she rejected him and he made his way to Indianapolis where he robbed a store to get some cash to pay for lodgings. He embarked upon a string of robberies and break-ins but was eventually arrested trying to steal a bicycle from a store. He escaped from the juvenile centre he was sent to after just one day. Following his recapture, a Catholic priest made an effort to get Manson onto the straight and narrow, pleading for him to be given a chance at the famous Boys Town in Omaha, Nebraska. Manson was there for only four days before he escaped with another boy with whom he carried out a couple of armed robberies. They were soon recaptured.

Incredibly, Charles Manson was only thirteen years old at this point.

Indiana School for Boys, his next stop, was a proper reform school, but it boasted a harsh and brutal regime – strict discipline, mistreatment by staff and sexual abuse. He escaped in 1951 with two other boys but, after another string of petrol station heists, was back behind bars again. This time, however, having driven a stolen car across a state line, he was sent to a federal institution, the National Training

School for Boys in Washington DC. Assessed by a caseworker, he was found to be illiterate and was described as 'aggressively antisocial'.

He committed his first crime of real violence following his transfer to a minimum security detention centre in October 1951. Just a month before his parole hearing, he held a razor to another inmate's throat while sodomising him. He wound up at the high security Federal Reformatory at Chillicothe, Ohio, where at last he seems to have come to his senses. For the next two years, he stayed out of trouble, for once in his life doing as he was told. It paid off when he was paroled in 1954. He was twenty years old and had no idea what life was like in the world outside the institutions in which he had so far spent half his life.

In January 1955, he married a waitress, Rosalie Willis, but although he claimed later to have at last found some kind of happiness with her, it was only a matter of time before he was in trouble again. He was arrested for driving a stolen car from Ohio to Los Angeles, once again a federal offence. He was lucky this time, getting off with only five years' probation but when he failed to appear to face a similar charge soon after, he was arrested and sentenced to three years' imprisonment in San Pedro in California. In prison he missed the birth of his child, Charles Manson Jr, but Rosalie had soon given up on Charlie and by 1957 she was living with another man and divorcing him.

Paroled in September 1958, he was earning his living as a pimp, but the next year he was given probation and a suspended ten-year sentence for attempting to cash forged US Treasury cheques. Failing to keep that probation, he went to the federal penitentiary on McNeil Island in Washington State for ten years. It was a horrific period for Manson. A man of small stature, he was raped on numerous occasions by other inmates, many of whom were black, a fact that contributed greatly to the racist views that would later colour his perverted philosophy.

He was finally released in 1967 into the new world of flower power and free love in San Francisco, capital of hippiedom. Manson, with his hypnotic stare and talk that seemed to be deep and meaningful, but was in reality shallow and meaningless, set himself up as a guru of sorts, surrounding himself with a coterie of easily-manipulated flower children, mainly middle class girls who had 'dropped out'. There were young malleable men, too, but the girls were Charlie's and they were all in love with him. Girls like twenty-one-year-old Patricia Krenwinkel who had been expensively educated and worked in a good job in insurance in Los Angeles. After meeting Charlie on a beach, she gave it all up. Or Leslie Van Houten, a nineteen-year-old acid freak. Or twenty-two-year-old Linda Kasabian who left her husband and two children for him. Susan Atkins was a twenty-one-year-old topless dancer who was into devil worship. She became Manson's right-hand woman, filling his head with Satanic nonsense, persuading him that he was the devil, a dangerous thing to tell a man like Charles Manson.

They all had one thing in common – LSD – and Charlie used it to control them.

Manson had learned to play guitar in prison and, fuelled by the success of his favourite band, the Beatles, in America, harboured his own dreams of becoming a pop star. His break seemed to arrive when a couple of the girls hitchhiking one day were picked up by Beach Boy Dennis Wilson and went back to his place. Soon after, the entire Family, as the group was now calling itself, had moved into Wilson's mansion and was costing him a fortune. To Manson's delight, however, Wilson paid for studio time for him to record some of the songs he had written and he provided introductions to producers and music industry people. The Beach Boys even recorded a Manson song, *Cease to Exist*, changing the words to the less dramatic *Cease to Resist* and renaming it *Never Learn Not to Love*. Nothing came of it all, however, and when Wilson had tired of them, he threw then out. They moved to a couple of ranches in the desert where Manson began to develop his crazed philosophy. He prophesied a racial war that would be called Helter Skelter, after a track on the Beatles' recently released *White Album*. Manson and the Family would seek shelter in a bottomless pit in Death Valley and when it was all over, the Family, by this time enlarged to 144,000 members, would emerge to rule the world.

In the meantime, they killed their first victim, Gary Hinman, a musician. Manson wanted him to hear some of his songs, but also learned that Hinman had recently inherited a large sum of money. Susan Atkins and Bobby Beausoleil were sent to steal the money, but ended up holding Hinman hostage for two days. When they could not find the money, they stabbed him to death. Atkins dipped her finger in the dead man's blood and scrawled 'political piggie' on the wall. A short while later, Beausoleil was arrested after a fingerprint was discovered at the murder scene. He was sentenced to life imprisonment but, loyal to the end, implicated neither Manson nor Atkins.

Manson moved his attention to successful music producer Terry Melcher, son of the movie star, Doris Day. When Melcher refused to have anything to do with the weird little hippie guru, Manson was furious. He decided on revenge with an act that would also show the blacks how it was done.

On 8 August, he ordered Charles 'Tex' Watson, Patricia Krenwinkel, Susan Atkins and Linda Kasabian to go to Cielo Drive and 'totally destroy everyone in it as gruesome as you can.' What he did not know was that Melcher had by this time moved out and the house was now being rented by film director, Roman Polanski and his pregnant actress wife, Sharon Tate.

When they arrived at the secluded house, they cut the phone lines and climbed over the wall into the grounds. Seeing a car's headlights approaching, the girls ducked into some bushes. Watson pulled out a gun, approached the car and shot dead its driver, eighteen-year-old Stephen Parent, who had been visiting William Garretson, a caretaker living in the nearby guesthouse on the property. Watson turned back to the house and cut a hole in a screen at an open window. He instructed Kasabian to go to the gate to look out for anyone coming while he, Atkins and Krenwinkel climbed in through the window.

Wojciech Fryokwski, a friend of Polanski, awoke on the couch in the living room to the large figure of Tex Watson looming over him. 'I'm the devil, and

I'm here to do the devil's business,' Watson hissed at him. The other occupants of the house were wakened and brought in – Sharon Tate, Jay Sebring, America's top men's hair stylist and twenty-five-year-old Abigail Folger, heiress to a coffee fortune.

Watson tied Tate's and Sebring's necks together and threw the other end of the rope over a roof beam. It was done in such a way that they would choke if they tried to escape. Folger offered them money, thinking they were robbers. She went to get her purse and they took the seventy dollars she had in it. Of course, they were not robbers, they were killers and the killing started when Watson plunged his knife into Folger a number of times. Frykowski, having desperately worked his hands free from the towel they had used to tie him up, tried to make a break for the door, but Watson caught him and hit him on the head a number of times with his gun. He then fired two bullets into him. At this point, Linda Kasabian appeared, trying to bring a halt to proceedings, she later said, by shouting that someone was coming.

Folger, bleeding but still on her feet, ran to the pool area where Krenwinkel cornered her, stabbing her repeatedly, along with Watson. Frykowski, trying to crawl across the lawn, was also stabbed by Watson and was later found to have fifty-one stab wounds. Meanwhile, in the house, Sharon Tate was pleading for her life and that of her unborn baby. Shouting at her coldly that she didn't care about her or her baby, Atkins stabbed her sixteen times. Manson had asked them to leave a sign when they left. Atkins grabbed a towel and wrote the word 'pig' on the front door in Sharon Tate's blood.

The following night it was the turn of Leno LaBianca, a supermarket executive, and his wife, Rosemary. This time, Manson went himself, 'to show them how to do it'. Manson broke in and woke the sleeping couple, tying them up and covering their heads with pillow cases. He left at this point, instructing Krenwinkel and Leslie Van Houten to go into the house and kill the couple. Watson began stabbing Leno with a chrome-plated bayonet, but in the bedroom, Rosemary was putting up a fight. Watson stabbed her, however, and she fell. Returning to the living room, he carved 'war' on Leno's stomach. In the bedroom, Krenwinkel was stabbing Rosemary with a kitchen knife and Watson ordered Van Houten to stab her, too. Rosemary LaBianca was stabbed a total of forty-one times.

Using the couple's blood, Krenwinkel wrote 'Rise' and 'Death to pigs' on the walls and misspelled 'Healther Skelter' on the refrigerator door. She stabbed Leno a further fourteen times, even though he was already dead, leaving a carving fork sticking out of his stomach. Before she left, she stuck a steak knife in his neck.

The LAPD were baffled by the killings and critically failed to make any connection between the death of Sharon Tate and her celebrity friends and a hard-working couple. The Tate killings had been attributed to a drug deal gone awry. Neither was any connection made with the murder of Gary Hinman, despite the writing on the wall at all three murder scenes.

When Helter Skelter failed to materialise, the Family began to drift apart. Susan Atkins went back to prostitution to earn money and was eventually arrested. While incarcerated, however, she boasted to another prisoner about the Family and the killings. The prisoner told the police and on 15 October, police raided the ranch on which the Family were living, arresting more than twenty of them, including Charles Manson whose longest period of freedom in many years was at an end.

Linda Kasabian was granted immunity in exchange for her testimony against the others but it was one of the strangest trials in American legal history. The girls and Manson played jokes throughout, even all arriving in court with their heads shaved at one point. When Manson carved a cross into his forehead, the girls all copied him. In an act of perverse defiance, that cross would later be fashioned into a swastika.

Throughout the proceedings the girls maintained that Charlie was innocent, but it made little difference to the outcome. When the verdict was announced on 25 January 1971, Manson, Krenwinkel and Atkins were found guilty on seven counts of murder and Leslie Van Houten on two counts. Sentenced to death, their sentences were commuted to life when the US Supreme Court declared execution unconstitutional in 1972. Tex Watson was also given a life sentence in a separate trial.

On 23 May 2007, Corcoran State Prison inmate number B33920 was denied parole for the eleventh time. Charles Manson had made his first application in 1978 and will again be able to make an application in 2012. Manson has been at Corcoran since 1989, having been transferred to its Protective Housing Unit from San Quentin State Prison. A great deal of his time in prison has been spent in the 'hole' – solitary confinement – for infractions of the rules. He is now seventy-five years old, balding, with an unkempt grey beard and his grey hair cut short at the sides. His eyes stare frighteningly as ever from a recent photograph and the swastika he carved into his forehead sometime in the 1970s is still visible.

Of course, the parole hearings are empty gestures. Charlie Manson will never be released. He will end his days in prison for the horrific crimes he ordered others to commit, crimes which contributed to the end of the hippie dream of the 1960s. Some suggest that he is exactly where he wants to be, having spent more than two-thirds of his life in institutions of some kind.

DAVID BERKOWITZ
'SON OF SAM'

David Berkowitz, self-styled Son of Sam and one of the scariest killers America has ever known, has been locked up since he was sentenced to 365 years in 1977. Responsible for the deaths of six people, he was heavily influenced by the occult in his murders. In prison, however, he has become a born-again Christian. He wrote in 2002 to the Governor of New York that he wanted his parole hearing to be cancelled, explaining that with God's help, he had long ago come to terms with his situation and accepted his punishment. He believed that he should remain in prison for the rest of his life.

Berkowitz has at last found a purpose to his life, even if it has to be fulfilled within the confines of the Sullivan Correctional Facility in Fallsburg, New York. But life has not always been like that for him. He was put up for adoption just a week after he was born Richard David Falco in Brooklyn in 1953. Adopted by hardware store owners, Nathan and Pearl Berkowitz, he had a troubled childhood. He was of above average intelligence but school held no attractions for him. Petty theft and pyromania, on the other hand, thrilled him. A bully with a mean streak, who was always big for his age, his neighbours and the local kids became wary of him

When his adoptive mother died of breast cancer when he was thirteen, Berkowitz was devastated and became increasingly introverted and reclusive. Home life was strained by his father's new wife who he disliked intensely. However, his stepsister was interested in the occult and she would spark a similar fascination in him. Later, he would pursue that interest rather more enthusiastically.

He enlisted in the US Army in 1971, serving in South Korea and receiving an honourable discharge in 1974. The following year, he attacked two women with a knife on Christmas Eve. He had always felt uncomfortable and inadequate in the company of women, feeling that they despised him and considered him unattractive. Now he wanted revenge.

Around 1974, he began hearing voices as he lay in bed at night in his filthy apartment. The voices were telling him to kill and he began to scrawl messages all over the walls, messages such as 'Kill for my Master!'

He obeyed those voices for the first time on 29 July 1976.

At around one in the morning, eighteen-year-old Donna Lauria and her friend, nineteen-year-old Jody Valenti were chatting outside Donna's apartment block in Jody's car. Suddenly, Donna spotted a man standing beside the car's passenger door. He pulled out a pistol from inside a paper bag in his hand and fired five bullets into the interior of the vehicle. Donna died instantly when a bullet hit her in the neck. Judy experienced horrific pain as a bullet tore into her thigh but retained the presence of mind to slam her hand down hard on the car's horn. The man turned and fled.

The officers who arrived to investigate the incident were puzzled. There seemed to be no motive for the attack whatsoever. Had it been a case of mistaken identity or an opportunistic psychopath?

Three months later, on 23 October, he struck again. Rosemary Keegan drove Carl Denaro home from a party at a bar in Queens. Parked near his house at around 1.30 a.m., they sat in her Volkswagen Beetle and talked. Suddenly, the side window of the car seemed to explode and bullets were whizzing past them. Keegan pressed her foot down on the accelerator and sped from the scene back to the bar. Denaro had been hit in the head but survived following an operation to have a piece of his skull replaced by a metal plate. They saw nothing of their attacker.

Once again, it was a motiveless incident but police did not connect it with the first shooting, initially, because the two incidents had occurred in different boroughs of the city and were investigated by different police agencies.

Towards the end of the evening of 26 November, sixteen-year-old Donna DeMasi and eighteen-year-old Joanne Lomino were chatting outside Lomino's house after walking home from a movie when a man suddenly approached and began to ask in a high-pitched voice, 'Can you tell me how to get…?' He left the phrase incomplete, however, instead pulling out a revolver. He shot each of them once and then while they were on the ground fired several more bullets seemingly at random, hitting a nearby building before running away. A neighbour came rushing out and saw a blonde man run past with a gun in his hand.

The girls survived, but Joanne Lomino was rendered paraplegic by the bullet which had hit her spine.

On 30 January, engaged couple Christine Freund and John Diel were in Diel's Pontiac Firebird, which was parked in Queens, when their car was shot at. Christine, hit twice, died two hours later in hospital while her companion was unharmed.

A task force named Operation Omega was assembled to deal with the thousands of leads that were coming in from the panicked populace of New York. Two detectives, Sergeant Joe Coffey and Captain Joe Borelli investigated the background of the victims, but found nothing to link them apart from the fact that they were mostly attractive young women.

On 8 March, Virginia Voskocherian was shot in the face and killed instantly by a man who approached her as she walked home from college. As he ran away, the shooter passed a man who was just coming round the corner of the street. 'Hi, mister!' he shouted as he ran past. The killer on this occasion was described by some as a teenager of about sixteen to eighteen years of age, although others gave a description that applied more to the man who was finally arrested. The bullet that killed Virginia Voskocherian was fired from the same gun as the one that had killed Donna Lauria the previous July, confirming that it was still the same perpetrator. They issued a description of the suspect – a white male, twenty-five to thirty-six years old, six feet tall, of medium build and with dark hair.

The next victims were a couple of young lovers shot as they kissed near the Hutchinson River Parkway at three o'clock on the morning of 17

April. A car pulled up alongside theirs and someone opened fire from inside. Eighteen-year-old Valentina Suriani died at the scene and her twenty-year-old boyfriend, Alexander Esau, died later in hospital.

Now the letters started. At the latest murder scene a letter was found, addressed to Captain Borelli. Complete with misspellings, it read:

Dear Captain Joseph Borrelli,
I am deeply hurt by your calling me a wemon hater. I am not. But I am a monster. I am the 'Son of Sam.' I am a little brat. When father Sam gets drunk he gets mean. He beats his family. Sometimes he ties me up to the back of the house. Other times he locks me in the garage. Sam loves to drink blood. 'Go out and kill,' commands father Sam. 'Behind our house some rest. Mostly young – raped and slaughtered – their blood drained – just bones now. Papa Sam keeps me locked in the attic too. I can't get out but I look out the attic window and watch the world go by. I feel like an outsider. I am on a different wavelength then everybody else – programmed too kill. However, to stop me you must kill me. Attention all police: Shoot me first – shoot to kill or else keep out of my way or you will die! Papa Sam is old now. He needs some blood to preserve his youth. He has had too many heart attacks. 'Ugh, me

hoot, it hurts, sonny boy.' I miss my pretty princess most of all. She's resting in our ladies house. But I'll see her soon. I am the 'Monster' – 'Beelzebub' – the chubby behemouth. I love to hunt. Prowling the streets looking for fair game – tasty meat. The wemon of Queens are prettyist of all. It must be the water they drink. I live for the hunt – my life. Blood for papa. Mr Borrelli, sir, I don't want to kill anymore. No sur, no more but I must, 'honour thy father.' I want to make love to the world. I love people. I don't belong on earth. Return me to yahoos. To the people of Queens, I love you. And I want to wish all of you a happy Easter. May God bless you in this life and in the next.

Another letter was delivered to the famous reporter Jimmy Breslin who wrote for the *New York Daily News*. The killer wrote:

Hello from the cracks in the sidewalks of NYC and from the ants that dwell in these cracks and feed in the dried blood of the dead that has settled into the cracks. Hello from the gutters of NYC, which is filled with dog manure, vomit, stale wine, urine, and blood. Hello from the sewers of NYC which swallow up these delicacies when they are washed away by the sweeper trucks. Don't think because you haven't heard [from me] for a while that I went to sleep. No, rather, I am still here. Like a spirit roaming the night. Thirsty, hungry, seldom stopping to rest; anxious to please Sam. Sam's a thirsty lad. He won't let me stop killing until he gets his fill of blood. Tell me, Jim, what will you have for July 29? You can forget about me if you like because I don't care for publicity. However, you must not forget Donna Lauria and you cannot let the people forget her either. She was a very sweet girl. Not knowing what the future holds, I shall say farewell and I will see you at the next job? Or should I say you will see my handiwork at the next job? Remember Ms Lauria. Thank you. In their blood and from the gutter – 'Sam's creation' .44.'

The *Daily News* immediately renamed the killer they had been calling the '.44 Caliber Killer.' They called him 'Son of Sam'.

The name 'Sam's creation' had actually come from an incident in which Berkowitz had shot a dog belonging to a neighbour, Sam Carr. The dog had kept Berkowitz awake at night and he had sent a series of poisonous letters to Carr. The police had been informed, but nobody considered that he might actually be 'Son of Sam'.

It was not over. On 26 June, in Queens, Salvatore

Lupo and Judith Placido were shot and wounded in their car. Five weeks later, on Sunday 31 July, just over a year since the murder of Donna Lauria, 'Son of Sam' claimed his last victims. Stacy Moskowitz was shot and died later in hospital while her boyfriend Bobby Violante was hit twice in the face, but survived.

This time, however, Sam committed a fatal error. When he returned to his Ford Galaxy which had been parked in front of a fire hydrant, he found he had been given a ticket for the violation. Angrily ripping it from his windscreen, he threw it to the ground. However, he was seen doing this by a woman who when she saw him again later, thought that he might have something up his sleeve resembling a gun. She informed the police who traced the ticket and ran a check on the vehicle, coming up with the name David Berkowitz, a man living in the New York suburb of Yonkers.

On 10 August, officers waited outside Berkowitz's apartment building at 35 Pine Street. A man walked out of the building towards the Ford Galaxy and climbed in. Before he could start the engine, however, a police officer approached the car from the rear, pointing a gun at Berkowitz and screaming 'Freeze!'

The man turned slowly, a smile of acceptance on

his face. He was ordered out of the car and told to put his hands on the roof.

'Now that I've got you,' said the officer, 'who have I got?'

'You know,' the man replied in a soft voice.

'No, I don't. You tell me.' Said the officer.

He paused and, the smile still on his face, laughed, 'I'm Sam. David Berkowitz'.

PETER SUTCLIFFE
THE YORKSHIRE RIPPER

Peter Sutcliffe, the Yorkshire Ripper, was at last locked up at Parkhurst Prison on the Isle of Wight on 22 May 1981, bringing to an end five years of terror in which he had killed thirteen women and left seven others for dead. The women of Yorkshire could again feel safe on the streets of their county's towns and cities. For the Ripper, however, it was the beginning of a torrid time.

At his trial he had been found to be sane but soon after arriving at Parkhurst, he was diagnosed as suffering from schizophrenia. However, all attempts to have him removed to a secure psychiatric facility were blocked. On 10 January, he was attacked and seriously wounded in prison by a thirty-five-year-old Glasgow criminal, James Costello. Costello plunged a broken coffee cup twice into the left side of Sutcliffe's face, leaving wounds that required thirty stitches.

In March, 1984, he was finally transferred to Broadmoor Hospital under Section 47 of the

Mental Health Act, but twelve years later he was the victim of another vicious attack when Paul Wilson, a convicted robber, attempted to strangle him with the electrical flex of a pair of headphones. He was saved only by the intervention of two other inmates.

In March 1997, he was attacked again, by fellow inmate Ian Kay. This time, he lost the sight of his left eye and his right was seriously damaged.

Sutcliffe could conceivably be released in the near future – his name was noticably absent from a 2006 Home Office list of prisoners who should never be released.

He seemed an unlikely candidate for a serial killer, a quiet man who appeared devoted to his wife Sonia. Born in 1946 in Bingley, to John and Kathleen Sutcliffe, he was something of a disappointment to his parents and especially to his sports-mad father who wanted young Peter to succeed at sport. Unfortunately, he failed in that as well as in his school work and left school, aged fifteen.

He worked in a number of jobs over the next few years, but seemed to settle down at the age of twenty when he met Sonia Szurma, a girl of Czech parentage. In 1974, they married and all seemed well apart from the fact that Sonia began to suffer a series of miscarriages. After a while they were devastated by the news that she would never be able to have children.

Peter Sutcliffe was never what he seemed on the surface to be. He claimed to be devoted to his wife but he frequented prostitutes, often in the company of his brother-in-law, Trevor Birdsall. The two of them would spend evenings drinking and cruising the red-light districts of Yorkshire in Sutcliffe's beloved white Ford Corsair. By now he was a lorry driver and earning good money.

He attacked twice before he actually killed. The first was in Keighley. A woman who had fallen out with her boyfriend was angrily banging on the door of his house. Suddenly, Sutcliffe leapt from the shadows and dealt her a crushing blow to the head with a hammer. She crumpled to the ground where he struck her with the hammer twice more before lifting her skirt. When a neighbour emerged from his house to ask what all the noise was, Sutcliffe calmly told him everything was fine and to go back indoors. As the man closed his door, Sutcliffe fled the scene. The police were baffled by the randomness of the attack and by the lack of motive – no money had been taken and she had not been sexually assaulted.

The second of what could be seen as warm-up

exercises came a month later, on Friday 15 August. As usual, he was out drinking in the pubs and clubs of Halifax. Forty-six-year-old Olive Smelt, who had been doing the same with her friends while her husband had stayed home to look after the kids, had been dropped off close to her house. Sutcliffe, seated with Birdsall in the Corsair, spotted her walking along the road. He told his companion he would only be a minute, got out and disappeared into the darkness. As Olive negotiated a dark alley, she heard a voice behind her say, 'Weather's letting us down, isn't it?' and then all went dark as she was hit on the back of the head by Sutcliffe's hammer. Hitting her again on the ground, he took out a knife and slashed her lower back. Luckily for Olive, he heard the engine of an approaching car, leapt to his feet and took off back to the Corsair. He climbed in as if nothing had happened.

Both attacks left police puzzled, but it would be another three years before they would identify them as having been carried out by the same man.

In the early hours of 30 October, twenty-eight-year-old mother of four, Wilma McCann was very drunk. She had been enjoying herself in Leeds but was struggling to get home. She was seen by a number of people, including a lorry driver who stopped to give her a lift but thought better of it when he saw the state she was in. At 1.30 a.m. someone saw her being picked up. It was the last time she was seen alive. Next morning a milkman found her lying on her back in a recreation ground only a hundred yards from her house. She had been hit twice on the back of the head with something heavy before her assailant had launched a frenzied knife attack on her, stabbing her fifteen times in the neck, chest and abdomen. She had not been raped, but there was semen on her trousers and underwear. As her purse was missing, the officers investigating put it down to a mugging gone wrong. One hundred and fifty officers were thrown at the case but despite thousands of interviews with local people, it remained firmly unsolved.

The first prostitute Sutcliffe killed was Emily Jackson who lived in Leeds and went on the game periodically when money was hard to come by. She had been having a drink with her husband in the Gaiety pub on 20 January 1976, before leaving him to see if she could drum up a bit of business. He remained there until closing time but when she did not return, he thought she would follow later. Instead, her body was discovered the next morning, a stone's throw from the Gaiety, her legs spread apart and her breasts exposed. Two shattering blows to the head with a hammer had forced her to the ground where she was subjected to an even more frenzied and horrific knife attack than Wilma McCann, having been stabbed fifty-one times. This time, however, he was using a new implement from his toolbox, a Phillips screwdriver that he had sharpened specially for the task.

Police knew now that they were dealing with a serial killer. But, at least they finally had a clue. The killer had stamped on her thigh, leaving the imprint of a size seven Dunlop Warwick Wellington boot.

Around this time, Sutcliffe had a lot of time on his hands, having been sacked from his job as a delivery driver. If his days were empty, however, his nights remained busy. On 9 May, he offered twenty-year-old prostitute, Marcella Claxton, £5 to have sex with him. He drove her to a large, secluded open space where she told him that she had to urinate first. As she crouched down she did not hear him come up behind her and deal her two crashing blows to the head with the hammer. She slumped to the ground and as she drifted in and out of consciousness, she saw him masturbating over her. Inexplicably, however, he did not kill her. When he had finished, he bent down and placed a £5 note in her hand, warning her not to go to the police. He jumped in the Corsair and sped off.

Claxton crawled to a nearby phone box, blood

pouring from her wounds, and dialed 999. She then slumped to the floor of the kiosk to await the ambulance. Just as well she did, because she spotted Sutcliffe drive past a couple of times looking for her, no doubt to finish what he had started.

Police now had a good description of the man the media were calling the Yorkshire Ripper, comparing him to the killer who had stalked the streets of Whitechapel in London almost a hundred years previously. The same panic that had broken out then, now hit the streets of the red-light districts of Leeds and many of the working girls left town. It was just too dangerous.

Sutcliffe finally got a job in October 1976, driving a lorry, and all went quiet. On 5 February 1977, however, Irene Richardson was killed in the customary manner. The knife attack was so savage that her intestines spilled out. When officers found tyre tracks they believed they had a major breakthrough in the case, but their mood changed when they learned that these could belong to any one of 100,000 vehicles. They were no closer.

The size seven Wellington boot made a reappearance on 23 April. It was found on a bed sheet in a flat belonging to a prostitute named Patricia Atkinson. He had stabbed her with a chisel after striking her with the hammer.

Meanwhile, the Sutcliffes were doing well. His job was paying well and Sonia, who had been training to be a teacher, was likely to start work in a school at the beginning of the autumn term. They became homeowners, spending £15,000 on a property in Bradford. After they had first looked at the house, Sutcliffe dropped Sonia off, telling her he was going for a drink. Instead he drove to Chapeltown, Leeds's red-light district.

His next victim was not a prostitute and this fact seemed to make the case more relevant to people. Prostitutes, they reasoned, take a risk every time they climb into a car driven by a stranger. Jayne MacDonald, on the other hand was a sixteen-year-old girl who was merely walking home. Sutcliffe had dragged her into a playground on 26 June after being felled by three savage blows to the head. He stabbed her repeatedly and left her with her breasts exposed.

There was revulsion and the officers involved in the investigation had to deal with a flood of information. Meanwhile, a huge number of interviews and house-to-house calls were being carried out. There was optimism when a white Corsair kept coming up as having been seen in the area but at the time taxi drivers in the north of England drove Corsairs. There were thousands of them. By the time they started checking, however, Sutcliffe had replaced the white Corsair with a red one.

On 1 October, Jean Jordan climbed into Sutcliffe's car in Manchester's Moss Side area, a down-at-heel suburb of the city. Again he paid her £5 and they drove off to find a quiet spot. Once there, the hammer was produced and he hit her with it no fewer than thirteen times, in a raging frenzy. He left her broken body and drove home. But the £5 note she had slipped in her handbag nagged at him. It had been brand new and could probably be easily traced back to him. Eight days after he had killed her, he returned to her body, which he had concealed well enough for it not yet to have been discovered. Her handbag was nowhere to be found, however, and he became enraged, stabbing her corpse repeatedly and attempting to decapitate her. She was found the following day and her handbag and the £5 note were found five days later, a short distance away. The note was traced to a batch that had been distributed to companies in the Bradford and Shipley area. It could have gone to anyone of 8,000 men, every one of whom – including Sutcliffe – was interviewed.

After attacking and failing to kill a prostitute in mid-December, he murdered Yvonne Pearson on 21 January 1978. She would not be found for two months. He killed another prostitute, Helen Rytka on 31 January, having sex with her as she lay on the ground. On 16 May, he killed Vera Millward who had gone out to the local shops. She was found in the grounds of Manchester Royal Infirmary, her skull crushed by three hammer blows, her body viciously slashed and stabbed. He had even stabbed her in the eye. Noises had been heard, but it was that kind of area. Once again, tyre tracks were found that matched those found previously.

There were eleven months when nothing happened, although during that time Sutcliffe's beloved mother died. In April 1979, however, he murdered Josephine Whitaker while she walked home from visiting her grandparents. He felled her with the hammer before stabbing her twenty-five times in the breasts, stomach, thighs and even her vagina.

His next victim was a young student who had been drinking in the same Bradford pub as the Ripper earlier on the evening of 1 September 1979. Barbara Leach was killed by one blow of the hammer – he was getting good with it – and then repeatedly stabbed. She was found covered up by an old piece of carpet.

The police campaign to find the Ripper intensified with £1 million being spent on posters and newspaper adverts. But they were being distracted by a belief that their perpetrator was from the Newcastle area, following a cassette tape they had received that was purportedly from the Ripper. The hoaxer, John Humble, would be jailed in 2006 for eight years for perverting the course of justice.

Sutcliffe, like many other men, had been interviewed by the police a number of times in connection with the enquiry. Ironically, his workmates started calling him 'the Ripper' but Sonia provided him with alibis for every night on which the Ripper had killed.

His next victim was not attributed to the Yorkshire Ripper until after he was in custody. When he had struck forty-seven-year-old civil servant Marguerite Walls, she had not fallen to the ground but had begun to scream loudly. He had to strangle her and this led police to believe that she had not been killed by the Yorkshire Ripper.

He failed to kill his next two victims, attacked on 24 September and 5 November, but on 17 November, with a single blow to the head, he murdered Jacqueline Hill, a student at Leeds University.

He was finally caught on Saturday 3 January as he talked to prostitute Olivia Reivers in his car that was parked on the driveway of the British Iron and

Steel Producers Association. Two policemen in a passing patrol car decided to investigate the brown Rover and when they found that it had been fitted with false number plates, Sutcliffe was arrested.

At Dewsbury police station, they noticed that he resembled very closely many of the descriptions of the Yorkshire Ripper and began questioning him about it. The next day when they returned to where he had been arrested, they found the tools of his murderous trade – the hammer, knife and rope. He had managed to dispose of them somehow during the arrest. Another knife was found hidden behind a toilet cistern at the police station where he had placed it the previous day.

When he was stripped they also found the uniform of his trade. Under his trousers he wore a v-neck sweater, the sleeves covering his legs and the space for the neck exposing his genitals. There was padding at his knees to make it easier for him when he knelt over his victims' bodies to mutilate them. Two days later he confessed to being the Ripper and detailed his many attacks. He would later say that God had told him to kill.

It was over for the women of Leeds, Bradford and Manchester, but, sentenced to life, it was just the beginning for Peter Sutcliffe.

DENNIS NILSEN

It was 8 February 1983 and there was a problem with the drains at 23 Cranley Gardens in the Muswell Hill area of north London. The tenants of the flats, into which the large house was divided, had been having trouble flushing their toilets for the last few days but when a plumber was called he was unable to resolve the situation. A drains specialist was summoned and he arrived that evening. He went straight to the manhole cover over the drains but when he lifted the cover he was almost overcome by the stench that emerged from within. He thought it smelled like decomposing flesh, a suspicion confirmed when he climbed down a few steps and saw what appeared to be piles of rotting white meat. Horrified, his first thought was that this was human flesh.

He returned next day with a supervisor but discovered that most of the material had been cleared from the drain. A tenant mentioned to them that she had heard constant footsteps during the night as a neighbour who lived above her had continually gone up and down the stairs. When they asked her who lived there, she told them he was a quiet thirty-seven-year-old Scottish civil servant by the name of Dennis Nilsen.

The police were called and a more thorough investigation of the drain was undertaken. They found a small six-inch square piece of flesh and some material that resembled the bones of human fingers.

That night when he came home from work at the Jobcentre in Kentish Town, a detective was waiting in the hall for Dennis Nilsen. He asked him if he knew anything about the drains and Nilsen replied by asking him upstairs to his flat. As they entered the flat, the stink of decomposing flesh was almost unbearable. The policeman asked him where the remainder of the body was, at which Nilsen calmly pointed to a cupboard and told him it was in there in a couple of plastic bags. Nilsen was arrested.

In the car taking him to the police station, the detective asked if the remains belonged to one body or two. Nilsen calmly replied that there had been fifteen or sixteen in total, three at Cranley Gardens and the remainder at the house he had lived in until the autumn of 1981, 195 Melrose Avenue in Cricklewood.

In the quiet suburbs of London, a mass murderer had quietly been indulging his obsession for killing young men and then keeping their bodies around for a while. Just for the company.

Dennis Nilsen was born at Fraserburgh on Scotland's northeast coast in 1945, his father a Norwegian soldier who was frequently drunk. His mother divorced the Norwegian when Dennis was seven and remarried. Dennis, however, formed a close attachment to his grandparents, especially his grandfather. But when his grandfather died, seven-year-old Dennis underwent a traumatic experience that possibly contributed to the direction his life would take. His mother took him in to the bedroom to see the corpse. He has, himself, admitted that it was at that point that his troubles began. According to Nilsen, he suffered a kind of emotional death with the loss of his grandfather. He became a desperate loner.

Having enlisted in the army in 1961 as a cook, in 1972 he changed uniform to that of a London policeman. He lasted only eleven months, however, and instead found work as a security guard. When he was arrested, he was employed by the Manpower Services Commission.

He had moved into the Melrose Avenue flat with David Gallichan who was ten years younger than Nilsen. They did not have a homosexual relationship, but when Gallichan tired of London and moved out, Nilsen was devastated. He felt betrayed and very lonely. It was a desperate loneliness would lead to the murders of fifteen young men.

On 30 December 1978, a year after the departure of Gallichan, Nilsen was drinking in the Cricklewood Arms where he befriended a young man. The two went back to Nilsen's flat and Nilsen and he climbed into bed together. The next morning, Nilsen realised with a sense of deep dread that the boy would be leaving soon after he woke up and after spending Christmas on his own, it would mean a solitary New Year for him. He strangled the boy with a tie but after a brief struggle he was still alive. Nilsen filled a bucket with water in the kitchen and, placing the semi-conscious boy on some chairs, dangled his head into the bucket and drowned him.

He carried the body into the bathroom and washed it, something that would become a signature of his killings. Returning to the bedroom, he put him to bed. Later, he went out to buy an electric carving knife and a large cooking pot but, unable initially to carve up the body which he actually found quite beautiful, he dressed it in clean clothes and underwear, laid it on the floor and went to sleep.

When he awoke, he ate some dinner and watched television. He thought about how he was going to dispose of the body and came up with an idea. He lifted the carpet, prized loose some floorboards and tried to slide it into the cavity under the floor. Rigor mortis had set in by this time, however, and he had to wait a while, with the body stood up against the wall, before it was again flexible enough to force into the space.

A week later, becoming curious, he lifted the floorboards, taking the decomposing body out again. It was a little dirty, so he gave it a wash, washing himself afterwards in the same water as he had used for the corpse. He became very aroused and masturbated over it. Then, he once again slid it into the space, nailed down the floorboards and tacked down the carpet. The body would remain there for seven months before Nilsen took it out into the garden and burned it, throwing pieces of rubber into the flames to conceal the rancid smell of burning flesh.

This young man, unknown at the time, turned out to be fourteen-year-old Stephen Dean Holmes who had been on his way home from a concert when he encountered Nilsen in the Cricklewood Arms. His identity would only become known in 2006, when in November of that year Nilsen confessed to his murder in an extraordinary letter sent from his prison cell to the *Evening Standard*.

When, in November 1979, Nilsen tried to strangle a young Chinese man in his flat, his intended victim escaped and actually reported the attack to the police. When officers arrived to question Nilsen about the incident, Nilsen told them that the Chinese man had been trying to 'rip him off'. They let it go and left him free to find other victims.

The next was twenty-three-year-old holidaying Canadian, Kenneth Ockendon who Nilsen also met in a pub, the Princess Louise in High Holborn, around 3 December 1979. They went back to the Melrose Avenue flat where they ate a meal. Later. as Ockendon listened to some music through headphones, Nilsen felt rejected and became angry. He strangled the Canadian with a flex and then sat down, put the headphones on and listened to music for hours. He washed the body before putting it to bed and lying beside it. In the morning, as he had to go to work, he stuffed the body in a cupboard.

The following day, he photographed it in various positions before climbing into bed and having sex with it. Like the last one, he slipped it under the floorboards but would, when he felt lonely, get it out and sit it beside him on the couch to watch television. Afterwards, he would clean it up, and put it back under the floorboards with a loving 'Goodnight'.

Martin Duffey, a sixteen-year-old trainee butcher, followed five months later, his corpse spending a fortnight in the cupboard before disappearing under the floorboards. Then Nilsen strangled a twenty-six-year-old Scottish man, Billy Sutherland, with his bare hands. Nilsen admits to remembering nothing of killing Sutherland, explaining that when he killed he entered a trance of some kind.

His next seven victims' names are all unknown. There was a Mexican or Filipino, a down-and-out, picked up in a doorway, and a further five who were killed between late 1980 and late 1981. They were mostly homeless or itinerant young men who were missed by no one. His eighth victim lay under his floorboards for almost a year, while the ninth and tenth victims were young Scottish men he picked up in Soho pubs. The eleventh victim was a young skinhead with a distinctive tattoo – a dotted line around his neck with the words 'Cut Here'.

The police were again informed of Dennis Nilsen's activity after a Scottish barman he picked up fought him off and fled the flat. Once again, however, they refused to get involved, putting it down to a homosexual contretemps.

Martyn Barlow was a twenty-four-year-old with learning difficulties whom Nilsen found outside his building. The man was in such a bad condition, very weak from epilepsy, that Nilsen took him to hospital. When he was released on 18 September 1981, he went back to Nilsen's flat to thank him for helping him. Nilsen responded by strangling him after they had eaten a meal together. He thought Barlow was a bit of a nuisance and he just fitted into the cabinet under the kitchen sink.

By now, of course, the question of hygiene was becoming pressing. There was a terrible smell at 125 Melrose Avenue which the neighbours began to complain about. Inside his flat, flies were hatching out in the putrefying flesh of the bodies he had stuffed into cupboards and under the floorboards. He began to carve the corpses up, undressing to his underpants to do so. The heads were boiled in his large cooking pot, stripping the flesh off the skull; he knew about butchery from his time as an army cook. He stashed body parts all over the garden.

In October 1981, having thoroughly cleaned out the old flat and removed the body parts from the garden and burned or buried them, he moved to Cranley Gardens and celebrated not long after, on 25 October, by taking a gay student, Paul Nobbs back to his new flat where they both got drunk and went to bed together. When Nobbs awoke the next morning, he discovered bruises around his neck. He was informed at University College Hospital that it appeared that someone had tried to strangle him. Had Nilsen exercised restraint for once in his life?

When John Howlett came back to his flat with him in March 1982, Nilsen, for once, wanted him to leave, not enjoying his company. He strangled him after an almighty struggle and having been forced to hit him on the skull to subdue him. He was then drowned and hidden in a cupboard. Later, he dissected the body, disposing of the flesh down the toilet and the bones in the dustbin.

Nilsen has no memory of killing Archibald Graham Allan. He does remember leaving him dead in the bath for three days, however, before carving up his body.

His final victim was twenty-year-old drug addict, Steven Sinclair, whom he met in Leicester Square. After strangling Sinclair with a piece of string, he bathed him as usual before carefully putting him to bed. He surrounded the bed with mirrors, took his clothes off and lay beside the dead body, looking at himself.

At his trial which began on 24 October 1983, Nilsen was charged with six murders and two attempted murders, although he had happily confessed to fifteen when arrested. At his trial he enjoyed being the focus of attention and although defence lawyers pleaded diminished responsibility and wanted the charges reduced to manslaughter, he was found guilty by a vote of ten against two. He was sentenced to life imprisonment.

In prison, Nilsen claims to have composed

more than eighty symphonic suites, painted and written poetry. He has also written an unpublished autobiography, *History of a Drowning Boy*.

JEFFREY DAHMER

It started innocuously enough, two police officers, Robert Rauth and Rolf Mueller, of the Milwaukee Police Department knocking on the door of Room 213, in a building called the Oxford Apartments. They had, a short while before, encountered a young black man who had come running towards them with a pair of handcuffs dangling from one wrist. Deliriously happy to have found them, he started ranting hysterically about a madman who had tried to kill him. Tracy Edwards gave them an address and they were now knocking on the door of that address.

The door swung open to reveal a tall, good-looking young white man with sandy hair. He calmly let them into the apartment, leading Rauth and Mueller to believe at first that there must have been some kind of mistake. But there was something about the place that made them uneasy. The smell. The smell of something rotting, like fish that had been left out too long.

The man gave his name as Jeffrey Dahmer and when they told him that Tracy Edwards was claiming that he had threatened him, he apologised. He had recently lost his job, he said, and was upset. He had also been drinking and things had just got a little out of hand.

The officers asked him for the key to the handcuffs but Dahmer suddenly became visibly nervous. He seemed to be playing for time, perhaps weighing up his options as he stalled them. Politely, but firmly, they insisted that he get the key. Suddenly, Dahmer became hysterical, screaming at them and looking as if he might get violent. The officers grabbed hold of him to subdue him and there was a struggle. He was no match for their training, however, and within seconds he was on the floor being cuffed and having his rights read to him. When they called in to run a check run on him, they quickly received the response that Jeffrey Dahmer had a conviction for sexual assault.

Now very interested in what had happened earlier, one of the officers asked Edwards to tell them what had happened. He explained that he had met Dahmer in a shopping mall about four hours ago and had come back to his apartment with him. As they sat on the sofa drinking beer and rum and coke, Edwards told them he began to feel drowsy. Dahmer tried to put his arms around him and he woke up and said he was going. He had already felt uneasy when he had seen male pin-ups on the apartment walls. He was more into women, he told the officers. Before he could get up, Dahmer had quickly put a handcuff on one of his wrists but he managed to fight off his attempt to put it around the other. He stopped struggling when Dahmer produced a large butcher's knife and held it against his chest. Seated like that, he spent the next hour watching the film The Exorcist. Seeming to get bored with the video, Dahmer calmly told Edwards that he was going to cut his heart out and eat it. But first he was going to strip him and take some pictures. As he stood up to get his camera, Edwards seized his chance, swinging a punch at Dahmer and kicking him. Dahmer was knocked off-balance and Edwards ran for the door. As Dahmer ran after him, offering to unlock the cuffs, Edwards did not hesitate. He flung open the door and threw himself down the stairs as fast as his feet could carry him.

While one officer remained with Dahmer, the other decided to have a look around the apartment. Going into the kitchen, he opened the refrigerator door and froze in horror. 'There's a fucking head in the refrigerator!' he screamed.

He was wrong. There were actually three heads, neatly wrapped in clear plastic bags. There were also plastic food bags containing human meat. In a cupboard in the bedroom there was a cooking pot containing decomposed hands and a penis. On the shelf above that there were two skulls. Male genitalia were preserved in formaldehyde and there was a variety of chemicals in containers – ethyl alcohol, chloroform and more formaldehyde.

In a filing cabinet they found three skulls as well as photographs that seemed to have been taken as victims died. There were also gruesome photographs of corpses. In one, a man's bloody head lay horrifically in a sink, while another depicted a victim cut neatly open from neck to groin. Others showed men in erotic and bondage poses. A kettle contained two more skulls and a blue plastic barrel hid three human torsos. There was a blood-stained electric saw – they had stumbled on a slaughterhouse.

Jeffrey Dahmer confessed to killing seventeen men, cooperating freely and seemingly glad to have a chance to get it all off his chest. He was yet another in a series of serial killers like John Wayne Gacy and Dean Corll, but the difference was that he did not just kill them; he also ate them. He was a cannibal and would most certainly have eaten Tracy Edwards' heart, as he had promised. The only foodstuffs in the apartment, apart from human meat, was a packet of crisps and a jar of mustard.

Jeffrey Dahmer was born in Milwaukee in 1960,

his family later moving to Akron, Ohio. The young Dahmer was a happy, normal little boy until at the age of six he underwent surgery for a double hernia. His father, Lionel, maintains that he was never the same little happy-go-lucky child again. He grew more introverted and strangely emotionless. It emerged at his trial that he took an unhealthy interest in dissecting animals, stripping the flesh off them and on one occasion putting a dead dog's head on the end of a stake. As he grew older, he became more tense and was inordinately shy. Soon, completely unmotivated, he started drinking.

He killed for the first time at the age of eighteen, his victim another eighteen-year-old, Steven Hicks, who had been hitch-hiking when Dahmer picked him up. He brought Hicks back to his house and killed him by smashing his skull with a weight because 'he didn't want him to leave.' He then masturbated over the body before burying it in the woods behind his house.

He did not kill for another nine years, enrolling in the army in the meantime and getting a posting to Germany. His drinking let him down, however, as it often did and he was discharged for drunkenness. Back in Milwaukee, he moved in with his grand-mother for a while, working at the Ambrosia Chocolate Company. He began to frequent the city's gay bars but as ever usually spent the evenings drinking alone. When he did actually get into a conversation with anyone, his drinking companion more often than not ended the evening in a drugged coma. He was experimenting with the chemicals that would later enable to do what he wanted to his victims in the privacy of his own apartment. One of his drinking companions wound up in hospital and the proprietor of the bar in which he had collapsed barred Dahmer.

He was also beginning to get into trouble with the police. He was picked up for a number of minor offences – drunkenness, disorderly conduct and so on. His father wrote later that his son had become 'a liar, an alcoholic, a thief, an exhibitionist, a molester of children. I could not imagine how he had become such a ruined soul...there was something missing in Jeff...We call it a "conscience"... that had either died or had never been alive in the first place.'

Then, on 8 September 1986, two twelve-year-old boys reported him to the police. He had exposed himself and masturbated in front of them. When he was picked up he claimed merely to have been urinating. He got a year's probation.

He stayed out of trouble during that year, but just a few days after the end of his probation, he murdered again. He picked up twenty-four-year-old Stephen

Tuomi in a gay bar. They went to a hotel and went to bed together. Dahmer claimed to remember nothing, apart from waking up in the morning to find Tuomi dead. He had been strangled.

He wondered how on earth he was going to get the body out of the hotel but quickly arrived at a solution. He slipped out and purchased a large suitcase into which he crammed the corpse. He took a taxi to his grandmother's house where he lived in a basement flat. He dismembered the body, stuffed the various bits into plastic rubbish sacks and put them in the dustbin. As he relaxed afterwards, he pondered on how much he had enjoyed it, how exciting it had been. He realised at that moment that the only way he could satisfy his sexual urges was to kill. From then on, that was his life's work.

Between 16 January 1988 and 19 July 1991, he would kill fifteen young men, more often than not black. They would be invited back to his apartment, given a drugged drink and either strangled or stabbed to death. The body would then be dismembered and bagged for eating, the parts that he did not need being left out with the rubbish. He told police that by eating the flesh of his victims, he believed they would come alive again in him. He experimented with seasoning and meat tenderisers. Eating human meat gave him an erection, he said, and his fridge contained strips of human flesh.

He further explained that before his victims died, he sometimes tried to perform a kind of lobotomy on them. After drugging them, he would drill a hole in their skulls and inject hydrochloric acid into their brains. He was trying to create a functioning zombie-like creature that he could exercise ultimate control over and control, after all, was really what it was all about. Needless to say, most died during this procedure, but he claimed that one survived for a few days.

By March 1988, he had claimed his third and fourth victims, fourteen year-old Native American, Jamie Doxtator and twenty-five-year-old Richard Guerro.

Soon the smells and the drinking became too much for his grandmother who threw him out. He moved to an apartment in Milwaukee, at 808 N. 24th Street and the day after he moved in, he picked up thirteen year-old Laotian boy called Sinthasomphone, who agreed to pose for photographs for fifty dollars. By grim coincidence, he was the older brother of a boy Dahmer would kill in 1991. But, he did not kill Sinthasomphone and, when the boy returned home, his parents realised he had been drugged. The cops picked Dahmer up on charges of sexual exploitation of a child and second-degree sexual assault. He pleaded guilty, claiming he thought the boy was older.

His arrest did not put him off his stride, however. As he awaited sentencing, on 25 March 1989 he killed Anthony Sears, a handsome black male model. Dahmer boiled the skull to remove the skin and painted it grey. He still had it when he was arrested.

In the style of the true psychopath, Dahmer put on a superb performance in court, charming and manipulative. The prosecution sought a prison sentence but he got off with five years' probation. He was also ordered to spend a year in the House of Correction under 'work release', which meant he went to work during the day and returned to jail at night. In spite of a letter from Dahmer's father, pleading with the judge not to release him without treatment, he was released after just ten months and went to live again with his grandmother, before moving into his rooms in the Oxford apartments in May 1990.

Exactly a year later, a naked fourteen-year-old Laotian boy, Konerak Sinthasomphone, was found wandering on the streets of the Milwaukee neighbourhood in which Dahmer's flat was located. He talked to a couple of women, but was largely incoherent, having been given a drugged drink by

Dahmer. The police were called and took the boy back to Dahmer's flat to investigate. Dahmer told them, however, that Konerak was his nineteen-year-old boyfriend and that there had been a drunken row. The police thought it was probably no more than a domestic argument and handed the dazed boy over to Dahmer, while at the same time noting a strange smell in the apartment. A few hours later, Sinthasomphone became Jeffrey Dahmer's thirteenth victim.

He was indicted on seventeen charges of murder, later reduced to fifteen and against the advice of his attorney, pleaded guilty, claiming insanity. The argument was that no sane person could have done what he did. The prosecution, on the other hand, pursued the line that he was a murderous psychopath, a cold-blooded killer whose murders were carefully planned and premeditated.

The trial, starting with jury selection on 29 January 1992, was inevitably a circus. There was heavy security, and an eight-foot barrier of steel and bullet-proof glass was erected around the area where Dahmer would sit, protecting him from angry members of the Milwaukee public.

It took the jury five hours to decide that Jeffrey Dahmer should go to prison and not to a psychiatric hospital. He was found guilty on all fifteen charges.

On the day of his sentencing, he read out a statement from the dock that could have been taken as an apology of sorts for the horror he had created.

Your Honor, it is now over. This has never been a case of trying to get free. I didn't ever want freedom. Frankly, I wanted death for myself. This was a case to tell the world that I did what I did, but not for reasons of hate. I hated no one. I knew I was sick or evil or both. Now I believe I was sick. The doctors have told me about my sickness, and now I have some peace. I know how much harm I have caused…Thank God there will be no more harm that I can do. I believe that only the Lord Jesus Christ can save me from my sins… I ask for no consideration.

They obliged. He was locked up for a total of 957 years.

He would only serve two of those years, however. Sent to Columbia Correctional Institute in Portage, Wisconsin, he was segregated from the rest of the prisoners. This failed to prevent him being attacked by a razor-wielding Cuban inmate in the prison chapel, however. Dahmer behaved himself, becoming a born-again Christian and was gradually being integrated into the prison population.

On 28 November 1994, he was on a work detail with two other men, both highly dangerous. Jesse Anderson was a white man who had murdered his wife and blamed it on a black man. Christopher Scarver was a black schizophrenic murderer who suffered from delusions that he was God.

That morning, the three men were left alone to get on with their work. When the guard returned, he found Anderson dead, in a pool of blood. Beside him lay Jeffrey Dahmer, his skull smashed in with a broom handle. He died later in the ambulance taking him to hospital. He was thirty-four years old.

ROSEMARY WEST

Since the death of Moors Murderer, Myra Hindley, in 2002, the dubious honour of being the most hated woman in Britain has probably passed to Rosemary West who, with her notorious husband Fred, was convicted of murdering ten young women and girls, one of them her own daughter Heather, in pursuit of deviant sex.

Rosemary Letts was born in November 1953 in Devon to Bill and Daisy Letts. Daisy suffered from depression while Bill was a schizophrenic who demanded unwavering obedience from his wife and children, a control freak who took pleasure in beating them with a piece of wood or a leather belt for the slightest infraction. If Daisy tried to intervene, the beating would be transferred to her. If the kids stayed in bed too long, he would chuck a bucket of freezing cold water over them; any task they were given to do was inspected meticulously afterwards and if they had failed to meet his unreasonably high standards, they would have to do it all over again; they were not allowed to speak and play was forbidden. Money was tight too when Rose was growing up. Her father's temper and his psychotic episodes led to difficulties in holding onto jobs and he drifted perpetually from one menial job to another.

In 1953, Daisy's health inevitably collapsed under the strains of her depression, caring for her three daughters and one son, and the issues with her brutally violent husband. She went into hospital where she was treated with electroshock therapy, a controversial treatment that involves delivering electric currents into the brain in order to induce seizures in anaesthetised patients. At the time she was pregnant with Rosemary and it is unknown whether her unborn baby suffered some kind of trauma as a result. There was little doubt that she was different to Daisy and Bill's other children. As a baby, she developed the habit of rocking violently in her pram and as she got older would rock her head sometimes for hours. The family began to believe she was 'a bit slow' and dubbed her 'Dozy Rosie'. However, she became the favourite of her father's children, always doing his bidding and helping him. She was the only member of the family not to be regularly beaten.

At school, her size – she was grossly overweight – made her the butt of cruel jokes and she developed into an aggressive loner who lashed out at anyone who tried to tease her. Her reputation at school was not helped by the fact that academically she was a dead loss.

In the area of sex, however, her education was, if anything, ahead of others of her age. She had no qualms about provocatively walking around naked at home after having a bath and is said to have sexually molested her younger brother at a young age. She also began having sex with the older men of the village, her father having forbidden her from having a boyfriend. On one occasion, she claims to have been raped by an older man.

In 1969, Daisy Letts finally walked out on Bill, taking only Rose with her. They moved in with her daughter Glenys and her husband and, free of her father's rigid constraints, Rose started going out at night. Surprisingly, however, she moved back in with her father a few months later.

Around this time, she met Fred West.

She was waiting for a bus at Cheltenham bus station when a scruffy, dirty man with frizzy hair and simian features approached her. At first she was repulsed but Fred was a charmer and before long she had agreed to have a drink with him. At first, she resisted his advances, but one day she succumbed in the caravan where he lived with his two children, Anne-Marie and Charmaine. Soon she was pregnant. Her father was furious and reported West to Social Services. When nothing changed he turned up outside West's caravan, threatening him. There was a fight and when Fred won, Rose was impressed. She began to realise that Fred West could provide her with the means of escaping from the domineering and violent man who had controlled her life. The trouble was, she just moved on to a man who was exactly the same way.

Fred was a petty crook and sexual predator who had banged his head a couple of times when he was younger and had been left with a volatile temper and violent mood swings as a result. He also had one leg shorter than the other, a consequence of a motorbike accident. At the age of twenty, he got a thirteen-year-old girl pregnant but did not seem to accept that there was anything wrong with that. 'Doesn't everyone do it?' he asked.

He was not interested in 'normal' sex. His turn-ons involved bondage, sodomy and oral sex. When his partner of the time was unwilling to participate, he went elsewhere for it.

When Fred was sent to prison for theft and for non-payment of outstanding fines, Rose moved into the caravan to care for the two children, one of whom was not actually his, but whose mother had once lived with him. In 1970, with Fred still in jail, Heather was born. Rose, still only sixteen, was now caring for three young children, and resented the fact that two of them were not her own.

In summer 1971, there were only two after Charmaine disappeared, most probably murdered by Rose in a fit of temper. Her temper has been spoken of by various people who know her; Anne-Marie said that she became 'a kind of maniac' when angry. She explained Charmaine's disappearance by telling Anne-Marie that the girl's mother, from whom Fred had been estranged for a couple of years, had come to collect her.

When Fred came out of prison, he and Rose moved into a house at 25 Midland Road in Gloucester. Charmaine moved in with them – they put her body, minus fingers and toes, Fred's trademark – under the kitchen floor. It would remain there until it was dug up by police in 1994.

In the Midland Road house, Rose West launched a prostitution business, entertaining many of the West Indians who had settled in Gloucester. Fred had his fun, too, watching her have sex with strangers through a peephole in the wall, mixing business and pleasure, so to speak.

When Charmaine's mother Rena suddenly turned up, looking for her daughter, Fred decided that she would have to die. One night, he plied her with alcohol and strangled her. She was cut up and her body, minus fingers and toes, was buried in the countryside.

Meanwhile, Rose was accompanying Fred on expeditions to find girls to rape. When the girls saw another woman in the car, they relaxed. Fred would then threaten them with worse if they told anyone about what he had done.

Fred and Rose married in 1972 and five months later, another daughter, Mae was born. However, the Midland Road house was by this time becoming too small for their growing family and Rose's burgeoning prostitution business. They moved into what would become one of the most notorious addresses in British criminal history – 25 Cromwell Road, Gloucester. It was a much larger house, on three levels with a basement that offered huge potential for Fred West. Often in those days, basements were converted into rooms for entertainment. Fred was no different. He converted it into a room for entertainment. Unfortunately, Fred West's idea of entertainment involved torture and depraved sex.

The first visitor to the basement was Fred's own daughter, eight-year-old Anne-Marie. They explained that they were going to demonstrate to her how she could please her husband when she was older. They stripped her, tied her hands behind her back and Rose held her down while her father raped her. It would not be the last time, but she was threatened with a beating if she told anyone.

They took on a nanny, seventeen-year-old Caroline Owens who lived with them and during her time there rejected advances by both Fred and bisexual Rose. When she told them she was leaving, they stripped her, raped her and threatened to kill her if she whispered a word of it to anyone. It was her mother who found out what had happened, noticing bruising on her daughter's body. She squeezed the truth out of her and went to the police. When the case came to court, Fred's defence was that she had agreed to have sex with him. The magistrate believed him and he got away with a fine.

The next nanny, Lynda Gough did not survive for long. She was dismembered and put under the floor of the garage. No one looked for her.

The year that Fred and Rose's son Stephen was born, 1973, they killed fifteen-year-old schoolgirl, Carol Ann Cooper, but only after torturing and raping her for a week in the basement. Twenty-one-year-old student Lucy Partington also spent a week in the hellish basement after climbing into Fred's car in December, the same year. She ended up under the house. Fred went to a hospital in the early hours of 3 January 1974 with a serious laceration that required stitches. When Lucy Partington was dug up in 1994, police found a knife matching his cut beside her body. It is surmised that he sustained the injury while dismembering her body.

Fred started work on adding some more space to the house, enlarging the basement and joining the garage onto the house. It was all done, unsurprisingly, given what was buried there, under cover of darkness. The basement had to be expanded to accommodate three more bodies – fifteen-year-old Shirley Hubbard, nineteen-year-old Juanita Mott and twenty-one-year-old Swiss hitch-hiker, Therese Siegenthaler. Horrifically, some of these girls would have seen other victims still alive when they were brought back to 25 Cromwell Road. When Shirley Hubbard's remains were found, her head was entirely wrapped in tape with only a three-inch rubber tube inserted in her mouth to enable her to breathe. Anne-Marie was still being abused, but now she was not only being raped by her father; he was bringing home other men to rape her too.

Rose's temper was still there, and her jealousy knew no bounds where Fred was concerned. When a lodger, a prostitute by the name of Shirley Robinson, got pregnant by Fred, Rose insisted she had to go. She was killed in July 1977. That December, Rose gave birth to a baby, Tara, who was not Fred's, but the daughter of one of her West Indian clients. Louise came along in November 1978; this baby was Fred's.

As soon as Anne-Marie grew old enough to look after herself, she immediately moved out. But it was no problem to Fred. He turned his incestuous urges onto his daughters Heather and Mae. Meanwhile, Barry was born in 1980, and Rosemary Junior – again not Fred's – in 1982.

The killing continued. A seventeen-year-old Swansea girl, Alison Chambers, was abducted in summer 1979. Space being short under the house, she was buried in the back garden. When their daughter Heather made the fatal mistake of hinting to a friend about what was going on, Fred heard about it and she was killed and buried. He later claimed he had not intended to kill her, that she had been sneering at him and he wanted to wipe the smirk off her face. Rosemary told an inquiring neighbour the following day that she and Heather had had a 'hell of a row' leading some to believe that Rosemary may have initiated her death.

It ended with a knock at the door on 24 February 1994. Sullen, vastly overweight Rosemary West opened it to a couple of policemen who had come with a warrant to dig up the back garden as part of the search for Heather West. A girl they had abducted but not killed had told a girlfriend what had happened to her and the friend had gone to the police. The West children were taken into care as a massive investigation began. When one of the children joked that Heather was under the patio, the police decided to have a look.

In December 1994, Fred was charged with eleven murders and Rose with ten. By this time her ardour had cooled and she visibly pulled away from him when he tried to comfort her in court.

Fred hanged himself using strips of bed sheet on New Year's Day 1995 and Rose was left to face the music, being found guilty of ten murders and sentenced to life imprisonment.

After she had rejected him in court, he wrote to her, 'We will always be in love…You will always be Mrs West, all over the world. That is important to me and you.' He never got a reply.

IAN HUNTLEY

It is a beautiful but relatively ordinary photograph. Two little girls posing in Manchester United football shirts, smiling at the camera just before sitting down to enjoy food cooked on a barbecue by one of their dads, on a warm August Sunday in 2002. When they finished eating, they asked if they could go to a nearby sports centre to buy some sweets. Their parents said okay and they set out. Holly Wells and Jessica Chapman, both aged ten, were never seen alive again.

The party in the Wells's garden continued until someone wondered where the girls were. It was getting late and their parents began to worry. They went out and looked around the neighbourhood, thinking that perhaps they had met some friends and had forgotten the time, as kids often do. But there was still no sign of them. Eventually, they called the police and reported the girls missing.

By the time a police search was launched towards midnight, the girls' parents were understandably frantic. They had been ringing the mobile phone that Jessica carried everywhere with her, but there was no reply. The search that night revealed nothing and as more resources were poured into the small Cambridgeshire town of Soham, bolstered by hundreds of volunteers, the days turned into weeks. That photograph was distributed widely and appeals for information were made by both girls' parents. David Beckham, who the girls worshipped and whose name had been on the back of their football shirts that afternoon, made a televised appeal, but still they did not turn up. It was as if they had vanished from the face of the planet.

Police had pieced together the journey the girls had taken that Sunday by finding witnesses who had seen them. Twenty-nine-year-old Ian Huntley, who worked as caretaker of Soham Village College, told police officers that he had seen Holly and Jessica stroll past the house he shared with his girlfriend, twenty-nine-year-old Maxine Carr, the girls' teacher at the local primary school. He would have been one of the last people to see them before they vanished and as such, he immediately became a suspect. In order to eliminate him from their enquiries, investigators searched both his house and the college where he worked. Nothing was found, however, to connect him with the girls or their disappearance. Nonetheless, there were still those who found his behaviour a little odd, sensing that he was somehow a little too emotionally involved. He asked too many questions and at one point gave an interview to a television news reporter.

Uneasy about him, investigators decided to search his house and workplace again and at last came up with something. In a building at Soham Village College the burned remnants of the football shirts Jessica and Holly had been wearing were discovered, as well as their shoes. On the bin bag in which they were found were Ian Huntley's fingerprints. Huntley and Maxine Carr were arrested immediately on suspicion of murder.

Finally, on 17 August, thirteen days after the barbecue, a game warden found the little girls' partially burned bodies in a trench six feet deep close to the RAF Lakenheath airbase in Suffolk. They had probably died of asphyxiation.

The people of Britain were stunned. Having followed every minute detail of the investigation, people were horrified when their faint hopes that Holly and Jessica would be found alive were shattered. The nation went into mourning.

Meanwhile, evidence implicating Ian Huntley was piling up. Huntley knew the area where the girls were found. He had often gone plane-spotting there. When forensic scientists searched his car, they found fibres that matched what the girls had been wearing that day. Strands of Huntley's hair as well as fibres from his clothes, carpets and car were found on the football shirts. Finally, the last signal from Jessica's mobile phone was traced to an area adjacent to Huntley's home.

On 20 August, Ian Huntley was charged with the murders of Holly Wells and Jessica Chapman. Maxine Carr, meanwhile, was arrested for assisting an offender. Having provided him with an alibi, telling police that he had been alone with her when the girls disappeared, she was also charged with conspiring to pervert the course of justice. She had actually been visiting her mother in Grimsby when she said she had been with him.

Huntley and Carr maintained that they were innocent during those first days but they were remanded in custody until their trial, which began on 3 November 2003 at the Old Bailey in London.

The prosecution case rested on a huge amount of evidence that had been collected against Huntley. Adding to the evidence was the fact that he had scrubbed clean his red Ford Fiesta the day after the girls disappeared. Even more suspicious was the fact that he had replaced the lining of the car's boot with a piece of carpet. A throw that had covered the back seat had been disposed of. Furthermore, he replaced all four of the vehicle's tyres, even though their treads were still legal. He was reported to have offered the man who changed the tyres £10 to write down a fake registration number. His cover-up was to no avail, however. There were copious amounts of material on and underneath the Fiesta that could only have come from the area where Holly and Jessica's bodies were dumped.

Three weeks after the start of the trial, Huntley suddenly confessed. A statement by him was read out to the court in which he described how on that Sunday the girls had stopped at his house to talk to their teacher Maxine Carr. While they were there, Holly had a nosebleed. He led the girls to the bathroom, he said, to tend to the nosebleed and claimed that while reaching for some toilet paper, knocked Holly backwards into the bathtub which was half-filled with water. At this point, he said, Jessica began to scream and when he placed a hand over her mouth to stop her, he accidentally pressed too hard and suffocated her. Looking round at Holly in the bath, he realised that she was also dead. He panicked and decided to get rid of their bodies. He wrapped them up, put them in the boot of his car and drove to Lakenheath, cutting off their clothes, pouring petrol over them and setting fire to them before driving back to Soham.

Maxine Carr added her confession a few days later. She had lied about being with Huntley that day to protect him, not believing that he had carried out the murders. She knew that Huntley had a rape allegation against him from 1998, which had been dropped when police established that he was not with the young woman concerned at the time of the assault.

Huntley persisted in his claims that the girls' deaths were accidental and establishing this fact became the basis of the defence case for the remainder of the trial. It was a tall order.

Their first witness was Ian Huntley himself and the prosecution tore into him, accusing him of being a liar and suggesting that rather than trying to help with a nosebleed, it had been his intention to kill the two little girls from the moment he opened the door to them. When asked why he made no effort to resuscitate them or call for help, he told the court that he panicked. It was suggested that Huntley's motivation for killing the girls was sexual, although no evidence of sexual molestation could be proved due to the advanced state of decomposition of the girls' bodies when found.

The judge sent the jury out on 12 December, advising them to consider their verdict very carefully. Five days later they returned a verdict of guilty against Maxine Carr for conspiring to pervert the course of justice. She was sentenced to three years and six months in prison.

Ian Huntley was found guilty of murdering Holly Wells and Jessica Chapman and was given a life sentence for each murder.

It emerged afterwards that Ian Huntley had previously been in trouble for sexual offences. Between 1995 and 1999 he was accused four times of having sex with girls who were aged between thirteen and fifteen. There had also been three allegations of rape and one of indecent assault against a victim of eleven. He had never been convicted, however, because either the police failed to find sufficient evidence of his guilt or the victims refused to press charges.

Astonishingly, in spite of these incidents, he had still managed to get a job as a school caretaker. There was horror and anger at the way the system had failed. It also became clear that communication between the various offices handling the case was poor and some of the evidence regarding Huntley's previous sex accusations had been deleted during a process to clean out archives. Had everything been brought together, an escalation in Huntley's offending would have been noticed and he might have been stopped. It was discovered also that his name and date of birth had been entered incorrectly into the national crime database when he was being checked for his job at Soham. Thus, his record did not appear. If it had been done correctly, he would not have obtained the job at Soham and Holly and Jessica would not have died that day.

Maxine Carr was released from prison after serving twenty-one months. She was provided with a secret new identity in order to protect her from attacks by the public.

In September 2005, Huntley was scalded by boiling water thrown at him by another inmate, quadruple murderer, Mark Hobson. Then on 5 September 2006, he was found unconscious in his cell at Wakefield Prison, having taken an overdose. He had previously overdosed at Woodhill Prison in 2003 before his trial. He survived but as his cell was searched afterwards, a tape was found on which it is believed he had made a full confession. He had made the tape in exchange for the drugs with which he tried to kill himself and the prisoner who provided the drugs was planning to sell the tape to the media on his release. On 28 January 2008, Huntley was moved to Frankland Prison in County Durham, where in March 2010, he was attacked again by a fellow inmate, and although reports stated that his throat had been slashed, he was back in prison the next day.

STEVE WRIGHT

They called him the Suffolk Strangler or the Ipswich Ripper and for six terrifying weeks in late 2006, he went on a murderous rampage in the quiet East Anglian town of Ipswich, killing five prostitutes.

Wright's childhood had been fairly exotic. Born in 1958, he lived as a child in both Malta and Singapore where his father, a military policeman, was posted. However, while he was still young, his parents divorced and each remarried. Wright moved in with his father and his new wife. After he left school in 1974, aged sixteen, he became a chef on ferries sailing out of Felixstowe in Suffolk. Five years later he married and in 1983, his son Michael was born. However, he and his wife divorced in 1987 after which he worked in a succession of jobs including as a steward on the cruise-liner, the *QE2*, a lorry driver and a barman. At the time of the murders, he was working as a forklift truck driver.

He married again in 1992, a marriage that lasted less than a year and then had a child with a different woman later that year, while he was running a pub in south London. He was sacked from this job because of his gambling and excessive drinking. He also stole £80 from the till and it is known that he had such substantial debts around this time that he was declared bankrupt.

He twice tried to commit suicide, firstly by carbon monoxide poisoning and in 2002 he survived a deliberate overdose of pills.

In 2001, Wright started a relationship with Pamela Wright in Felixstowe and the couple moved to Ipswich in 2004. When Pamela started working nights, Wright became frustrated by their lack of sex. He had used the services of prostitutes since his days at sea, and as he became increasingly frustrated, he began to frequent the prostitutes of Ipswich's red-light district, in the middle of which he and Pamela conveniently rented a flat.

The first girl to be reported missing was nineteen-year-old Tania Nichol, an Ipswich girl who had disappeared on 30 October 2006. Forty-eight hours after she had last been seen, her mother called the police. On 8 December, her body was found by police frogmen in a river near Copdock Mill. She had not been sexually assaulted, but because of her lengthy submersion in the river it was difficult to establish the cause of death. Nichol had been using heroin since the age of sixteen when she left home to live in a hostel and like many of the 'working girls' in the area, she worked as a prostitute to fund her drug habit. When her habit had led to her being thrown out of her job in one of the town's massage parlours, she had been forced to take to the streets. Her mother had no idea she was a prostitute, believing her to be working as a barmaid or in a hairdressers.

Twenty-five-year-old Gemma Adams disappeared in West End Road in Ipswich just after midnight on 15 November, after last being seen outside a BMW dealership. Her partner reported her missing later that day. Gemma, a heroin addict since her teenage years, was found on 2 December in a river at Hintlesham, naked, but not sexually assaulted. She had once worked at an insurance company but had lost the job because of her drug habit.

Twenty-nine-year-old mother of one, Annette Nicholls was last seen in Ipswich on 8 December. Anyone connected with the world of prostitution was beginning to become edgy and her family, concerned at her absence, called in the police. She was found on 12 December, near the village of Levington. She was naked, like the others but also like them had not been sexually assaulted. There was one important difference, however, in that her body was laid out in the shape of a cross. Police were unsure how she died but believed that her breathing had somehow been hampered. An addict since about 2000, her son, Farron, was looked after by her mother.

Anneli Alderton was a twenty-four-year-old drug addict from Colchester in Essex, who was in the early stages of pregnancy. She was last seen on 3 December on the 5.53 p.m. train from Harwich to Manningtree, where she got off the train at 6.15 p.m. that evening to catch another train for Ipswich. Seven days later her asphyxiated naked body was found in woodland in front of Amberfield School near the village of Nacton, just outside Ipswich. She was laid out, like Annette Nicholls in a cruciform position.

The stories of the Suffolk prostitute murders were now headline news in the media. A local Ipswich business offered a reward of £25,000 for information leading to the arrest of the killer, a sum it later increased to £50,000. The Sunday newspaper, the *News of the World* offered £250,000 for information.

The strangler's fifth and last victim was a twenty-four-year-old mother of three, Paula Clennell, who disappeared on 10 December and was found on the same day as Annette Nicolls, also close to the village of Levington, southeast of Ipswich. Again naked but not sexually assaulted, she had been strangled. Also a drug addict, Clennell had moved to Ipswich from Northumberland ten years previously following the break-up of her parents' marriage. Ironically, she gave an interview about the disappearances and murders to *Anglia Television News* just days prior to her own death. She confirmed that like all the girls she was wary of climbing into strange cars, but she did it simply because she needed the money.

The police enquiry made little headway even though a huge task force, called Operation Sumac, had been assembled to investigate. Officers from neighbouring constabularies were drafted in and two hundred and fifty of the two hundred and seventy scientists employed at the Forensic Science Service in Huntingdon, Cambridgeshire worked full-time on the case, undertaking painstaking analysis of fibres, clothing and anything else that was found at the scenes of the murders. It was soon clear that the women had been killed elsewhere before being dumped in the locations where their bodies were found.

The DNA analyses provided rich rewards. By 17 December, the scientists had constructed a good DNA profile of the person they believed could be the murderer. Just before 8 p.m., it was sent to the national DNA database in the Midlands and thirty minutes later, a police officer waiting by a computer at Suffolk police headquarters received the information they had been waiting for. The DNA had matched a name on the database – Steven Gerald James Wright. The DNA obtained on his conviction five years earlier for stealing £80 from the pub in which he worked at the time would send him to jail for the rest of his life.

A surveillance operation was set up and Wright, already questioned twice during door-to-door enquiries, was questioned for a third time.

Nonetheless, three men were arrested in connection with the murders. The first, released without charge, was arrested in Felixstowe at 7.20 a.m. in the morning of 18 December. A day later, however, a supermarket worker, Thomas Stephens, was questioned, but again was released without charge. Finally, on 19 December, Steve Wright was arrested. His car and his clothes provided a substantial amount of incriminating material, including small amounts of his victims' blood. Two days later, he was charged with all five murders, appearing before magistrates in Ipswich on 22 December and being remanded in custody. On 1 May, he formally entered a plea of not-guilty and a trial date was set for 14 January 2008.

It was an unusual media frenzy for a British court. A special 'media pen' was created at the court while

Sky News went one better by erecting a shelter on the roof of a nearby building.

The prosecution case opened with pictures of two of the victims that had been deliberately posed and information that DNA linked Steve Wright to three of the victims – two had been washed clear of DNA evidence as they had been immersed in water. There was also fibre evidence that connected him to them. The defence, however, argued that as a frequenter of prostitutes, there was every likelihood that there would be links between him and some of the women. They claimed he had had sex with all of the victims, apart from Tania Nicholls whom he had picked up in his car with the intention of having sex with her but had changed his mind and deposited her back in the red-light area. But, police had him on record as having been stopped one night driving in the red-light district. He had claimed to have been unaware that he was in the red-light district – even though he lived in the middle of it. He claimed he had been unable to sleep and was just driving around.

It took the jury eight hours to find Wright guilty on all five charges of murder on 21 February 2008. He was sentenced to life imprisonment, with the trial judge, Justice Gross, saying that because of the element of premeditation and planning, in his case life should mean life.

JOSEF FRITZL

His lawyer tried to blame it all on the effects of a brutal childhood, and there is no doubt that the kind of upbringing endured by Josef Fritzl would have taken its toll on anyone, but would probably not have turned everyone into a criminal responsible for murder, incest, enslavement, rape and the deprivation of his daughter's liberty for twenty-four years, not to mention the incarceration of the seven children she gave birth to during those years of rape and astonishing brutality.

Fritzl was born in the Austrian town of Amstetten in 1935, three years before the *Anschluss*, the absorption of Austria into the Third Reich. After his father abandoned the family, his mother brought her son up alone. She was a strict disciplinarian, however, and the young Josef Fritzl often bore the bruises he received in vicious beatings by her. Of course, this brutality was inflicted against the even greater social brutality of the totalitarian and aggressively militaristic Nazi regime which had supplanted the authoritarianism of the previous Austro-Hungarian empire.

After the war, Josef Fritzl was an ordinary man. In fact, he was always an ordinary man – well turned out and the driver of a well-maintained Mercedes. His finances were always well organised and his home and other properties he owned were always in good order.

No one knew very much about him, however, not even the people with whom he worked. If only they had known what was really going on behind that veneer of ordinariness.

The gloss of respectability was smashed wide open in 1967 when, aged thirty-two, he was convicted of rape in Linz and sentenced to a year and a half in prison. He was also suspected of assault in two other cases in the area at that time. It has been reported that he also liked to indecently expose himself. Another rumour has it that he raped his wife's sister. These crimes and rumours would shamefully be ignored by the authorities later, allowing Fritzl to continue with his monstrous life of deceit and horror.

None of his various criminal acts seem to have concerned his wife, Rosemarie whom he married when he was twenty-one and she was just seventeen. She was a kitchen helper and during their marriage he would dominate her as he would his daughter and grandchildren later. She deferred to her husband, submissive to a fault, and does not seem to have been bothered when he went to prison in 1967 or when he would go on sex tourism holidays in Thailand. She asked no questions, especially when he began to spend a considerable amount of time in their basement, working, as he told her, on mechanical drawings.

He had been making his perverted plans for some time. His daughter Elizabeth was born in 1966 and he began sexually abusing her in 1977, when she was eleven years old. A year later, he began building a subterranean extension to the modest Fritzl house in Amstatten. The cellar he was building, however, far exceeded the size for which he had obtained planning permission. He cleverly added walls that would conceal a part of the structure. That part – fifteen-feet square, but only five-and-a-half-feet high – was reserved for his daughter.

Finally, on 28 August 1984, he put his plan into operation and began Elizabeth Fritzl's twenty-four-year nightmare. He ordered the eighteen-year-old girl to help him carry a new door down to the basement. She was used to obeying and immediately did as he was asked. She had already tried to escape him, but she had been picked up by police in Vienna after being on the run for a month. He feared she would eventually get away and he was going to prevent that happening. As she helped put the heavy door in place downstairs, little did she know she was helping him install the door to her own prison cell and that she would not see daylight again for twenty-four years. He sedated her with ether and locked the door with her on the other side.

Rosemarie Fritzl reported her daughter's disappearance to the police a day after the door in the basement closed behind her, but a month later, Josef Fritzl gave them a letter which he had forced Elizabeth to write. Postmarked Braunau, it said that she was staying with a friend and no longer wanted to live with her family. It warned them not to instigate a search for her or she would leave the country. Fritzl suggested that she had probably joined a religious sect and the police took his word for it. They never looked for her.

From that time on, letters would occasionally arrive at the Fritzl house from Elizabeth. One warned, 'Do not search for me; it would be pointless and would only increase my and my children's suffering. Too many children and an education are not wanted there.'

She lived alone in this tiny world for five years. There were no windows, no books and no fresh air. Just a bed on which her father raped her time and time again. Then, her first baby, Kerstin, was born in 1988. Stefan followed in 1990 and two years later,

Lisa. Fritzl smuggled Lisa out of the basement when she was still very young, pretending to anyone who asked, that she was Elizabeth's baby and that she had abandoned her. No one though to check on the truth of this story. The Fritzls adopted Lisa and she lived upstairs as their own daughter. It is thought that Fritzl would take certain children upstairs because he was worried their crying would be heard from above ground.

In the next twelve years, officials from the childcare section of the local social services department visited the Fritzl house at least twenty-one times but astonishingly, no one thought to follow up on any of the things they were told. Fritzl was often not there when he should have been, which should have aroused suspicion, but one would have thought his criminal record alone would have made them curious. They simply thought that he was a good, solid family man who deserved praise for taking in his wayward daughter's children.

His tenents noticed nothing untoward either, although they were warned that if they ever went anywhere near the cellar they would be evicted immediately. As a friend later said, no one stopped to wonder why he was so afraid of people going down there.

They followed the usual formula with Monika

who was born in 1994, taking her upstairs and adopting her. Three days after the birth of twins in 1996, one of them, Michael died, Fritzl callously disposing of his body in the household furnace. The other twin, Alexander moved upstairs when he was fifteen months old to add to the growing Fritzl family, or at least the one that everyone knew about. In 2002, Elizabeth gave birth to Felix who remained downstairs with his mother and sister, Kerstin, who had not seen daylight for the entire fourteen years of her life. Elizabeth Fritzl was now thirty-six years old and had spent half her life underground, a prisoner of the monster who was her father.

The routine was mundane. He spent hours down there, sometimes he stayed the night, playing with the children and talking to Elizabeth, when he was not raping her. The remainder of his time was spent buying and selling property and making a fool of Rosemarie in public. He once told someone when she was with him, 'We don't have sex any more; she's too fat.'

It was a secure dungeon. He was a good electrician and engineer and he had installed locks on the doors that could only be opened with the right access code. There was also a fail-safe mechanism that meant if he died or could not get to them, the doors would automatically open after a specified period of time.

He added some home comforts over time. She had an old television, a video recorder, hotplates to cook on and a fridge. It was a charmless, low-ceilinged, oppressive place in which to live and it is impossible to imagine what Kerstin, incarcerated there for her entire life, made of the bustling world she saw on television. It must have seemed like a fantasy world to her.

It appears that towards Christmas 2008, Fritzl was beginning to feel exhausted by the constant effort involved in keeping up his dreadful pretence. His time was filled with burning rubbish from the basement and shopping surreptitiously in order to provide for their daily needs. Furthermore, Elizabeth was getting older; she was forty-one by this time and he was becoming less attracted to her as her youth began to fade. He devised a plan whereby she would be released by the cult that had kept her prisoner for so long and return to the house.

The plan was rendered unfeasible, however, by the deteriorating health of Kerstin who was becoming increasingly ill and for whom he could not obtain the right medicines. Elizabeth begged him to let her go to hospital but, of course, it was impossible. There would be questions he would not be able to answer. When the girl fell unconscious in April 2008, however, he had no option but to take her to hospital. Hospital staff were immediately suspicious and the police were alerted. Within a few days, Elizabeth stepped through the prison door she had herself helped to install twenty-four years previously.

The children, eighteen-year-old Stefan, and five-year-old Felix were amazed by the new world they stepped into. They gazed in awe at the moon, screamed with excitement when they heard a police siren and flinched every time a car went past. The next day, there were extraordinary scenes as the downstairs family met the upstairs family for the first time. Elizabeth was reunited with her children, Lisa, Monika and Alex all of whom she had not seen since they were babies. She also fell into the arms of her mother. 'I'm so sorry,' Rosemarie said. 'I had no idea.'

However, the children were seriously damaged by their experiences. Stefan and Alex mainly communicated to each other through growls and other sounds while Felix seemed terrified of everything, never letting go of his mother.

Rosemarie moved into a psychiatric hospital with Elizabeth and her children as the authorities tried to socialise them and familiarise them with the world they had not known all those years. They later moved into an apartment, but after a time Elizabeth evicted Rosemarie. Some suggest she had suspicions that her mother had known all along what was going on beneath her feet.

Fritzl claimed that he did it to protect his daughter but she had been nothing more than a normal teenager who was behaving the way teenagers across the world behave. She had been sneaking out of the house to sit in bars with her friends but given what her father got up to when she was at home, she can hardly be blamed for that. At the time of her initial incarceration she was waiting to hear about a waitressing job in Linz. She had already enjoyed her first taste of freedom when she had spent six months training to be a waitress at Strengberg and was anticipating getting away for good.

On Thursday 19 March 2009, Josef Fritzl was found guilty of all charges and sentenced to life imprisonment. During the trial Elizabeth gave an eleven-hour video testimony but a few days before the end, she slipped into the courtroom, wanting to ensure, a representative said, that her father was finally going to be held accountable for his appalling actions. When Fritzl spotted her, he turned white and broke down.

For the first time, this cruel, unemotional monster wept.

PART TWO

HIGH PROFILE
EXECUTIONS

WILLIAM KEMMLER

The electric chair is an enduring symbol of American justice. No longer the only method of dispatch of the condemned, sharing that role with the increasingly preferred lethal injection, it still looms in the background of many great criminal cases. Amongst those who have sat uneasily on it are evil killers such as Ted Bundy, Lepky Buchalter and Charles Starkweather. The various electric chairs have taken on personalities of their own, given names that hide the gruesome nature of their purpose – Yellow Mama is Alabama's chair; Gruesome Gertie is the name given to the Louisiana chair by inmates and the most famous of all, Old Sparky has almost become a generic name, having been used for electric chairs in a number of states.

Until 1890, the favourite method of execution had been hanging, but a more humane method was needed to suit more enlightened times and the first beneficiary of this was William Kemmler, a convicted thirty-year-old murderer from Buffalo, New York.

Punishment had always been harsh in America. Although hanging was the most common method of execution, other forms were not uncommon in the early years of the republic – burning, beheading and pressing to death, for example. By the early nineteenth century, however, hanging was normal for capital crimes. It began also to be practiced behind prison walls rather than in public in the town square. People began to believe that execution should be as humane and dignified as possible, a far cry from the bloodthirstiness of previous times.

Towards the end of the nineteenth century, however, hanging was beginning to be thought of as an inhumane way of executing convicted criminals. There were endless variables for a hangman to consider, most notably the length of the drop. If it was too short, the condemned would not gather enough momentum for his neck to be broken and he would dangle on the end of the rope experiencing an excruciating, slow strangulation. It could sometimes take twenty minutes to die. If the drop were too long, the drop would be too violent and could result in the beheading of the condemned person. The knot used was also critical as was as its positioning. Americans considered themselves to be modern and progressive. Hanging, they thought, was barbaric and cruel.

In New York, in 1887, therefore, moves were undertaken to find a better way. A Buffalo dentist, Alfred P. Southwick, had seen a drunk man accidentally touch a live electric generator and believed that electricity might provide the answer. The man had died very quickly and, Southwick reckoned, relatively painlessly. He reasoned that death by electrocution would, therefore, provide a good alternative to hanging. It may have been his dentistry background, but he suggested the current could be conducted through the body of the condemned person while he was seated in a large chair. With Dr George Fell, Southwick conducted experiments and the two men took their findings to the authorities.

They approached the electrical giants of the day – Thomas Edison and Nikola Testa – who were, at the time, waging what was known as the War of the Currents. Edison promoted direct current – DC – while Testa and George Westinghouse advocated alternating current – AC. But they both initially feared that the association with killing a person would be an invidious one. Customers might become afraid of what they might consider to be 'dangerous' electricity, the one that kills. Nonetheless, Edison eventually decided to experiment with electrocution using DC electricity.

Two of his employees, Harold P. Brown and Arthur Kennelly, made the first electric chair, using AC and not Edison's DC. Edison claimed that it was the more lethal of the two forms of current. The fact that it was his rivals' version, of course, had something to do with his decision.

They proved its efficacy and the danger of the rival AC, by electrocuting numerous animals in public demonstrations. At these events, the term 'electrocution' was coined, meaning electrical execution. Edison, ever anxious to get at his rivals, tried to have the verb 'to Westinghouse' adopted to denote the execution of people using electricity, but it never caught on.

In 1889, the committee looking into execution adopted Edison's electric chair.

Its first victim would be William Kemmler, an illiterate Buffalo vegetable peddler. Kemmler had a relatively successful business, although he lived in a notorious Buffalo slum, mainly because he was an inveterate drunk who drank any profits he made. He was married to Tillie Ziegler who had left her first husband in Philadelphia to travel with Kemmler to Buffalo. But Kemmler was worried that Tillie was going to leave him and return to Philadelphia. No wonder; they fought and argued ceaselessly and Kemmler's drinking got worse.

On the morning of 29 March, he was trying to shift the effects of a pulsing hangover by drinking beer. He had been drinking heavily the previous night and was in a poisonous mood. When one of his employees, John Debella, arrived to take him to work, Tillie asked Debella if he would go to the market and do some shopping for her. Somehow, this enraged Kemmler and he began to accuse her of packing her trunk in preparation for leaving him. She shouted back at him that she had merely rearranged the contents of the trunk. Kemmler continued shouting, however, that she had been stealing money from him and that she was planning to run away with Debella. Tillie snapped and screamed at him that it was all true, but whether she was trying to be sarcastic or whether it was true is unknown.

Kemmler walked outside and fetched a hatchet from his barn. He came back in and started to hit his wife repeatedly with it until she lay dead. He then walked to a neighbour's house, covered in his wife's blood, and told him, 'I killed her. I had to do it. I meant to. I killed her and I'll take the rope for it.' But, of course, it would not be the rope that finished him off.

As he had confessed, and there was little doubt that he had murdered Tillie in a fit of rage, his trial was brief. He was found guilty on 3 May 1889, of first-degree murder and sentenced to death, the sentence to be carried out within three weeks. As he was the first man to be sentenced to death in New York State that year, he would also be the first man to die in the electric chair.

Almost at once, however, a temporary stay of execution was granted as his lawyer, W. Bourke Cockran, made an appeal based on the fact that electrocution represented cruel and unusual punishment, violating the 8th Amendment of the United States Constitution.

Although Cockran claimed to be working only for the benefit of humanity in opposing electrocution, he was actually working for Thomas Edison's great rival George Westinghouse. Meanwhile, the maker of the electric chair, Harold Brown, constantly described the current to be used in the electric chair as deadly AC, with each mention damaging Westinghouse's business prospects. When Edison testified at the appeal hearing, he was also diligent in reminding everyone that the AC current provided by a Westinghouse generator should be used.

Edison won the day, the appeal was denied and William Kemmler would be executed at New York State's Auburn Prison between 3 and 6 August 1890.

A call went out for official witnesses to the execution and hundreds turned up to volunteer.

Amongst those who were finally accepted were Southwick and Fell, who would be there to see their idea in action.

The execution was set for 6 August at 6 a.m. and as the time neared, Kemmler seemed calm. That morning, he dressed and had the top of his head shaved to accomodate the electrodes and provide a better contact for them. He walked resolutely to the execution chamber and when asked if he had any last words, he magnanimously replied, 'Well, gentlemen, I wish everyone good luck in this world. And I think I am going to a good place and the papers have been saying a lot of stuff that isn't so.'

As the warden fastened his arms to the chair with leather straps, Kemmler noticed that his hands were shaking and said, 'My God, warden, can't you keep cool? Take your time. Don't be in a hurry.' An electrode, in the form of a metal cap containing a sponge was placed on his head. Another was attached to his spine in order to provide a clear path through the body for the current. The increasing hum of the Westinghouse generator, located in the room next door, could be heard as it increased power. When it had reached 2,000 volts, the amount it was believed would kill a man, the executioner, Edwin Davis, pulled the switch that permitted the electrical current to flow to the chair. For seventeen seconds, electricity surged through William Kemmler's body. Those watching saw him strain against his straps and turn red. When Davis switched off the current, however, there was one slight problem. William Kemmler was not dead. They would have to try again, but the generator needed time to build up again to the requisite 2,000 volts and as they waited they had the agonizing sight of the condemned man fighting for breath and groaning in pain. At 2,000 volts, Davis again threw the switch and held it on for a full minute until smoke began to rise from Kemmler's head. It was horrific and those watching were appalled. The smell of burning flesh pervaded the small chamber and a strange crackling sound could be heard. This time there was no doubt. Kemmler was well and truly dead.

Reporters who had witnessed the event wrote sensational pieces about it, one saying that flames had shot out of Kemmler's mouth. There was considerable unease about it but although a large section of the public were outraged, legislators refused to repeal the law that permitted electrocution.

The next four executions in the electric chair in the spring of 1891, using a modified version of the one used at Auburn, went much better.

Meanwhile, although Thomas Edison won this

particular battle, he would lose the war. DC systems fell out of favour and AC became the national standard in the United States.

BRUNO HAUPTMANN

As stories go, it had everything. America's greatest hero who was also one of the most famous men in the world, ransom notes, assignations in dark cemeteries and the kidnap and murder of a beautiful child, for whom a life of privilege lay ahead. Even the defendant was from central casting – a German-born man who fought against the Americans in the trenches of World War One. No wonder they called it the 'Trial of the Century'.

Charles Lindbergh was an aviator, author, inventor and explorer, son of a US Congressman and world-famous for making the first solo non-stop flight across the Atlantic in his single-seat, single-engine monoplane, *Spirit of St Louis*. On the night of 1 March 1932, between 8 p.m. and 10 p.m., as Lindbergh and his wife Anne sat downstairs in their Hopewell, New Jersey home, someone scaled the wall of the house, using a home-made ladder and entered the window of the second-floor room where the Lindberghs' twenty-month-old son,

Charles Jr was sleeping. The child was snatched and the kidnapper left behind a ransom note on a radiator case near the window, which read:

Dear Sir!
Have 50,000$ redy 2500$ in 20$ bills 1500$ in 10$ bills and 1000$ in 5$ bills. After 2-2 days we will inform you were to deliver the Mony. We warn you for making anyding public or for notify the polise the child is in gute care. Indication for all letters are singnature and 3 holes.

Investigators found a three-piece home-made extending ladder which had broken as the kidnapper descended with the child. There was also a chisel and in the mud, heading in a southeasterly direction, was a set of footprints. However, these were never measured so that they could be matched up with potential suspects.

Rather than the news not being made public, it had flashed around the world by the next morning and hordes of people gathered at the Lindbergh house – reporters, cameramen, rubberneckers and souvenir hunters – and a great deal of evidence was destroyed by the milling onlookers.

Charles Lindbergh, meanwhile, made it clear to the New Jersey State Police that he wanted a free rein to negotiate with the kidnappers. The ransom would be paid and the baby would hopefully be returned safely. Only then, Lindbergh insisted, could the police move in. He and his wife made a radio broadcast stating that any arrangements that were made to hand over the ransom would remain confidential.

Finally, on 5 March a handwritten note arrived from the kidnappers. It told them that Charles Jr was being well cared for and warned them again to keep the police out of 'the cace' (*sic*). A further note, they went on, would give details of where the ransom was to be handed over.

Out of nowhere, a retired school principal, Dr John Condon became involved, writing in a newspaper that he would offer $1,000 of his own money to be added to the Lindberghs' cash and he would make himself available to go anywhere to hand over the ransom. He promised never to divulge the details. The kidnappers wrote to Condon and instructed him to get the money from Lindbergh and await further instruction.

At 8.30 p.m., on 12 March, a note was delivered to Condon instructing him to go to a specific location near a hot dog stand where, under a stone, he would find another note with instructions as to where he should go next. The note he found about forty-five minutes later told him to 'follow the fence from the cemetery direction to 233rd Street. I will meet you.' Condon did as he was told and as he walked towards the gate to the cemetery, he spied a figure motioning him over. The man had a handkerchief covering his nose and mouth and in a German accent, he asked Condon, 'Did you gottit my note?' He asked him if he had the money, but Condon replied that until he saw the baby there would be no money. The other man suddenly saw another man outside the cemetery and said 'It's too dangerous!' before turning and fleeing. Condon ran after him and when he caught him up the two sat on a bench. The man, who told Condon that his name was 'John', asked him if he 'would burn' if the baby was dead. When Condon became agitated, 'John' told him the baby was not dead. After telling Condon the baby was on a boat, 'John' left, saying that he would send Lindbergh the baby's sleeping suit. A few days later it arrived.

Lindbergh, becoming worried that the kidnappers might be running out of patience, ordered the money to be made ready even without proof that Charles Jr was still alive. On Tuesday 31 March, Condon was instructed in a note from 'John' that the money should be be handed over the following Saturday evening.

The money that was prepared consisted of gold notes which had distinctive round yellow seals and, being relatively rare, would be more easily traced.

On Saturday 4 April, at 7.45 p.m., a note was delivered to Condon's house telling him to go to a florist shop where he would find another note under a table outside the shop. Accompanied by Charles Lindbergh who was armed, he drove there and was directed to another cemetery. Lindbergh remained at a distance as Condon approached the cemetery. There was a shout of 'Hey, Doctor!' and Condon saw 'John' in the shadows. He handed him the $50,000 in return for an envelope giving directions to a boat called the *Nelly* where the Lindberghs would find their child. Sadly, no trace was ever found of a boat by that name.

On 12 May 1932, more than two months after Charles Jr had disappeared, a truck driver stopping to relieve himself in some woods to the north of Mount Rose, New Jersey, stumbled upon a baby's head and foot sticking out of the ground. It was the badly decomposed body of Charles Lindbergh Jr, buried in a shallow grave. It would emerge later that the child had been killed by a blow to the head, sustained, it was speculated, when the ladder broke back at the Lindbergh house on the night of the kidnap.

The world was horrified and the Lindberghs were, naturally distraught. Meanwhile, police tracked locations all over New York City where the marked gold ransom notes were turning up. Throughout the remainder of 1932, and into the next year the notes were found in numerous places. Finally, in summer 1934, a teller at the Corn Exchange Bank in the Bronx found one of the marked notes with a car's registration scribbled in the corner, probably by an attendant at a petrol station. When the attendant was questioned, he described the man who had paid with the note as of average size, with a German accent and driving a blue Dodge. The owner of the vehicle was Bruno Richard Hauptmann, a thirty-five-year-old carpenter who lived with his wife Ana in the Bronx.

The following morning, when Hauptmann was arrested, almost $14,000 was discovered in his garage. He told police officers that he had found it in a box given to him for safekeeping by a business associate, Isidor Fisch, who had returned to Germany and had recently died there. This story became known in the media as the 'fishy' story.

Hauptmann was further compromised, however, by a smudged telephone number found on a cupboard door in his house. It was the number of Dr John Condon. Furthermore, in his attic there was a plank of wood cut out of the floor. It matched the wood of the home-made ladder found at the Lindbergh house. He was indicted for murder and 2 January 1935 was set as the trial date.

It was a circus. Jack Benny, Walter Winchell and Damon Runyan were just a few of the celebrities who arrived in town for the trial and the courthouse in New Jersey was besieged by hundreds of reporters and cameramen. Miniature kidnap ladders and locks claimed to be of the Lindbergh baby's hair were amongst the souvenirs on offer on the streets outside the court.

The defence attorney, Edward J. Reilly, nicknamed the 'Bull of Brooklyn' pursued an odd defence, suggesting that the killers of the baby had actually been neighbours of Lindbergh who had been upset by Lindbergh's decision to ban them from hunting in a forest he owned. He also tried to place the blame on the Lindbergh domestic servants. Astonishingly, he also suggested that Dr Condon might himself have been behind the kidnapping.

One major piece of testimony was given by eighty-seven-year-old Amandus Hochmuth who lived near the Lindbergh estate. He claimed to have seen a man driving a green car with a ladder in it pass his house on 1 March 1932. When asked if that man was in the room, he immediately pointed his finger at Hauptmann. It was extraordinary because Hochmuth was almost blind.

It was stacked against Hauptmann from the outset. Lindbergh said his voice was the same one that he had heard shout 'Hey Doctor!' to John Condon on the night of 4 April 1932 even though it seemed a bit of a stretch to remember a voice that said only two words some two years ago.

However, John Condon was the most important witness, because he had actually met the kidnapper. When asked who 'John' was, he replied dramatically, 'John is Bruno Richard Hauptmann'.

The handwriting on the various notes was confirmed to be a match for that of Hauptmann and an expert in wood, confirmed the matching of the wood on the ladder and in Hauptmann's attic.

After one hundred and sixty-two witnesses had delivered their testimony and the lawyers had summed up their cases, the jury went out to deliberate over its verdict at 11.21 a.m. on 13 February. Eleven hours later, at 10.28 p.m., they announced that Bruno Richard Hauptmann was guilty of first degree murder. He was sentenced to die in the electric chair.

Hauptmann continued to protest his innocence to the end and his wife tried to have the case re-opened until her death in 1994. However, at 8.44 p.m., on 3 April 1936, as hundreds of people waited outside the prison walls, Bruno Richard Hauptmann felt the surge of 2,000 volts of electricity coursing through his body.

SACCO AND VANZETTI

It was 1919, the era of the 'Red Scare' in the United States, when Americans, not for the last time, lived in fear of their capitalist system falling to the communism that had killed the royal family in Russia and taken over the country. It was a time of suspicion and terror, when radicals and foreign nationals were rounded up and, without trial, locked up or deported, a kind of hysteria that ruined many lives. Two of the lives that were runined were Nicolo Sacco and Bartolomeo Vanzetti who, accused of murdering two men during an armed robbery in Massachusetts, were executed in 1927. Their case, however, highlighting many important issues and concerns about American society that are still relevant today, has become one of the most controversial cases in American legal history.

The issues are, firstly, did Sacco and Vanzetti actually have anything to do with the murders and, secondly, did they get anything approaching a fair trial?

The events that would lead the two men to the electric chair began with the theft of a couple of sets of vehicle licence plates on 22 December 1919 and 6 January 1920. Such thefts were usually the precursors to a robbery, the plates to be used on getaway cars. It was the kind of thing professional criminals did routinely.

Between 7.00 a.m. and 7.30 a.m., on 24 December, two men, one armed with a shotgun, the other with a revolver, attacked a payroll truck that was carrying $30,000 in Bridgewater, Massachusetts. The truck, containing three men, crashed into a telegraph pole as the bullets flew. It was soon apparent to the robbers that they had underestimated the response from the payroll guards. They fled in a car containing at least two more men.

Although there was no evidence to support it, the police chief of Bridgewater, Michael Stewart, suggested that the attempted robbery had been carried out by 'radicals' who wanted to use the money to fund their activities. His reasoning was that the robbers had been described as 'dark and foreign'. The getaway car had been a Buick Overland which led Stewart to suspect the involvement of an Italian named Mario Buda who lived in Cochesett. Buda shared a house with Ferrucio Coacci, also of Italian origin, who had recently been served with a deportation order. Both Broda and Coacci had alibis for the time of the robbery, however.

Four months later, on 15 April 1920 there was a more successful robbery at South Braintree, Massachusetts. Frederick A. Parmenter, paymaster for the Slater and Morrill Shoe Factories was being accompanied by a guard, Alessandro Beradelli, as he carried almost $16,000 for two hundred yards between two buildings. On Pearl Street, two men, dressed in dark clothing were leaning on a fence. One of them lunged at Beradelli as the other two passed. The other opened fire, hitting Beradelli three times and Parmenter once. Parmenter staggered towards some nearby workmen but was felled by another shot and Beradelli had two more bullets pumped into him as he kneeled in the gutter. A seven-seat Buick arrived at speed and the gunmen, carrying the payroll boxes, leapt into the car. A third man appeared from behind a pile of bricks and also jumped into the vehicle which sped away. As the car drove out of town, rubber strips with nails attached were tossed from its windows with the intention of puncturing the tyres of any pursuing vehicles. It vanished on a road leading to thickly wooded countryside.

The following day, Chief Stewart visited Ferrucio Coacci, already in trouble for missing a deportation hearing. He found him packing his trunk, apparently in a hurry to leave the United States. He was not arrested.

Two days after the robbery, the getaway car was found in a wooded area. That same day, Mario Buda took his Buick Overland to a garage to be repaired and Stewart, still suspicious of the Italian, asked the garage owner to let him know when he came to pick up the car. On 5 May, Buda arrived on a motorcycle and sidecar, with a friend, Ricardo Orciani. Two other men of Italian origin, Nicola Sacco and Bartolomeo Vanzetti, arrived with them on foot. The garage owner pointed out to Buda that his vehicle did not have the correct 1920 licence plates and while he explained this to the men, his wife phoned the police. Eventually, unable to drive the car away, Buda left the garage with Orciani as they had come, and Sacco and Vanzetti caught a trolley bus back to Brockton where they lived. At Campello, two police officers boarded the bus and arrested Sacco and Vanzetti, recognizing them from the Garage owner's description. When they were searched Vanzetti was discovered to be carrying a loaded .38 Harrington and Richardson revolver and Sacco a .32 Colt automatic.

When questioned, they lied about where they had just been and how they had obtained the weapons.

When the names Buda and Coacci were mentioned to them, they denied knowing them. When asked about their political beliefs, they were vague. They were locked up for the night, probably thinking they had been picked up because of their anarchist beliefs or for draft-dodging. The robbery was not mentioned until the following day when Frederick Katzmann, the District Attorney, questioned them.

Meanwhile, Ferrucio Coacci was arrested and even though he managed to establish the alibi that he had been at work at the time of the robbery, he was deported. Mario Buda sailed for Italy three days later.

Sacco had been at work on 24 December, but had not been at work on 15 April. He was arrested and charged with robbery and murder. Vanzetti, who sold fish from a handcart for a living, was charged with robbery and murder but was also charged with assault with intent to murder for the failed robbery.

Sacco and Vanzetti had both immigrated from Italy in 1908, seeking the opportunity that America offered. They were both from prosperous families, Sacco, seventeen at the time, from Foggia and Vanzetti, twenty, from Cuneo. They would meet for the first time in 1917.

Sacco first settled in Massachusetts where he

trained as a shoe edger. He married an Italian girl, Rosina and had a son, Dante, in 1913. He was a hard-working family man who was earning good money and had even managed to save some. Although steady in his work and family life, in his politics Sacco was a rebel. He followed the teachings of the leading Italian anarchist thinker, Luigi Galleani, and engaged in fund-raising activities for the cause. At the outbreak of World War One, both Sacco and Vanzetti moved to Mexico with other Italian anarchists to escape being called up to fight. Galleani taught them that the war was for capitalists and not ordinary people. Missing his family, however, Sacco returned home a few months later.

Vanzetti's first years in America were spent in a variety of menial jobs. After the armistice, he returned to America from Mexico and began peddling fish from a handcart. He never married, did not drink and rented a room from an Italian family. Like Nicola Sacco, he read voraciously and he believed passionately in the same politics.

Anarchists were popularly seen as bomb-throwing agitators who wanted to see the eradication of all forms of government and laws. There were actually several different types, however, and they ranged from versions of communism, to syndicalism, to pure anarchism. Men such as Luigi Galleani, who

Sacco and Vanzetti followed, advocated the use of violence and that included the use of bombs. Galleani had even written a bomb-making manual.

The trial of Vanzetti for the failed robbery opened on 22 June 1920 at Plymouth, Massachusetts, with Judge Webster Thayer presiding and Frederick Katzmann prosecuting. His defence team was led by J. P. Vahey who advised him not to take the stand as the prosecution would very quickly expose his radical views to the jury. His defence rested, instead, on sixteen witnesses, all Italians, who had seen him selling fish at the time of the robbery. The prosecution, on the other hand, brought forward witnesses who claimed to have seen him at the robbery. Importantly, it was revealed that when arrested, Vanzetti had shotgun shells on him. Ridiculously, one witness identified one of the robbers as a foreigner from the way he ran.

He was found guilty and sentenced to fifteen years in prison, even though the customary jail term for attempted armed robbery was eight to ten years.

The trial for the successful robbery at South Braintree began on 31 May 1921, with the same judge and prosecutor. The prosecution produced eleven witnesses who placed Sacco and Vanzetti in the area at the time. Only one of them had actually seen the shooting. They also produced testimony from experts that the type of bullet that killed Baradelli was 'consistent' with being fired by Sacco's Colt pistol. There was no certainty that the bullet had actually come from Sacco's weapon. The prosecution also argued that Sacco and Vanzetti behaved like guilty men. They focused in particular on the way they had fled the garage when Mario Buda was unable to drive his car away. The defence argued that in fact they wanted the car in order to dispose of incriminating anarchist literature. The guns they were carrying were explained away in the light of an incident that had occurred shortly before they were arrested. A fellow anarchist, Andrea Salsedo, had fallen or was pushed to his death from a window while in the custody of Department of Justice officials. Sacco and Vanzetti feared that if they fell into those officers' arms, the same fate would await them.

Katzmann played on the jury's patriotism in a savage cross-examination of Nicola Sacco, emphasizing his flight to Mexico and his draft-dodging. He was encouraged in this by Judge Thayer who was outrageously biased against the two Italians throughout the proceedings.

On 14 July 1921, Nicola Sacco and Bartolomeo Vanzetti were found guilty of murder and sentenced to death on very little evidence.

The appeals process was long and torturous and

lasted six years. However, Massachusetts law gave Judge Thayer total control of the process and it was, consequently, a lost cause from the outset.

Remarkably, even a confession by another man, Celestino F. Mederos, in 1825, failed to change matters. He had been a member of a band of robbers known as the Morelli Gang whose leader bore a remarkable resemblance to Nicola Sacco.

There were protests across the globe about the verdict and the treatment of the two men. Amongst the notable people who campaigned for a retrial were George Bernard Shaw, Dorothy Parker, Upton Sinclair and H. G. Wells. There were demonstrations in cities around the world.

It was to no avail, however, and when the last appeal was finally exhausted, Bartolomeo Vanzetti said eloquently to Judge Thayer, 'I would not wish to a dog or a snake, to the most low and misfortunate creature of the earth – I would not wish to any of them what I have had to suffer for things that I am not guilty of. But my conviction is that I have suffered for things that I am guilty of. I am suffering because I am a radical, and indeed I am a radical; I have suffered because I am an Italian, and indeed I am an Italian…If you could execute me two times, and if I could be reborn two other times, I would live again to do what I have done already.'

Nicola Sacco and Bartolomeo Vanzetti died in the electric chair on 23 August 1927 but their case is still being tried on film, in books and in music, more than eighty years later.

JULIUS AND ETHEL ROSENBERG

The trial and execution of the Soviet spies Julius and Ethel Rosenberg in Sing Sing Prison in New York on 19 June 1953, can only be viewed against the background of the remarkable and frightening times in which it took place. It was the time of the second 'Great Red Scare', a period of suspicion and fear of communism in the United States. The first such phenomenon occurred in America between 1917 and 1920 and produced its own martyrs, the Italian-American anarchists Nicola Sacco and Barolomeo Vanzetti who died in the electric chair in 1927. The second wave of communist hysteria featured the invasion of South Korea by Chinese and North Korean forces, an invasion that led to the Korean War; numerous revelations by lapsed communists and spies; the detonation of the Soviet Union's first atom bomb; the witch-hunt mentality of McCarthyism and a pervasive anti-semitism. It would produce another two tragic characters – Julius and Ethel Rosenberg.

It has all the elements of a Cold War spy story – passwords, codebooks, mysterious assignations and a cast of undesirable characters relentlessly promoting their own agendas.

In Canada in 1945, a clerk attached to the Russian Embassy, Igor Gouzenko, defected to Canada, taking with him GRU – Soviet military intelligence documents that implicated British physicist, Alan Nunn May, in spying for the Soviet Union. May was arrested and confessed. Around the same time, a partially burned KGB codebook was discovered in Finland, leading to the cracking of codes used by the Russians. One document decoded was a report on the progress of the Manhattan Project at Los Alamos, the United States' effort to develop the atom bomb during World War Two. It was written by another British physicist, Klaus Fuchs. Fuchs was persuaded to confess.

In his confession, he mentioned a courier who was known to him only as 'Raymond'. Raymond, it transpired, was an American laboratory chemist named Harry Gold who had worked at the Manhattan Project. Gold, in turn, named his Soviet contact as 'John', in reality an NKVD agent, Anatoli Yakovlev who asked Gold to not only pass on to him Fuchs' documents, but also to collect other documents from an American soldier who worked at Los Alamos. He could not recall the soldier's name but remembered he had a wife whose name was Ruth, and he roughly identified where he lived. Shortly after, the soldier, David Greenglass, was arrested and under interrogation implicated his own wife Ruth as well as his brother-in-law, Julius Rosenberg.

Julius Rosenberg was born into a poor Jewish family in the Bronx, New York, in 1918. He joined the Young Communist League while still young and rose through its ranks. Graduating from college with a degree in electrical engineering in 1939, he enlisted in the US Army Signal Corps, working on radar equipment.

His wife Ethel was born Ethel Greenglass three years before her husband, also to poor Jewish parents in the Bronx. She worked as a secretary at a shipping company where she became active in labour disputes. This led to her joining the Young Communist League where she met her future husband when he was eighteen. The couple had two sons, Robert and Michael.

During the next five years, while Julius was in the Signal Corps, the Rosenbergs lived better than at any time in their lives, modestly but comfortably. In 1945, however, Julius's Communist Party membership from 1939 was discovered and he was thrown out of the army. The family fell on hard times.

In 1942, Julius had been recruited as a spy for the Soviet Union by the Soviet spymaster, Semyon Semenov. When Semenov was ordered back to the USSR, Rosenberg reported to Alexandre Feklisov.

Julius was arrested on 17 July 1950 and on 11 August, Ethel was also arrested. They were each held on $100,000 bail but they did not have the money to gain temporary freedom. They were held, therefore, in the New York House of Detention.

No matter what can be said about the Rosenbergs, no one could doubt their love for each other. In the van as they were being transported to the courthouse, they held hands and kissed through the wire that separated them. Once when they were allowed to meet, their guards, embarrassed by the passion of their greeting, had to separate them. Later, when they were separated on Sing Sing's death row by a wall and were allowed to see each other only once a week, Ethel would sing to Julius through the wall.

Their trial opened on 6 March 1951 and included a third defendant, Morton Sobell, an engineer working for General Electric, also accused of conspiring to pass secrets to the Soviet Union.

It is worth noting the extraordinary events occurring in the background around this time, events that created a kind of anti-communist hysteria in the United States. In January 1950, Alger Hiss was convicted of perjury in the famous Hiss/Chambers spy trial; in February, Senator Joseph P. McCarthy gave a speech at Wheeling, West Virginia, in which he claimed that there were two hundred and fifty subversives working in the State Department; in March, British spy Klaus Fuchs was convicted and sentenced to fourteen years for passing secrets to the Russians; in June, the Korean War began.

Irving R. Kaufman was the judge at the trial and the prosecutor was United States Attorney, Irving H. Saypol who had secured the conviction of Alger Hiss. Both these men had been desperate to secure their roles at this high-profile trial. Assisting Saypol was Roy Cohn who would later become famous as Senator McCarthy's right-hand man.

The case against Sobell was based largely on testimony provided by a man called Max Elichter that he had delivered a can of microfilm to Julius Rosenberg. Sobell and Elichter had attended college with Rosenberg. However, it was the Greenglasses and Harry Gold – already sentenced to thirty years – who were the basis of the case against the Rosenbergs. In a piece of testimony straight out of a spy novel, Gold described how half of a Jello box had been given to him to present to David Greenglass when they met in Albuquerque. Greenglass had the other half and when they put them together each could be sure he was talking to the right man. Gold also had a phrase to be used as code – the highly incriminating, 'I come from Julius'.

David and Ruth Greenglass testified that Julius had encouraged David to become a member of the Communist Party and had asked Ruth to urge David to steal atomic secrets while working at Los Alamos. In 1950, when everything began to unravel with Harry Gold's confession, Julius told David and Ruth to go to Mexico with their children. He even gave the Greenglasses $4,000 to pay for the trip. David Greenglass, who would later be sentenced to fifteen years in prison, had cut a deal with the prosecution whereby he would testify against the Rosenbergs in exchange for immunity for his wife, Ruth.

David Greenglass's testimony also directly implicated Ethel. They claimed that she typed out David's notes about Los Alamos that contained names of scientists engaged on the Manhattan Project, and details and sketches of the bomb's design. A sketch of a device designed to focus energy for the detonation of the bomb was of particular use. This testimony would prove fatal to Ethel, even though in reality, the information in question was of a much lower grade than that already provided to the Soviets by Klaus Fuchs. However, the Rosenbergs' attorney made a curious error of judgement during the testimony, requesting that, in order to preserve 'the secret of the atom bomb' it should be given in secret, with no members of the public present. Thus, the jury was convinced that the material being handed over to the Soviets must be vitally important. It was such an extraordinary decision by the attorney that the judge asked him if he was sure that was what he wanted.

The defence case consisted purely of testimony from Julius and Ethel. It did not go well from the beginning, any sympathy the jury might have had for them quickly waning, especially when Julius refused to answer the question of whether he had ever belonged to a group that had discussed the Soviet system. He pleaded the Fifth Amendment, refusing to answer on the grounds that it might incriminate him. On the stand, Ethel seemed cold and arrogant but like Julius, she denied each allegation put to her. Like him, she pleaded the Fifth on certain questions, but it was not only out of principle that they refused to answer – they simply did not want to implicate others.

The jury was sent out on 28 March 1951 and at 11 a.m the next day they returned with a verdict of guilty for each of the three defendants. On 5 April, Judge Kaufman announced that Julius and Ethel Rosenberg would die in the electric chair during the week of 21 May 1951 and that Morton Sobell would spend thirty years in prison.

Turning to the Rosenbergs, Kaufman seemed to place the blame for the entire Korean War firmly on their shoulders. 'I consider your crime worse than murder,' he said '...I believe your conduct in putting into the hands of the Russians the A-Bomb years before our best scientists predicted Russia would perfect the bomb has already caused, in my opinion, the Communist aggression in Korea, with the resultant casualties exceeding fifty thousand and who knows but that millions more of innocent people may pay the price of your treason. Indeed, by your betrayal you undoubtedly have altered the course of history to the disadvantage of our country. No one can say that we do not live in a constant state of tension. We have evidence of your treachery all around us every day for the civilian defense activities throughout the nation are aimed at preparing us for an atom bomb attack.'

There was horror in many quarters at the death sentence and it was not just communists around the world who protested. Committees to secure justice for the Rosenbergs were established in Britain, France and Italy. Support was forthcoming from prominent scientists such as Albert Einstein and the chemist Harold Urey.

Eventually, after appeals and a false dawn when

Supreme Court Judge, William Douglas called a stay, the execution was scheduled for 11 p.m. on 19 June. In a desperate attempt to win more time, the Rosenbergs' attorney pointed out that it was a Friday and that the Sabbath would already have begun when they were executed. To his horror, the problem was solved by bringing the time forward to 8 p.m.

Julius went to the chair quietly but Ethel had to be electrocuted a second time before she was dead, smoke reportedly rising from her head during the process.

Ultimately, it is clear that Julius Rosenberg was engaged in spying for the Soviet Union. Former Soviet Premier, Nikita Khrushchev writes about Rosenberg's spying for Russia in his memoirs and his Soviet contact, Alexandre Feklisov has admitted recruiting him and working with him. But, the arguments over the case rage on. Some argue they were innocent and some insist on their guilt. Others state quite simply that their death sentence was too harsh a penalty for their crime, especially in the light of the comparatively lenient fourteen-year sentence given to Klaus Fuchs in Britain when the secrets he passed were so much more vital to the development of the Soviet atomic bomb.

DEREK BENTLEY

On 30 July 1998, the British Appeal Court finally ruled that the 1952 conviction of Derek Bentley for murder was unsafe. Tragically, the decision came too late for his sister Iris who had campaigned on her brother's behalf for forty-five years. She had died in 1997. Even more tragically, it was forty-five years too late for Derek Bentley himself. He was hanged at Wandsworth Prison on 28 January 1953.

His problems had begun in 1938 when, aged five, he had fallen from a lorry, banging his head on the pavement. Following that incident, he suffered from epilepsy. He had then received a serious head injury when a V-1 flying bomb had blown up the house the Bentley family was living in. Slow to learn, he failed the eleven-plus examination and attended a secondary modern school but not long before he was due to leave school at fifteen, he was arrested for theft and sent to Kingswood Approved School. At this time, his IQ was estimated to be around seventy-seven and he was unable to read or write.

Released from Kingswood, he found work with a

furniture removal company, in March 1951. When he injured his back, however, he had to leave the job, working next for Croydon Corporation and then as a dustman. He moved on to street-sweeping but was even sacked from that. When it came time for him to do National Service in February 1952, he was deemed unfit due to the injuries he had received during the war.

On the night of 2 October 1952, in the company of sixteen-year-old Christopher Craig, nineteen-year-old Bentley was climbing the gate of the Croydon warehouse that belonged to confectionery manufacturers and wholesalers, Parker & Barlow. As the two boys shimmied up a drainpipe onto the roof of the warehouse, Bentley was carrying with him a knife and a knuckle-duster he had been given by Craig. Craig, meanwhile, could feel the dead weight of a Colt .455 Eley revolver in his pocket.

Their progress had not gone unnoticed, however. A little girl, looking out of the window of her room across from the warehouse, spotted the boys and ran downstairs to tell her parents what she had seen. Her father put on a coat and walked to the nearest telephone box to phone the police.

By the time the first patrol car arrived, the boys were on the roof, hiding behind a lift-housing, but they had been spotted by Detective Constable

Frederick Fairfax who climbed the drainpipe and made a lunge for Bentley. The boy managed to slip out of his grasp but as he did so, police officers, looking up anxiously from below, heard him shout the fatal words: 'Let him have it, Chris!' Craig pulled the trigger, firing a bullet that wounded the policeman in the shoulder. Fairfax still managed to arrest Bentley, however. Bentley made no attempt to escape and remained with the stricken officer for some thirty minutes, completely unrestrained.

Reinforcements soon arrived and began to climb onto the roof but Craig continued to fire at anything that moved. PC Sydney Miles emerged onto the roof through a door at the top of some stairs. As he did so, he was hit in the head by a bullet from Craig's gun. He died instantly. A terrified Craig continued to fire his weapon until he ran out of ammunition. He leapt from the roof, a height of about thirty feet, and landed on a greenhouse roof below, fracturing his spine and breaking a wrist.

The two boys were charged with the murder of Constable Miles but the case contained a number of tricky questions. The most important was whether Derek Bentley should have been charged at all. His learning difficulties presented one issue, but there was also the fact that he had neither fired a gun nor had one in his possession that night. However, four policeman had been murdered in London the previous year and the press seethed with stories of young men joining gangs and terrorizing the populace of the capital.

Medical reports found Bentley to be of low intelligence, but concluded that he had been of sound mind on the night of the murder and was fit to stand trial. Although it existed in Scottish law, English law did not yet recognise the concept of diminished responsibility due to 'retarded development'. Insanity was the only defence and Bentley, it was claimed, was not insane.

Both boys pleaded not guilty when their trial opened at the Old Bailey on 9 December 1952, the Lord Chief Justice, Lord Goddard, presiding. Interestingly, however, the case against Christopher Craig was not as cut and dried as it had first appeared. The bullet exhibited in court had no traces of blood on it and there was increasing debate whether a bullet from the .455 revolver had actually been the one that had killed the policeman. There were many other doubts and inconsistencies. The prosecution failed to establish how many shots Craig had actually fired and a ballistics expert cast doubt on whether he could have hit the policeman, given that he had sawn off the gun's barrel, making it wildly inaccurate and, in addition, was using the wrong calibre bullets.

The case against Bentley was more complex and several issues preoccupied the jury. The words 'Let him have it, Chris,' caused problems. Some suggested they had never even been uttered and been invented later to bolster the prosecution case. The prosecution, on the other hand, took them to mean that the two boys had 'common purpose' and in that case, they were both guilty of murder.

Of course, if he did say those words, Bentley may just have been telling Craig to hand over the gun.

There is, of course, also the fact that Bentley, although possibly not under arrest, was being detained by PC Fairfax at the moment the fatal shot was fired. Understandably, Fairfax was somewhat preoccupied at the time with his wound and avoiding Craig's gunfire, but if he had read Bentley his rights and thrown a charge at him, Bentley would, undoubtedly, have had a strong case against being accused of the murder that was about to be perpetrated.

For Lord Goddard, it seemed enough that the two had gone together to rob the warehouse and the fact that Bentley had a knuckle-duster and a knife did not help his case in his Lordship's eyes.

The jury took a mere seventy-five minutes to find both boys guilty of murder. Craig, at sixteen, legally a minor was ordered to be detained at Her

Majesty's Pleasure while Derek Bentley, being nineteen, was sentenced to death. The jury had added a recommendation of mercy for Bentley when they had delivered their verdict but the Lord Chief Justice did not pass this on to the Home Office. In mitigation, Lord Goddard probably thought there was no possibility that Bentley's sentence would actually be carried out and, consequently, thought the recommendation unnecessary.

Sadly, however, Bentley's appeal was rejected on 13 January 1953, leaving the Home Secretary of the time, Sir David Maxwell-Fife as Bentley's last resort for clemency. However, after reading psychiatric reports, he recommended that the execution should go ahead. A petition asking for mercy was signed by two hundred MPs. Bizarrely, however, Parliament was constitutionally prevented from debating whether he should be hanged until after he actually had been hanged.

There are numerous theories as to why the execution of Derek Bentley was allowed to proceed. Some said the Home Office let it happen to increase the case for the abolition of the death penalty, that Derek Bentley was sacrificed for that cause. Of course, the fact that the dead man was a police officer added to the difficulty of giving Bentley a reprieve.

Some have suggested that armed police officers were at the scene before the fatal shot was fired, although the official version says that they did not arrive until after the death of PC Miles. Was he killed by a police bullet and then the matter covered up and the boys blamed? It was a case that would not go away and that continued to make the British people and the British justice system uneasy during the years following Bentley's execution.

Christopher Craig was released from prison after serving ten years, but for Derek Bentley it took forty-six years to obtain a release of some kind, even though it was too late. His remains were removed from the grounds of Wandsworth Prison and re-buried in a family grave.

ERIC EDGAR COOKE
THE 'NIGHT CALLER'

When asked why he did it, he replied that he liked to hurt people. That much was obvious from the one-man crime spree during which he terrorised the Western Australian city of Perth between 1959 and 1963. During that time, he committed at least twenty-two violent crimes and murdered at least eight people.

It should have been no surprise he turned out bad. Born in Perth in 1931, with a cleft palate, he was the victim of numerous beatings as a child from his alcoholic father, often for no reason. At the age of sixteen, for example, he ended up in hospital after he tried to intervene when his father was beating his mother. He explained it away by telling doctors that he had been beaten up by a gang of boys. He was bullied at school because of his appearance but several operations failed to improve matters and he was left with a facial deformity and an inability to speak clearly.

Rejected by everyone around him, he became a loner and started to spend his nights committing acts of pointless vandalism and petty crime. At one point, he was sent to jail for burning down a church just because they had rejected him for a place in the choir.

Aged twenty-one, he joined the Australian Army but three months later, when his juvenile record was discovered, he was discharged. He did learn something about how to fire a gun, however. It was a lesson that the inhabitants of the city of Perth would live to regret.

A year later, he married British immigrant, Sally Lavin, a nineteen-year-old waitress, and with her he would have seven children. He found work as a lorry driver but none of this stopped his criminal sidelines, however, and he was arrested several times for looking in people's bedroom windows and for other petty criminal acts. In 1955, he was given two years' hard labour for car theft and he would return to prison in 1960. In between those prison terms, he continued breaking the law. He also killed for the first time when he murdered a divorcee in the course of a break-in, but he got away with it. His real killing spree began, however, on a summer's night, 27 January 1963.

A couple, Nicholas August, a married man, and

a barmaid, Rowena Reeves were enjoying a drink in August's car in the early hours in a secluded part of the Perth suburb of Cottesloe. Peering into the darkness, Rowena suddenly saw a figure watching them. August leaned out of his window and yelled 'Bugger off!' at the man who he presumed to be a peeping tom. When the figure did not move, August angrily chucked an empty bottle at him. Rowena noticed that the man had something in his hand and to her horror realised it was a gun, which was aimed straight at them. Thinking fast, she pushed August's head down as a bullet flew into the car, grazing his neck and hitting her in the arm. August sat up quickly, turned the key in the ignition and pressed his foot down hard on the peddle. The car sped past the man, almost hitting him. It was a shame they missed him; it would have saved several lives that night if they had not.

August and Reeves survived, although, having lost a considerable amount of blood, she was unconscious by the time they got to the nearest hospital. The next few people that Eric Cooke encountered were not quite so lucky.

A little later that night, fifty-four-year-old retired grocer, George Walmsley, wondered who could be at his door at that time of night. Puzzled, he sleepily made his way to the front door. No sooner had he opened it than he lay dead on the floor with a bullet hole in the middle of his forehead.

It was 04.00 a.m. as Cooke made his way round the corner from where he had claimed the life of George Walmsley. There, asleep on the verandah of the boarding house where he had a room, he found John Sturkey, a nineteen-year-old student. Cooke shot him between the eyes without even bothering to wake him up.

He next pumped a bullet into the forehead of Brian Weir, an accountant who had been asleep in his bed. Weir, who lived alone, was discovered the next morning when he failed to turn up for work. His sheets were soaked with his blood and he survived,but was seriously brain-damaged. He became the Night Stalker's fourth victim of that night when he died from his injuries three years later.

The next day the media went into a frenzy. Perth was just not used to this kind of thing. It was a city were the residents prided themselves on being able to leave their doors unlocked and their windows open. Crime was negligible and murder was unheard of, unlike some of the other cities of Australia with their gangland killings and turf wars. A huge reward was offered for information leading to the capture of the man they were calling the 'Maniac Slayer'.

Just as the randomness of the killings terrified the people of Perth, so it baffled the police. No one had any idea where the killer would strike next and just in case it was anywhere near their neighbourhood, people began to stock up on guns and ammo and sleep with loaded weapons by their bedside. Windows and doors were now double-locked all the time.

On 16 February, Cooke raped and strangled twenty-four-year-old social worker Constance Madrill and left her naked on the lawn of a west Perth house. The different method of this murder led police not to link it with the recent killings. They suggested, without any grounds to support their theory, that it had been carried out by an Indigenous Australian.

For the next six months nothing happened and the city began to breathe a little more easily. On 10 August, however, an eighteen-year-old student, Shirley McLeod, was shot dead as she was babysitting. The baby she had been caring for was left unharmed. It was a different gun, but investigators were certain it was the same man and drastic steps were taken. Every male in Perth over the age of twelve was fingerprinted and there was talk of closing down certain secluded roads and alleyways at night.

Just when the city's terror had reached its peak, they caught him. A couple were picking flowers in some woods in the Mount Pleasant area of the city when they came upon a rifle concealed in some bushes. They called the police who discovered that it was a .22 Winchester, the same weapon that the killer had recently used. It was a remarkable stroke of luck. Without any doubt, he would be returning to collect the weapon at some time and all they had to do was wait. For two weeks the area was put under tight surveillance before Eric Cooke finally turned up. They grabbed him, cuffed him and at last took him into custody.

After initially denying having anything to do with the killings, Cooke began to catalogue an astonishing series of crimes. He claimed some two hundred and fifty break-ins and car thefts, recalling tiny details in a way that amazed the officers interrogating him. He described abusing women while they slept and hit-and-runs that he had deliberately staged, running people over and then speeding off.

Even the Winchester had been obtained in a break-in. The owners were seated in the lounge watching television as he crept out of their house with the gun and ammunition. Initially, he planned to sell it, but used it instead on the babysitting student, He claimed, however, not to recall anything about that murder. When he woke up next morning to see it on the news, he realised that he must have done it. Regarding Constance Madrill, she had wokenup as he searched her house for valuables. He hit her and then strangled her with the electrical cord from a lamp. He had then raped her as she lay dead on the floor. His intention had been to steal a car and take her body somewhere to be disposed of. But he could only find a bicycle and was forced to dump her in the middle of the lawn.

He explained away his murderous night of the previous summer by saying he did it because he 'wanted to hurt somebody'. When Nicholas August had thrown the bottle at him he had lost his temper and the remainder of his killings and woundings that night had been just opportunistic; his victims really were in the wrong place at the wrong time. He suggested that he was probably just a cold-blooded killer.

One murder to which he confessed was the 1959 killing of thirty-three-year-old Patricia Vinico Berkman, lover of local radio star Fotis Hountas. She had received multiple stab wounds to the head as she lay in bed in her apartment in South Perth. Furthermore, he claimed to have killed wealthy twenty-two-year-old socialite Jillian Brewer later that same year. A twenty-year-old deaf-mute,

Darryl Beamish had confessed to killing her but later claimed that he had been forced to make the confession. Nevertheless, he was found guilty and given the death sentence. Cooke, however, cast doubt on that verdict by recalling tiny details about the flat. He also solved a mystery about the murder. When the woman's body was found, all the doors to the flat were locked from the inside and there was no sign of forced entry. Cooke explained that he had stolen one of Jillian Brewster's keys when breaking into the flat a few months previously. The appeal court judges did not believe Cooke's confession, but at least Beamish did not hang; his sentence was commuted to one of life imprisonment.

Eric Edgar Cooke had no such luck. He was hanged in Fremantle Prison on 26 October 1964, the last man to be hanged in Australia.

TIMOTHY EVANS

The duty sergeant was unsure whether to believe Timothy Evans or not. The small, rather insignificant man had walked into the police station in Merthyr Vale on 30 November 1949 and told him that he had put his wife's body down a drain in London. They drove him across to the police station at Merthyr Tydfil where he made a statement to a couple of astonished detectives. They contacted the police at Notting Hill in London and several officers were sent round to the address he had given, the flat where he used to live. It took three of them to lift the manhole cover outside the house – something he claimed that he did alone – but they found nothing beneath it. The address they were at would become one of the most chilling addresses in British criminal history – 10 Rillington Place, the home of serial killer, John Reginald Christie.

The news that nothing had been found was sent back to South Wales and Evans was informed. He insisted on making another statement in which he said that his wife's death had actually been the result of an unsuccessful attempt at aborting her unborn baby. Notting Hill police paid another visit to Rillington Place to have a look around Evans' flat. Christie was brought in for questioning while his wife was interviewed at their flat.

But police were still baffled. Had a crime been committed or not?

Before Timothy Evans had been born in Merthyr Vale in 1924, his father had walked out and was never seen again. As a child, Evans was slow in learning to speak and had difficulties at school which were not helped by the considerable amount of schooling he missed after developing a tubercular verucca on his right foot. As a result, he could neither read nor write anything more than his name by the time he was an adult and nowadays would be described as having learning difficulties. Even at an early age, he had a reputation for his temper and also seems to have been a compulsive liar, concocting elaborate lies about himself, a habit that he still possessed as an adult.

His mother remarried and in 1935, when Evans was eleven, the family moved to west London to make a fresh start. Evans worked as a painter and decorator while still at school, and in 1937 returned to Merthyr Tydfil briefly to work in the mines. His troubles with his foot forced him to give up the work, however. By 1939, he was back in London with his mother.

In 1947, aged twenty-three, Evans married eighteen-year-old Beryl Thorley and they moved into a second-floor flat at 10 Rillington Place where their neighbours two floors below, on the ground floor, were a middle-aged couple, Reg Christie and his wife Ethel. In 1948, Beryl gave birth to their first child, a daughter that they named Geraldine.

On 2 December 1949, police officers made another, more thorough search at 10 Rillington Place, still not actually knowing what they were looking for. However, an officer searching outside in the small back garden that came with the Christies' flat, made a grim discovery – the decomposed bodies of Beryl Evans and baby Geraldine, hidden in a wash-house behind some wood.

Evans was driven back to London where he identified the clothing taken from his dead wife and daughter. Charged with their murders, he made two statements admitting to having killed them.

The trial opened on 11 January 1950, Justice Lewis presiding and Christmas Humphreys prosecuting. Evans was defended by Malcolm Morris. He was tried only for the murder of Geraldine, even though it was widely accepted that he was really being tried for Beryl's death as well. Evans had by this time returned to his second Merthyr Tydfil statement and was now blaming everything on his neighbour, Reg Christie who, he claimed, had killed his wife while performing an abortion on her. When called to testify, however, Christie gave an engaging performance, diverting attention from his criminal record that included a conviction for assault on a woman, onto his record in World War One where he had been rendered unable to speak for three years by a mustard gas attack. He said that he saw Beryl leave with her baby around noon on the eighth and never saw her again. Later, Timothy Evans came home and he and his wife Ethel went out for the evening. Around midnight, he claimed, he and his wife heard a loud thump from above them. As the man in the second floor flat was away, it could only have come from the Evans' flat on the third floor. It was followed by the sound of something heavy being dragged across the floor.

The following day, Christie told the police, Evans told him his wife had gone to Bristol and the day after that, he came home saying that he had packed in his job and was selling up and moving to Bristol to join her.

Timothy Evans was found guilty and sentenced to death. His appeal was rejected and on 9 March

1950, he was hanged at Pentonville Prison.

In March 1953, a new tenant, a Jamaican named Beresford Brown, moved into the ground floor flat at 10 Rillington Place, recently vacated by Reg Christie who had given up his job, sold all his furniture and moved back to Sheffield, as he had told friends, to join his wife who had gone on ahead several months previously. While stripping wallpaper in preparation for redecorating the flat, Brown came upon a door that had been covered up by the wallpaper. It appeared to lead to a pantry. Opening the door slightly, he shone a torch into the space beyond. There, to his horror he saw the body of a woman, seated and hunched forward, clad only in a bra, stockings and suspenders. He immediately called the police and when they arrived, they discovered another two women's bodies. They were the bodies of three prostitutes that Christie had lured back to the house and killed while he lived there – Kathleen Maloney, Rita Nelson and Hectorina MacLennan. Searching the remainder of the flat, under the floorboards of the living room they found the remains of Ethel Christie. Christie had strangled her on December 14 1952. She had been in poor health and Christie claimed later that he had merely put her out of her misery.

A massive manhunt was launched for Christie

which ended about a week later when he was apprehended on the Embankment of the River Thames, not far from Putney Bridge. He confessed to the murders of six women and to the murder of Beryl Evans for which Timothy Evans had hanged two years previously.

It had happened in September 1949. To her dismay, Beryl was pregnant again. She and Timothy were already struggling financially and she would now have to give up her part-time job as well. There was also the fact that the flat was just not big enough for another child. She spoke to Timothy about an abortion, but he, a Roman Catholic, would not hear of it.

When she mentioned her predicament to Reg Christie, he hinted that he had gained some medical experience during the war and told her that he could perform an abortion if she wanted. He spoke to Evans about it, but he remained opposed to the idea. Nonetheless, Beryl went ahead. On the morning of 8 November, she went down to Christie's flat to have the abortion. That night when Evans returned from work, an edgy Christie met him on the stairs of the building and told him that it had all gone disastrously wrong – Beryl had died during the procedure. He impressed upon Evans not only that he would be in serious trouble for attempting to abort a child but that Evans's rows with his wife, which had been a feature of their marriage, would lead to him being suspected of murder. The slow-witted and infinitely suggestible Evans agreed. Christie offered to dispose of the body down the drain outside and suggested that he would also find a home for Geraldine. Evans helped him carry the body down to the vacant first floor flat. On 10 November when Evans returned from work, Christie informed him that he had placed the child with a couple in Acton. He had, of course, killed her.

Christie now suggested to Evans that he get out of London. In this, he had a stroke of luck as Evans had just lost his job and, there was, therefore, nothing to keep him there. He sold his furniture for £40 and on 15 November took the train to the home of his aunt and uncle in Merthyr Vale. He told them that Beryl had returned to her parents. On 23 November, anxious about Geraldine, he returned to London, but Christie told him he could not see her until she had properly settled in with her new parents. Evans returned to Wales where his aunt and uncle had become suspicious. They had written to Beryl's parents and learned that she was not there.

The problem for Timothy Evans was that everyone – the police and even his own solicitors

– had presumed he was guilty from the outset, a presumption not helped by his confessions, of course. But vital pieces of evidence were also ignored. One involved some workmen who had been using the wash-house to store tools all that week. They stated categorically that when they left the wash-house on 11 November there was nothing out of the ordinary there. Police should have noticed that this was in direct contradiction of Timothy Evans' statement. He said that he put Beryl's body there on November 8 and Geraldine's two days later, ready for disposal in the drain. Furthermore, a carpenter had taken up some floorboards on 11 November and had given them to Reg Christie on the 14th. Christie had used these pieces of wood to conceal the bodies. Evans had already left Rillington Place earlier that day. No statement was ever taken from the carpenter.

Police did call the workmen back to provide second statements, but this time, they gave the investigators the version they wanted, the one who had last used the wash-house, saying on this occasion that he had not really paid any attention to it.

There were many other factors that should have made the police think twice about Timothy Evans' guilt. A friend of Beryl's visited on the day of the murder and was certain that when she tried to open her door, someone was pushing it closed from the inside. It may have been around the time that Christie killed Beryl. Police suggested to her, however, that she had actually visited the day before. Furthermore, vital evidence was lost and contradictory statements by Christie were not seized upon.

Christie's trial for the murder of his wife opened at the Old Bailey on 22 June 1953. He related the story of her poor health and how he had strangled her on 14 December 1952, to end her misery.

He was found guilty and sentenced to death. On 15 July 1953, he was hanged on the same gallows as Timothy Evans.

Christie had not confessed to the killing of Geraldine Evans and the police still believed there were no grounds to believe that there had been a dreadful miscarriage of justice. An inquiry headed by John Scott-Henderson QC upheld Evans' guilt of both murders, even though Christie had confessed.

A campaign was launched to obtain a posthumous pardon for Evans. In 1955, the Home Secretary was petitioned by a group of newspaper editors and the first of dozens of books about the case was written. In 1961, a parliamentary debate failed to establish a second enquiry into the case. Another prolonged campaign finally resulted in the Home Secretary of the time recommending Timothy Evans be given a Royal Pardon. It was granted. His body was removed from Pentonville Prison and reburied in Leytonstone in London.

In 2004, Evans's half-sister, Mary Westlake, launched an attempt to overturn a decision by the Criminal Cases Review Commission not to quash her half-brother's conviction. She argued that he had never been declared innocent and a pardon is only a forgiveness for crimes actually committed. The judges decided the costs involved in such a case would be unjustified, but accepted that Timothy Evans did not murder either his wife or his daughter.

CHARLES STARKWEATHER

The night before his execution, spree killer Charles Starkweather was asked whether he would like to donate his eyes. Starkweather sneered back at the questioner, 'Why should I. Nobody ever gave me anything.'

It was 1958 and America was changing. President Eisenhower and Vice President Richard Nixon ran the country admittedly, but Elvis Presley had exploded out of Memphis with the new, dangerous sound of rock and roll and just a few years earlier James Dean had invented the teenager, and splashed teenage angst on the country's cinema screens. Now there was Charles Starkweather, another anguished Dean-like figure in the full glare of the media but this time the discomfort he created in ordinary Americans was for real and not fictional.

Charlie Starkweather was not lying when he claimed no one had ever given him anything. The third of seven children, he was born into poverty in

Lincoln, Nebraska in 1938. The family did not go without but that was mainly due to the hard work of Charlie's parents, Guy and Helen Starkweather. Guy worked as a carpenter while Helen was a waitress.

It was school where young Charlie had problems. He had a speech impediment and bowed legs, differences that the other kids loved to pick up on. He was constantly teased about them and he hated it. It may have been for that reason that he never really tried and, although not stupid, he came to be considered a slow learner. What was never picked up, however, was that he was severely short-sighted, an ailment that was not picked up until he was fifteen.

He was big and strong for his age and as a result was constantly getting into bother for fighting with the other boys. Soon, he had earned a reputation for being one of the hardest kids in Lincoln. Also, like many young American men of the time, he became a James Dean obsessive. He copied the actor's mannerisms, his tics and wore the same clothes, leather jerkin, tight jeans and cowboy boots. He swept his hair back in the James Dean style. But, he was acutely aware that he was no James Dean. Instead, he was trapped in poverty and going nowhere. He feared he would end up like his parents, having to work every hour there was in unrewarding menial jobs, in order to keep a roof over the heads of a wife and a brood of kids. The thought of it terrified him.

When Charlie's friend, Bobby Von Busch started going out with Barbara Fulgate in 1956, Charlie began to take an interest in her younger sister, Caril. Charlie was at this time sixteen while Caril had recently turned thirteen. She was a pretty girl and they had a lot in common. She had a rebellious streak and, like Charlie, she was failing at school. Being so young, of course, she thought Charlie was the coolest thing on two legs; she loved his cars and the reputation he had around town for being tough. She worshipped him and Charlie loved the attention she lavished upon him.

Quitting school at sixteen, Charlie found work in a warehouse not far from the school Caril attended so that he could see her every day. But things turned sour at home after Caril was involved in a minor accident while illegally driving Charlie's car. As part owner of the car, Guy Starkweather, Charlie's father, had to pay for the damage to the other car. He was furious and after a fight broke out between Charlie and Guy, Guy threw his son out of the house. He took a room in a boarding house where Bob was living with Barbara Fulgate and began telling people that he and Caril were going to get married.

When he spread a story that Caril was pregnant, her parents were furious. Meanwhile, his efforts to escape the life of drudgery offered by Lincoln were hardly helped when he quit the warehouse job and started working as a dustmen. Not only was the work not what he saw himself doing with his life, the pay was poor. He was locked out of his room until he could pay rent he owed and he could hardly support Caril and a family on it. He was even unable to afford a cheap stuffed dog that he had seen in a petrol station the previous day and knew that Caril would love. The attendant refused him credit and Charlie seethed with indignation about it. He would one day get back at these small-minded people who seemed to be doing better than him.

He began to realise that the only way he was going to break free was to steal what he wanted. Therefore, in the early hours of 1 December 1958 he took a 12-gauge shotgun he had stolen from a cousin of Bob Von Busch and drove to the petrol station where the stuffed dog was for sale. Inside, the attendant who had refused him credit the previous day was on duty alone. Robert Colvert, married with a pregnant wife, was working on a car when Starkweather walked in, bought a packet of cigarettes and drove away again. Not far along the road, however, he turned the vehicle round and drove back. He bought some gum and once again drove off into the night. He parked the car down the road, tied a bandana around his face and put a hunter's hat on his head, covering his distinctive red hair. This time he walked into the petrol station carrying the loaded shotgun. Sticking the gun into Colvert's back, he ordered him into the office and told him to open the cash drawer. He scooped up the cash and put it in a sack but when he ordered Colvert to open up the safe, the other man told him he did not know the combination. Starkweather accepted that but for some reason decided to take Colvert for a drive. Arriving at a property owned by a local character known as 'Bloody Mary', Charlie ordered him out of the car. He later claimed that Colvert then made a grab for the gun and in the ensuing scuffle, it went off. Colvert collapsed to the ground and as he tried to get up again, Charlie finished him off with a shot to the skull.

The police thought the murder had been committed by someone passing through and Charlie was off the hook. For once, however, he had money. Furthermore, he felt on top of the world, like he could do whatever he wanted and get away with it. He told Caril about the robbery but said that someone else had shot Colvert. It is unlikely that she believed him but they now possessed a unique bond.

Before long, however, things were even worse than prior to the murder when he lost both his job and his room. Meanwhile, Caril's family were doing everything to split up their daughter and the loser she followed around like a puppy dog.

On the afternoon of 21 January, Charlie drove to the Fulgate house, a squalid rubbish heap of a property. In the car was a .22 rifle he had borrowed. He later told police officers that he was actually hoping to go hunting with Caril's stepfather Marion Bartlett, in an effort to make friends with him. However, Caril's mother, Velda angrily told Charlie that she wanted him to stop seeing her daughter. An argument ensued and Charlie left. When he returned to argue his case, he was literally kicked out of the house by Marion. He went back again but this time he brought his gun. When Marion came at him with a hammer, Charlie shot him in the head. Velda came screaming at him with a knife and he shot her in the face. In a rage, he then smashed their two-year-old toddler's skull with the rifle butt before throwing a knife at her that stuck in her throat. He finished off Marion Bartlett who was still alive by stabbing him in the throat.

Caril and Charlie tried to clean up the house and dispose of the bodies outside as best they could. They then stayed there for a week, pretending to anyone that asked that the family had flu. When Charlie's friend Bob Von Busch became suspicious, he went to the police. They visited and gave the house a cursory check but said everything was in order. Bob and his brother went to see for themselves, however, and discovered the bodies, hidden in outhouses and in the chicken coop. There was no sign of Charlie and Caril. They were long gone.

They had headed for a farm twenty miles outside Lincoln, owned by Charlie's friend, seventy-two-year-old August Meyer. For some reason, that has never really been clear, Charlie shot Meyer in the head and killed him. They stole money and guns and went to bed. Next day when their car got stuck in mud as they tried to leave, they hitched a ride from seventeen-year-old Robert Jensen and sixteen-year-old Carol King. As soon as they were in the car Starkweather pulled out a gun and demanded money. He ordered Jensen back in the direction of Meyer's farm where he shot him six times in the head. Carol was also dispatched with a bullet to the head. She was later found half-naked with stab wounds in the abdomen and pubic area, but she had not been raped. Charlie later said the killing and stabbing of Carol King was the work of Caril, claiming she was furious that he seemed attractive to the girl.

They drove off in Jensen's car, incredibly driving back to Lincoln where they cruised past the Bartlett house. Seeing the police cars outside the property, they knew that the bodies had been found. They spent the night sleeping in the car in a wealthy part of town. The next day, the mayhem at the Meyer farm was discovered. Charlie and Caril, now the subjects of a massive manhunt, were wanted in connection with the murders of six people.

There would be more.

When they woke up Charlie selected a house to rob, the home of wealthy industrialist, C. Lauer Ward. That morning, Ward's wife Clara and her fifty-one-year-old maid, Lillian Fencl, were at home. Lillian Fencl was horrified when she opened the front door to find a disheveled young man pointing a gun at her. The maid had a hearing problem and to make himself understood, Starkweather had to scribble notes to her. He wrote one ordering her to put the Wards' dog Queenie in the basement and to carry on preparing breakfast and when Clara Ward walked into the kitchen, he reassured her they would not be hurt. He called Caril in from the car and after drinking some coffee, she fell asleep in the library. Meanwhile, Mrs Ward was trying to remain calm and do as she was told. He ordered her to make breakfast for him and ate it in the library. He was getting a kick out of ordering this wealthy woman around.

At around 1 p.m., when Clara Ward went upstairs to change her shoes, Starkweather followed her. He claimed later that when he walked in she was pointing a gun at him. He pulled out a knife and threw it at her and it stuck in her back. He then stabbed her in an uncontrollable frenzy. When her poodle Suzy barked at him as he dragged her body into the bedroom, he broke the dog's neck with the butt of the gun.

Around this time, he telephoned his father and told him to let Bob Von Busch know that he was going to kill him for trying to interfere in his relationship with Caril. He then wrote a letter addressed 'to the law only', a confession of sorts, but mainly a self-justification.

They loaded up the Wards' black 1956 Packard with food and valuables before tying Lillian Fencl to a bed and stabbing her to death. Later each of them blamed the other for killing her. When C. Lauer Ward walked in from work that evening, they shot him dead.

The discovery of their bodies the next day sparked outrage and the National Guard were even called out to hunt for the killers. Jeeps, armed with mounted machine guns, began to patrol the empty streets. Spotter planes droned in the sky, searching for the black Packard.

Charlie and Caril made for Washington State, crossing into Wyoming next morning. At the side of the highway, they spotted a Buick in which travelling salesman Merle Collison was catching up on some sleep. He was shot in the head, neck, arm and leg, a shooting for which Charlie blamed Caril. But unable to work out how to release the car's emergency brake, Charlie summoned help from a young geologist who was passing. When the man stopped, Starkweather informed him that if he could not work out how to start the car, he would be killed. The young man suddenly realised that the man next to Starkweather was not asleep; he was dead. He made a grab for the gun. Just at that moment, as the two men struggled, a police car, driven by deputy sheriff William Romer pulled up behind the Packard. Caril immediately jumped out of the car shouting it was Charlie Starkweather and that he was a killer. Charlie pulled himself free of the other man and leapt into the car and sped off, officer Romer in hot pursuit, joined along the road by Sheriff Earl Heflin who had seen Starkweather's car fly past. Heflin pulled his gun and fired at the Packard, shattering its back window. Suddenly, the car in front stopped in the middle of the highway; Starkweather thought he had been shot. There was blood around his ear, but it had been made by a piece of flying glass. The officers approached the car and Charlie Starkweather was arrested.

The choice was now stark for Starkweather and Caril Fulgate – the gas chamber in Wyoming or the electric chair in Nebraska. They chose Nebraska to where he and Caril were extradited in January 1958. They were both charged with first-degree murder and murder while committing a robbery.

Starkweather's lawyers entered a plea of 'innocent by reason of insanity', but Starkweather insisted that he was sane. He also said initially that Caril was innocent but changed his tune when he learned that she was saying that she had been held hostage by him. He began to implicate her, claiming she was responsible for some of the murders and all the mutilations.

Caril was found guilty, but, being only fourteen, was spared the electric chair. Sentenced, instead, to life imprisonment, she was paroled in 1976, still maintaining that he had kidnapped her and that she was innocent. Starkweather was also found guilty and he was sentenced to die in the electric chair. The sentence was carried out on 25 June 1959.

Charles Starkweather had finally escaped from

JAMES HANRATTY

The place was known as Deadman's Hill, an appropriate name, given the events that took place there on 22 August 1961, events that would lead to one of the most controversial executions in British legal history.

That evening, the Morris Minor belonging to Michael Gregsten, a thirty-seven-year-old scientist at the Road Research Laboratory at Slough, was parked at Taplow Meadow, outside Maidenhead. In the car with him was twenty-two-year-old Valerie Storie, a fellow employee at the laboratory, with whom he was having an affair. The two were kissing in the front seat when there was a tap at the window. Turning, they saw a large, black revolver pointing at them through the window. A voice with a heavy cockney accent snarled, 'This is a hold-up. I am a desperate man; I have been on the run for four months. If you do as I tell you, you'll be alright.'

He opened the back door of the car and climbed in, ordering Gregsten to drive further into the field in which they were parked. They stopped and for the next two hours he talked to them. At 11.30 p.m., he said he was hungry and ordered Gregsten to start the car. They set off in the direction of London and drove around the city's northern suburbs aimlessly for a while. He told him stop at a milk-vending machine and then sent Gregsten into a shop to buy cigarettes for him. They then stopped at a petrol station to fill up before going on their way again. Meanwhile the terrified couple tried to persuade him to take money in exchange for letting them go, but he turned them down.

They drove through the town of St. Albans before joining the A6 at about 1.30 a.m., heading in a southerly direction. Their abductor told them he was tired and wanted to sleep. Twice he ordered Gregsten to turn off, but changed his mind. Finally, at Deadman's Hill, he ordered him to pull into a lay-by and stop.

Gregsten, increasingly concerned about what the man had in mind for them, at first refused, but when he was threatened with being shot, he did as he was told and pulled over. The man told them that he was going to sleep, but first he would have to tie them up, all the while the increasingly anxious Gregsten and Storie pleading with him not to shoot them. He firstly tied Storie's hands behind her back, using Gregsten's tie and then, having seen some rope in a bag in the car's boot, ordered Gregsten to pass it over to him. However, as Gregsten made to do so, without warning the man pulled the trigger of his revolver, firing two bullets into Gregsten's head, killing him instantly. A hysterical Storie asked him why he had done it and he replied coldly that Gregsten had moved too quickly.

He ordered Valerie Storie into the back of the Morris Minor, lying on top of Gregsten's body which had fallen there and proceeded to rape her, before ordering her to drag Gregsten's body from the car. He wanted to drive the vehicle, but seemed either unaware of how to drive this model, or simply had never learned to drive. When she was unable to explain how it worked, he angrily ordered her out of the car. She pleaded for her life, seated on the ground next to the body of her lover, even pulling out a pound note and offering it to him if he would take the car and go. Instead, he unloaded his gun into her, firing a total of seven shots, five of which hit Storie and would leave her paralyzed for the rest of her life. She fell backwards and pretended to be dead. She then heard him get into the car and drive off, gears crunching and engine racing. She lay there motionless for three hours, terrified in case he came back, and a few hours later passed out.

Sydney Burton, a farm labourer passing on foot,

found her and Gregsten at 6.45 a.m. the next day. He ran off and found a student, John Kerr, who was seated further along the A6, carrying out a road census. Kerr succeeded in flagging down a car and the emergency services were summoned.

With great presence of mind, John Kerr managed to write down barely conscious Valerie Storie's account of what had happened, scribbling it on one of the census forms he had been using earlier. When the police arrived, Kerr handed this vital, first-hand evidence, taken immediately after the incident, to one of the officers. It was never seen again. The investigation had already got off to a less than satisfactory start.

When Valerie Storie was interviewed later that morning, before undergoing surgery at Bedford Hospital, there were immediately some strange elements to the case. It seemed odd, for instance, that the gunman claimed he had been 'on the run for four months', but was dressed immaculately in a three-piece suit and clean, well-polished shoes. Police were also puzzled by the randomness of the attack; there was no motive that they could see.

The gun turned up two days after the attack under the back seat of a 36A London bus. It was loaded again, but, having been carefully wiped clean, it revealed no fingerprints. Decades later, it would be used to provide DNA evidence. When an appeal went out to hotel and boarding house managers, asking them if they had seen any guests behaving strangely in recent days, they received a report from one who said one guest had not left his room for five days after 22 August, the day of the murder. The man was picked up, giving his name as Frederick Durrant, but on investigation he was revealed to be Peter L. Alphon. He provided an alibi for the night in question, however, and was released.

Valerie Storie helped in the creation of an Identikit picture of the killer's face, but a few days later she provided police officers with an entirely different description. It was not helpful.

Then, on 7 September, a man claiming to be the A6 murderer, as the media were now calling him, attacked Meike Dalal in her Richmond home. On 23 September, she would identify him as Peter Alphon.

Meanwhile, two cartridge cases were discovered in a room at the Maida Vale Hotel. They matched the bullets that had killed Michael Gregsten and wounded Valerie Storie. They also matched the bullets in the gun found on the bus. According to the hotel manager, William Nudds, the room's last occupant had called himself James Ryan and that Ryan had asked where he could get on the 36A bus, the route on which the gun had been found. Peter Alphon had also stayed at the hotel, but in room 6 and not the one in the basement where the bullets had been found. Under questioning, Nudds changed his story, claiming that Alphon had actually been in the basement room and Ryan in number 6, but they had swapped rooms during the night.

When police took the unusual step of naming Peter Alphon as a suspect in the murder of Michael Gregsten, Alphon gave himself up, but Valerie Storie failed to identify him as the killer. By this time, Nudds had yet again changed his statement, saying that what he had first said about James Ryan was true. He claimed that, realizing that Alphon was the main suspect, he wanted to assist the police in bringing him to justice.

James Ryan was actually an alias of James Hanratty, a car thief and burglar. He rang the police and told them that as he had no alibi for the night of the murder, he had fled, but, he maintained, he was not the killer. Arrested eventually in Blackpool, he was identified by Valerie Storie in an identity parade – principally because of his cockney accent – and charged with the murder of Michael Gregsten and the rape and attempted murder of Valerie Storie.

His trial opened in Bedfordshire on 22 January 1962 and Hanratty initially defended himself by claiming to have been in Liverpool on the day of the murder. He recalled handing his suitcase to an attendant with a withered arm at Liverpool Lime Street station's left luggage counter. The man was introduced as a witness, but claimed never to have seen Hanratty. Unknown to the defence team, however, there was another man with a deformed hand working there and he did remember a man he thought might have been called something like 'Ratty'. He was never brought forward by detectives. Doubt remained as to Hanratty's whereabouts on the evening of the 22nd.

Suddenly, however, he changed his alibi, saying he had actually been in Rhyl in North Wales that night, having travelled there to sell a stolen watch. It was a foolish move because at that point there really was no evidence linking him with the crime. A woman who ran a boarding house in Rhyl, recognised Hanratty and said he had stayed sometime during the week of 19 to 26 August, but her records were chaotic and little could be worked out from them. The prosecution accused the boarding house owner of merely lying to gain publicity for her establishment. Nonetheless, the defence lawyers established that Hanratty could have stayed there on the night in question.

Valerie Storie's testimony was, of course, critical.

Seated in her wheelchair, she was still traumatised by the event and the questioning by the defence was, consequently, less rigorous than it perhaps might have been. She insisted that James Hanratty had killed Michael Gregsten but her belief was still based on nothing more than his cockney accent.

The jury entered a unanimous verdict of guilty after retiring for nine and a half hours. James Hanratty was sentenced to death and, on 4 April 1962, he became the 8th last man to be hanged in Britain.

Doubts lingered, however. Many still believe that Peter Alphon was the killer and one theory suggests that he confessed to a man called Jean Justice that he was paid £5,000 to end the affair between Gregsten and Storie. The gun went off entirely by accident, he claimed.

On 22 August 1962, the anniversary of the murder, Alphon is reported to have visited Hanratty's family and offered them compensation for their son's death. They showed him the door. Then, in May 1967, he staged a press conference in which he confessed to the murder and spoke about the involvement of a man called Charles France who hated Hanratty for having an affair with his daughter.

There is much to support the fact that Alphon was the A6 murderer. He resembled the Identikit pictures, even more than Hanratty; when stressed, he spoke with a cockney accent; he had no alibi; he had a motive and he was not a good driver. An investigative journalist proved also that Alphon did receive substantial cash payments between October 1961 and June 1962. But the police have continued to refuse to investigate Alphon's alleged involvement.

With the arrival of DNA testing, new hope arrived for James Hanratty's supporters who over the years had even included Beatle John Lennon and his artist wife Yoko Ono, who made a short film about the case. However, comparing DNA taken from material used as evidence proved inconclusive. Finally, James Hanratty's body was exhumed in 2001 in order to obtain DNA from it. It was compared with mucus found in the handkerchief in which the revolver had been wrapped before being left on the 36A bus, and with semen found on Valerie Storie's underwear. DNA samples from both sources matched Hanratty's, the first time evidence had been found linking him with the crime scene. Still, concerns remained about contamination of the materials used. Judges reviewing the case, however, regarded the contamination theory as 'fanciful'. They concluded that James Hanratty had, in actual fact, been guilty of murder and rape.

On the eve of his execution, James Hanratty told his family, 'I'm dying tomorrow, but I'm innocent.

Clear my name.' They never let him down and even now they continue to fight on his behalf.

GARY GILMORE

'Let's do it!' he said, looking at the white screen where there were five holes through which poked the barrels of five rifles. Then to the priest who had given him the last rites, he said quietly in Latin the words for, 'There will always be a father'. Suddenly the air was filled with the sound of gunshots and a few seconds later, his head slumped forwards. He raised his right hand slightly and let it drop as blood slowly seeped through his shirt, dripping onto the floor. A doctor approached, checked him and said that he was still alive, but within twenty seconds, he was dead. After an incredible months-long media circus, at 8.07 a.m. on 17 January 1977, Gary Mark Gilmore had at last got his wish and been executed.

It was a miserable life, half of it spent behind bars, that he at last left behind.

He was born in 1940 in Waco, Texas, to a couple who travelled around the western United States, his father selling advertising space, before settling finally in Portland, Oregon in 1952. His father had been a conman and much of the ad space he sold did not exist. He was also violent and abusive, especially where his son Gary was concerned. It created in the young boy a hatred and distrust of authority that would eventually turn him into a killer.

Within a couple of years, Gary Gilmore's long history of criminality had begun, with offences such as shoplifting, assault and car theft. At the age of fourteen, although he was a highly intelligent kid and a talented artist, he dropped out of high school and hitch-hiked to Texas. After a few months he returned to Portland where he resumed his criminal activity, starting a car-stealing ring with some acquaintances. He was soon under arrest, but his father hired a lawyer who got him off with a caution. If nothing else, his father's actions showed Gilmore that the legal system could be manipulated if you knew what you were doing. Two weeks later, however, he was in court again on another charge of stealing a car. This time, they were not so lenient. He was sent to the Maclaren Reform School for Boys for a year and spent the next few years in and out of jail until, at the age of eighteen, he was sent to the Oregon State Correctional Institution, again for car theft. Following his release, it was not long before he was back behind bars, now adding armed robbery to his substantial rap sheet. During this

JOHN STRAFFEN
John Straffen had the claim of being the longest-serving prisoner in the United Kingdom, having been in continuous custody since 23 April 1952 for murder. He eventually died behind bars in Broadmoor on 19 November 2007, aged 77.

BRUNO HAUPTMANN
Richard 'Bruno' Hauptmann was the man accused of
the kidnap and murder of the baby of the famous aviator
Charles Lindbergh. Despite using every tactic in the books,
investigators of this crime failed to get Hauptmann to confess
and he eventually went to the electric chair on 3 April 1936
in New Jersey State Prison.

JULIUS AND ETHEL ROSENBERG

The Rosenbergs were executed early in the morning on Saturday 20 June 1953 for conspiring to pass atomic secrets to Russia during World War Two. The couple were the first civilians in American history to be executed for espionage, despite desperate pleas written by Ethel to save their lives. Neither said a word as they faced their final minutes.

JAMES HANRATTY
There has been much controversy over the conviction and execution of James Hanratty. This controversy was mainly concerned with the question of the correct identity of the suspect and Hanratty's body was exhumed on 22 March 2001 so that a DNA sample could be taken for analysis.

GARY GILMORE
Gary Gilmore was the first person to be legally executed
in the US since 1967, ending a four-year lapse in which the
death penalty was outlawed. He is believed to have murdered
two people but was only convicted of one. Gilmore was fairly
unique in that he refused all attempts to appeal against his
stay of execution. His final words – 'Let's do it!'

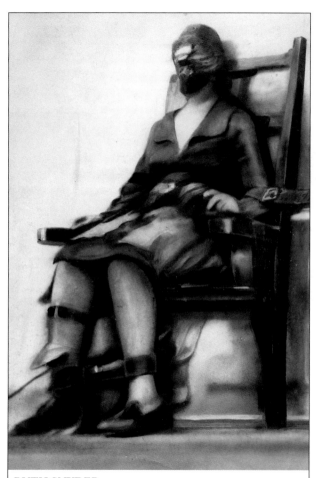

RUTH SNYDER
Ruth Snyder and her lover Judd Gray were found guilty of the premeditated murder of Ruth's husband. Judd Gray was executed first on 12 January 1928, followed just minutes later by Ruth. A clever reporter from the *New York Daily News* smuggled a camera into the death chamber by strapping it to his ankle, and managed to snap Ruth's last minutes.

JOSEF FRITZL
For twenty-four years the daughter of Austrian Josef Fritzl and three of the children she bore him were imprisoned in three tiny underground cellars. Having been sentenced to life imprisonment at a secure institution for mentally ill offenders, Fritzl now knows what it is like to have your freedom taken away.

LINDA CARTY

Linda Carty, a rape victim who claims she was framed for murder by career criminals, has been on death row in central Texas since 2002. Here a life-size cardboard cut-out is about to be placed on the Fourth Plinth in Trafalgar Square in yet another effort to prove her innocence.

incarceration, however, his father Frank died and on hearing the news, Gilmore went mad, wrecking his prison cell and trying to kill himself with a broken light bulb, the first of numerous suicide attempts. He was not permitted to attend his father's funeral and as a result became increasingly difficult to handle.

Prolixin is an antipsychotic drug that is used in the treatment of psychoses, such as schizophrenia. They decided to give it to Gary Gilmore to try to calm him down and reduce the violence he was displaying towards both prison warders and other inmates. Prolixin reduced him to a shambling, drooling zombie and horrified his mother when she next visited him. Eventually she persuaded the authorities to stop prescribing the drug to him but he would never forget its dehumanizing effects.

At twenty-four he was released from prison, but when he was arrested for robbing a man of just $11, the state of Oregon decided enough was enough. He was sentenced to fifteen years in Oregon State Penitentiary.

Gilmore was a habitual rule-breaker in prison and spent a large proportion of his sentence in solitary confinement. He used this time to his advantage, however, reading voraciously and writing poetry. He also developed his artistic skills to such an extent that he began to win art competitions. The authorities looked approvingly on this aspect of his character and he was granted early release in 1972 so that he could attend art school at a Eugene college. Needless to say, however, he blew the opportunity. On registration day at the college, he was getting drunk in a bar.

A month later, he was under arrest yet again for another armed robbery. In court, he made a moving plea for leniency. He explained how he had been in jail for all but two years since the age of fourteen:

...you can keep a person locked up too long' ... there is an appropriate time to release somebody or to give them a break...I stagnated in prison a long time and I have wasted most of my life. I want freedom and I realise that the only way to get it is to quit breaking the law...I've got problems and if you sentence me to additional time, I'm going to compound them.

The judge was not listening, however. He sentenced him to nine years. Gilmore was furious and took his rage out on the prison authorities, becoming even more violent and trying on a number of occasions to end his life. When they threatened him with Prolixin again, he begged them to come up with an alternative. That alternative was the harsh regime of the maximum-security penitentiary at

Marion in Illinois. He was allowed no family visits, but began a correspondence with a cousin, Brenda Nichol, who began working for his release, certain that a stable environment such as the one her family could offer him, would sort him out.

In 1977, she met him at the airport in Provo, Utah. At the age of thirty-seven, he carried his entire worldly possessions in a tiny sports bag.

They found him a job in his Uncle Vern Damico's shoe repair shop and he also worked installing insulation in houses. But, after being institutionalised for so long, Gilmore found it hard to settle and began to drink heavily in the bars of Provo. He finally found a girlfriend, however. Nicole Barrett was an attractive nineteen-year-old who had already been married and divorced three times. He moved in with her in the town of Spanish Fork, near Provo but it was not always good between them, especially when he was drinking, which was most of the time. Nicole feared the violent side she knew he had and eventually she and her two children moved out.

He searched everywhere for her, ranting to his cousin Brenda that he might kill her when he found her. She stayed out of sight, however, and he could not locate her.

Gilmore's blue Mustang that he had bought from a used car dealer was the bane of his life. It was always breaking down. On the dealer's forecourt was a ten-year-old white Ford pickup truck that he really wanted but he still owed money on the Mustang and the dealer had no interest in selling him another one on credit. Deep in debt and determined to have the truck, he went about getting money the only way he knew how, by stealing it.

On Monday 19 July 1976, he persuaded the used car dealer that he would be in a position to pay for the white pickup within a few weeks. The man warned him that if any payments were missed it would be immediately repossessed. They shook on it and Gilmore drove off in his new vehicle, heading for Nicole's mother's house but not finding his girlfriend there. Her younger sister April had always liked Gilmore and asked him if she could come for a ride in the truck.

At around 10.30 p.m. that night, he stopped the truck and told April he had a phone call to make. He got out, leaving her in the truck. He walked around the corner out of her sight, towards a Sinclair petrol station. He noted that it was quiet and only the attendant, a young Mormon named Max Jensen, was there. Gilmore quickly walked into the building and pulled out a .22 Browning Automatic. He ordered Jensen to empty his pockets and then pushed him into the toilet where he told him to lie down with his arms under his body. Gilmore put the barrel of the gun to the terrified young man's head and saying, 'This one's for me,' and pulled the trigger. Putting the barrel to the man's head again, he said, 'This one's for Nicole.'

Blood pooling on the floor and some even getting on his trousers, he turned and left the petrol station, neglecting to pick up a wad of cash on the counter. He and April went to see the film *One Flew Over the Cuckoo's Nest* and he dropped by his cousin Brenda's house for a short time. She noticed that he was agitated and thought there was something wrong. He and April spent the night in a hotel.

The next day, Tuesday 20 July, he had a problem with the pickup truck and took it to a garage near his Uncle Vern's house. He left the truck to be repaired, saying there was something he had to do. Walking towards his uncle's house, he saw the City Center Motel next door and had an idea. He went in.

Twenty-five-year-old Ben Bushnell, manager of the motel, lived on the premises with his wife and their baby son. He was walking into the foyer as Gilmore walked through the door with his gun in his hand. Gilmore ordered him to hand over the cash box and then lie down on the floor. He shot him in the head as he lay there. Bushnell was not dead, although he was fatally wounded and as he lay there trying to move, his wife Debbie walked into the foyer. Gilmore ran out, removing the cash from the cash box and stowing the box under a bush as he went. A little further on he was doing the same with his gun when it went off, a bullet ripping into the fleshy bit of his left hand between the thumb and palm.

Back at the garage he collected his truck, but the garage owner noticed he was bleeding. After Gilmore drove off, he heard about the shooting at the motel on a scanner he had and called the police, passing on the make, model and registration of Gilmore's pickup.

When Gilmore called Brenda and told her he had been shot and needed bandages and painkillers, she instead phoned the police, giving them her cousin's location. Meanwhile, Ben Bushnell's wife was being told that her husband had died.

Gilmore was arrested outside Nicole's mother's house and the next day, when he asked his cousin why she had turned him in, she replied, 'You commit a murder Monday, and commit a murder Tuesday. I wasn't waiting for Wednesday to roll around.'

At first, he denied having killed the two men, but his alibis did not stack up and his stash of stolen guns had been found. Eventually, he confessed, saying that if he had not been stopped, he would have carried on killing.

At his October trial, the prosecution concentrated on the murder of Ben Bushnell, the one which provided the strongest case and the jury took just an hour and twenty minutes to find him guilty of first degree murder. He was sentenced to death and was asked whether he wanted to be shot by a firing squad or hanged. He chose to be shot.

Until a few months previously, death sentences were customarily commuted to life. No one had been executed in the United States since the US Supreme Court had declared capital punishment to be a cruel and unusual punishment in 1972. This had been overturned in July 1976 by the Supreme Court judges and execution was now permitted. Astonishingly, however, the authorities were reluctant to carry out the punishment, even though Gilmore insisted that he wanted to die, to the extent that he dismissed his defence team and would not even allow an appeal to be brought. He had to argue his case in front of the Utah Supreme Court, insisting that he did not wish to spend the remainder of his life on death row. 'It's been sanctioned by the courts,' he said, 'and I accept that.'

His execution date, 15 November, came and went with protest groups and the American Civil Liberties Union trying to stop the execution. Gilmore became globally famous as his case raged on and he received thousands of letters, many from young women.

Meanwhile, he and Nicole staged a joint attempt at suicide. She smuggled pills into the prison, hidden in a balloon in her vagina. The two swallowed them at the same time, but both survived and she was banned from visiting him.

His story was sold to a film producer for $50,000 which Gilmore asked to be distributed amongst the family, some also going to the families of his two victims.

Another execution date, 6 December, passed, after his mother requested a stay. Gilmore had been on a hunger strike and she said he did not know what he was doing. That stay of execution was overturned ten days later but when Gilmore learned he would have to wait another month to be executed, he tried to kill himself.

On the night of 16 January the courts were still wrestling with the legal problems of his execution. There was a stay of execution and then that was set aside. Eventually the US Supreme Court declared that the execution could go ahead. Gilmore, meanwhile, was partying in prison with his family, drunk on three miniatures of whiskey that his Uncle Vern had managed to smuggle in. At one point country singer Johnny Cash phoned him and sang a song to him.

At 8 a.m. following morning he was strapped to a chair in a prison building and a paper target was taped over his heart. A black corduroy hood was then slipped over his head.

His was the first of 1,194 executions that have been carried out in the United States since 1977.

TED BUNDY

The problem was, he just looked and sounded nothing like a sex killer. Not only a sex killer; one of the worst the United States had ever known. How could this clean-cut, handsome, well-groomed man who spoke articulately and intelligently possibly be the same man who bludgeoned young women into unconsciousness and strangled them? How could he possibly be the kind of man to rape and even have sex with their corpses long after death? To grotesquely apply make-up to their dead bodies at the places in the mountains where he had dumped them and lie beside them? To decapitate them with a hacksaw? It did not seem possible, but it was. Bundy murdered thirty young women although some say he killed more, possibly as many as one hundred.

His first murder victim was twenty-one-year-old student Lynda Healy. For some time, he had been looking in windows, watching women undress, graduating to beating them on the head with a piece of wood. In January 1974, he had attacked eighteen-year-old Sharon Clarke at home. He beat her repeatedly with a crowbar until she was unconscious and then thrust a piece of wood inside her vagina, causing dreadful internal injuries. He did not kill her, however. On 1 February, he battered Lynda Healy into unconsciousness before carrying her out to his car. He drove her to Taylor Mountain, about twenty miles to the east of Seattle, where he forced her to take off her pyjamas and raped her. He then beat her to death.

In the next six months, he killed seven more times. On 12 March, nineteen-year-old Donna Manson was abducted walking to a jazz concert on the Evergreen State College campus, in Olympia, Washington. Her body was never found. On 17 April, eighteen-year-old Susan Elaine Rancourt disappeared as she walked across Ellensburg's Central Washington State College campus at night. On 6 May, twenty-two-year-old Kathy Parks vanished from Oregon State University in Corvallis while innocently walking to another dorm hall to have coffee with friends. On 1 June, twenty-two-year-old Brenda Carol Ball disappeared from the Flame Tavern in Burien, Washington. On 11 June, eighteen-year-old Georgeann Hawkins disappeared from behind her sorority house at the University of Washington, and on 14 July, twenty-three-year-old Janice Ann Ott and nineteen-year-old Denise Marie Naslund were abducted several hours apart from Lake Sammamish State Park in Issaquah, Washington.

Three of the girls were taken to Taylor Mountain. The last two were raped at a house near to the park in which they were abducted, the second being raped in full view of the other girl. It was a new thrill for him.

The method he used to abduct Janice Ott and Denise Naslund was generally the way he always did it. Calling himself by his own Christian name, he approached them with his arm in a sling asking for help to unload his sailing boat from his car. When they arrived at the car park, however, they would discover that there was no boat. Ted told them that they would have to help him get it from his house which was nearby. Many young women he asked that day sensed there was something not quite right and refused to help. The two girls he killed that day seem to have been eager to help the handsome young man. On other occasions, he would seek help in carrying books or a box to his car, but when they arrived there, he would grab a crowbar and smash them on the skull with it before bundling them into the vehicle.

In 1946, Ted Bundy had been born to an unmarried mother who moved to Seattle to escape the social stigma of having an illegitimate child.

There she married a cook who worked in a hospital and from whom the young Theodore Robert took his surname, Bundy. At a relatively early age Bundy began to steal and he was a habitual liar, which may have been a consequence of learning that he was illegitimate. It seems to have had a profound effect on him.

In his late teens, he fell in love with a fellow student, Stephanie Brooks. The two were engaged and Bundy went to Stanford University to study Chinese, possibly in an effort to impress Stephanie and her wealthy family. It did not work out, however – his grades were poor and he felt lonely and homesick. Not long after his return, Stephanie broke off the engagement, leaving him devastated. He became solitary and moody.

While working as a busboy in a hotel, he befriended a drug addict and with him drifted into a career of theft, stealing for thrills more than anything else. He meandered through various jobs, at one point working for the Republican Party during an election campaign.

One night, however, he met a woman named Meg Anders and they became lovers. But at the same time, he was spending a lot of his evenings spying through the windows of women's college dorms. He was now studying psychology at university and eventually obtained his degree. He moved on to law, but was unable to find a law school that would take him. Around this time, he also rekindled his affair with Stephanie Brooks now living in San Francisco, even though he was still in a relationship with Meg Anders. Stephanie found that he was no longer the gauche, immature young man she had known. There was a new-found air of confidence about Bundy that she found attractive. Manipulative as ever, however, no sooner had he snared her again than he dumped her, dishing out some of the medicine she had given him.

After the disappearances of Janice Ott and Denise Naslund in July 1974, Investigators at least had a description, the name 'Ted' and a make of car, a Volkswagen Beetle. Several people, including Meg Anders, passed his name to police but they were inundated with tip-offs and this clean-cut college student just did not seem the type. They ignored the tips. Meanwhile, bodies were turning up on patches of wasteland and on Taylor Mountain.

Finally, Bundy found a college that would take him, the University of Utah law school in Salt Lake City. Once established there, he started killing again. On 2 October, Nancy Wilcox disappeared, having last been seen in a Beetle. On 18 October, he murdered seventeen-year-old Melissa Smith, daughter of the Midvale police chief. She was found nine days later, raped, sodomised and strangled. Seventeen-year-old Laura Aime, disappeared after leaving a Halloween party on 31 October. She was found, naked, beaten and strangled a month later in American Fork Canyon in Utah's Wasatch Mountains.

On 8 November, Carol DaRonch only just escaped from his clutches. He approached her in a mall, told her he was a police officer and told her someone had been trying to break into her car. When he asked her to accompany him to the police station, she got into his car, but when they had driven only a short distance, he pulled over and tried to put a pair of handcuffs on her. As he did so, he pulled out his crowbar but she caught it in mid-air, managed to get the door open and fell out onto the highway. Bundy sped off.

An hour later, however, seventeen-year-old Debby Kent disappeared from Viewmont High School. A small key was found in the car park which later turned out to be the key to the handcuffs that had been attached to the wrist of Carol DaRonch.

Bundy started killing in Colorado in 1975. Caryn Campbell disappeared from Wildwood Inn at Snowmass, where she was holidaying with her fiancé and his children. She vanished walking from the elevator to her room, a distance of fifty feet. Vail ski instructor, Julie Cunningham disappeared on 15 March and Denise Oliverson vanished from Grand Junction on 6 April. Using crutches, Bundy asked her to help him carry some ski boots to the Beetle.

As more women disappeared, Bundy's name kept appearing on lists of suspects, but it remained to be investigated.

Suddenly, however, they had him. He was picked up after failing to stop for a police officer and in the car they found the tools of his trade – a ski mask, a crowbar, handcuffs, trash bags and an icepick. Soon, they linked him to the Carol DaRonch incident. While investigations continued into the murders, he was convicted of kidnapping and sentenced to fifteen years in prison. Bundy sobbed as sentence was pronounced.

They found strands of hair in his car that matched that of Melissa Smith who he had killed the previous October. He was extradited to Colorado to stand trial for murder. But, sensationally, they let him escape on 7 June when he leapt from the window of the Pitkin County Courthouse in Aspen. He was on the run for almost a week before being recaptured and would have got away, but for a couple of diligent police deputies.

Six months later, however, on 30 December, he

was out again, having acquired a hacksaw blade and $500 in cash. He escaped through a roof space above his prison cell and stole an MG in town. When its engine gave out in a blizzard in the mountains, he hitch-hiked to Vail and travelled by bus, train and plane to Tallahassee in Florida, renting a room in a boarding house under the name Chris Hagen. In Florida, Bundy established a new identity for himself, even obtaining a false birth certificate and social security card in his new name. Shoplifting and stealing purses and credit cards kept him in funds.

The boarding house in which he had a room was close to the sorority houses of Florida State University and it was not long before he began to have the old familiar urges.

On the evening of 15 January 1978, a student spotted a man lurking in front of her sorority house. As she was about to telephone the police, a fellow student, Karen Chandler staggered out of her room with blood pouring from a serious wound, screaming hysterically that she and her roommate, Kathy Kleiner had been attacked by a madman. Karen and Kathy lived, but two other students, twenty-year-old Lisa Levy and twenty-one-year-old Margaret Bowman were not so lucky. Bundy had battered Lisa Levy with a piece of wood and then strangled her. He had bitten her on the buttocks and nipples and had sexually assaulted her with a bottle of hairspray.

The night was young, however. A few blocks away he broke into a house in which student Cheryl Thomas was sleeping. He beat her savagely, but she survived. At the foot of her bed police found a ski mask. The evidence was there, but forensic science was not as advanced as it is today and Bundy was, of course, completely unknown to the Florida authorities.

On February 9, he travelled to Lake City in Florida where he abducted, raped and murdered twelve-year-old Kimberly Leach. Three days later, he stole another VW Beetle and drove west across the Florida panhandle, and on 15 February he was stopped by a Pensacola police officer who called in a check on Bundy's registration. When he was informed that the car was stolen, he tried to arrest Bundy. There was a scuffle but Bundy was subdued. As the officer drove him to the police station, the killer moaned, 'I wish you had killed me.'

Bundy skillfully conducted his own defence at his trial, charming the jury with his winning personality and using the law to make the case last for as long as possible. It came as little surprise, however, when in February 1980, he was found guilty and sentenced to die in the electric chair.

Awaiting execution, he confessed to many details of murders that had been unknown or unconfirmed. He even offered to help in the search for another serial killer, the so-called Green River Killer, and the investigators in that case did talk to him but he provided no real insights.

His appeals succeeded in beating death warrants for 4 March, 2 July and 18 November 1986, but when they were finally exhausted, he confessed to the eight murders in Washington State for which he had been the prime suspect. He further confessed to the murders in Idaho, Utah and Colorado. He did not do this out of the goodness of his heart, however. He was hoping he could obtain another stay of execution. He failed.

He, apparently, contemplated suicide in the days before the execution but decided against it. Therefore, on the morning of 24 January 1989, Ted Bundy was strapped into the electric chair at State Prison at Starke, Florida. Asked if he had any last words, he said, 'I'd like you to give my love to my family and friends'. The switch was thrown at 7.06 a.m. and the crowds waiting outside the prison that morning cheered as the news spread that Ted Bundy was dead

RUBEN MONTOYA CANTU

Ruben Cantu's last request for bubblegum was denied, another disappointment for a kid who never had much of a chance in life and who never had any chance when it came to his death. Firstly, he shot a police officer, never a good idea, even though the officer was off-duty and pulled out his weapon first without identifying himself. Secondly, Sam Millsap, the Bexar County District Attorney who presided over his case just happened to be, in his own words, 'a lifelong supporter of the death penalty.' The problem was, Ruben Cantu, executed by lethal injection in August 1993, was innocent of the crime for which he died.

He had been a painfully quiet kid, always eager to please, who sucked his thumb much longer than he should have. But his upbringing might have had something to do with that. His mother had married at the age of thirteen to a man twenty-four years older than her. Ruben was the fourth of the five

244

children that Aurelia and Fidencio 'Fred' Cantu brought into the world.

Fred was a maintenance man at Market Square, a popular tourist attraction and his long hours at work meant that Aurelia brought up her four sons and one daughter pretty much on her own. When Ruben was fourteen, the couple separated, Aurelia moving with the children close to the ranch owned by her parents at the small town of Floresville. Ruben, however, chose to stay with his father. They lived in a trailer park on Briggs Street in the downmarket southern outskirts of San Antonio. It was a rough place where drugs were readily available and the nights were frequently punctuated by the sound of gunfire. The southern part of San Antonio was the territory of a gang known as the Grey Eagles, a bunch of tough kids who ruthlessly protected their turf, keeping out rivals and running rackets in the area. Like most other local kids, Ruben became a member, even though he was small for his age, had learning difficulties and was forced to take special classes at school. Before long, he was indulging in the pastimes of the gang members – taking drugs and stealing cars.

By the time he was fifteen years old, Ruben was working in a car-theft ring, stealing cars to order and sometimes driving them to the Mexican border, absent for days, but returning with as much as $3,000. Not bad money for a fifteen-year-old. In the midst of the horrific poverty with which he was surrounded, Ruben was doing okay, able to buy video games, videos and all the drugs he wanted. Life was good, or at least as good as it could get in southern San Antonio.

It was a time of corruption and bad practice in the San Antonio police department. Police officers were accused of being involved in drug trafficking and vigilantes even began to supplant the police in certain areas, unable to rely on official solutions to law-breaking. Ruben Cantu was taught by his environment that police officers were not to be trusted and given the way his life turned out it was the correct thinking. It was said in the area in which he lived that he was a master of the art of silence, of never snitching on anyone, no matter what the situation. However, he was never arrested, even though his older brothers were regulars at police headquarters on drug and theft charges. For that reason, police officers disliked him and were desperate to implicate him in something. They would get their wish.

It was a violent murder on 8 November 1994, Briggs Street where Ruben lived with his mother, that would finally give the authorities their chance to nail the quiet kid who was involved in all kinds of criminal activity. Nineteen-year-old Juan Moreno had recently left a Mexican ranch in Zacatecas to seek his fortune in the United States. He and his friend, twenty-five-year-old Pedro Gomez, a father of three, also from Mexico, were building a house for Moreno's brother and wife but a water heater had recently been stolen from the unfinished property and Gomez and Moreno had decided to sleep there at night in order to deter thieves. That night, they had eaten dinner and had gone to sleep inside what was a shell of a house. Living conditions for the two men were pretty harsh. Water was stored in empty beer cans and the only light was from a bare low-wattage bulb that was powered by electricity from a neighbour's supply. They went to bed that night wearing their clothes, but in their wallets was around $1,000 in cash.

Suddenly they were both woken by the light being switched on and found themselves confronted by a couple of young Latinos, probably teenagers, the older of whom was wielding a .22 calibre rifle. They wanted money and Gomez quickly handed over his wallet, containing $600. Foolishly, however, as he did that, he turned over his mattress, beneath which lay a concealed .38 calibre revolver. He leapt to his feet, the gun in his hand. The teenager with the rifle opened fire immediately, pumping nine bullets into

Gomez who fell to the floor dead. The boy then turned his weapon on Moreno, shooting him at least nine times. The two teenagers fled.

Juan Moreno had not been killed, however, and somehow made it outside where he called for help. He was discovered at midnight by a police officer in the seat of his pickup close to death, his wallet untouched. He gave investigating officers a description of his assailants, saying he thought they lived nearby, but, in reality, they could have been any young Hispanic male in the area.

Homicide detective James Herring tried to interview Moreno the day after the murder at Wilford Hall Hospital on the Lackland Air Force Base. Moreno, however, was in a critical condition and on a ventilator. He had received massive facial injuries and eventually would lose a lung, a kidney and part of his stomach as a result of his injuries.

Six days later, police made another visit to Moreno's bedside. He was still barely able to talk, but provided more details, describing his attackers as two Latin-American males, one thirteen or fourteen and the other nineteen. He said that he had seen the younger one in the neighbourhood. A teacher at South Antonio High School told a beat officer that there was a rumour going round that Ruben Cantu, a pupil at the school had been involved in the killing.

Detective Herring was passed this information and went back to the hospital to show Moreno five photographs of Hispanic men, Ruben Cantu's amongst them. Moreno failed to identify Cantu.

For a time it appeared as if the Gomez murder case was going to be closed without resolution. That changed on 1 March 1985, however. Ruben Cantu was shooting pool for 35 cents a game at the Scabaroo Lounge, not far from where he lived. Playing on another pool table was an off-duty police officer, Joe De La Luz. As usual, De La Luz was wearing two revolvers under his civilian clothes. Tragically, Ruben Cantu was also armed and both men had had a few drinks.

Their versions of events differed. Officer De La Luz maintained that there was a dispute and Cantu shot him four times, completely unprovoked. 'I remember a person standing in front of me firing an unknown calibre weapon at me,' he later said. Ruben Cantu, on the other hand, stated that the two had argued over a game of pool they were playing and that he had only pulled his weapon after De La Luz had shown him the gun he was wearing in his waistband. He said he had no idea that De La Luz was a police officer but never denied shooting him.

Yet, he was never charged with the shooting, even though he had admitted it and had done it in front of a poolroom full of witnesses. The fact that police officers carried out an illegal search of Cantu's home on the night of the shooting was going to make it difficult for them to bring a successful prosecution. Instead, they reopened the Briggs Street murder case which Cantu had not been connected with. It seemed that as they were unable to nail him for the shooting of a police officer, they were going to get him for another murder, even though he had not even been there.

On 2 March, a detective turned up at Juan Moreno's brother's house where Moreno was recovering from his injuries. Again, he showed him a picture of Ruben Cantu and again he failed to identify him as the killer of Pedro Gomez. During their conversation, however, the officer let slip that Cantu had shot a police officer. The next day, a second detective was sent to show Moreno a set of photographs. This time Moreno picked Cantu out of the four pictures he was shown, although he said in a later interview that 'They told me they were certain it was him, and that's why I testified...That was bad to blame someone that was not there.'

There were no fingerprints, no murder weapon and no confessions and fifteen-year-old David Garza, arrested as Cantu's accomplice that night, refused to name Cantu as being involved, even when told it would help his case. At the trial, Moreno refused to budge on his implication that his friend had been shot by Cantu. He was asked to point him out in court and had no hesitation in doing so. He provided an emotional testimony that swayed the jury and they found Ruben Cantu guilty of murder in the first degree.

When it came to the sentencing phase of the trial, Officer De La Luz was introduced as a witness. Cantu's gang activities, an impending charge for the possession of marijuana and De La Luz's testimony condemned him. De La Luz testified that Cantu had fired his weapon at him completely without provocation. It came as no surprise when Ruben Cantu, silent as usual throughout the trial, was sentenced to death. He wrote to the people of San Antonio days after his sentence, saying, 'My name is Ruben M. Cantu and I am only eighteen years old. I got to the ninth grade and I have been framed in a capital murder case.'

It was to no avail, even though the Texas Court of Criminal Appeals found the identification process improperly suggestive. Significantly, however, not one of Cantu's appeal lawyers attempted to bring Juan Moreno back from Mexico, to where they assumed he had returned, to confirm his identification.

Ironically, he was in San Antonio all the time.

Moreno has said that he knew what he was doing was wrong, that he was only giving the police officers what they wanted. District Attorney Sam Millsap has since said, 'It is troubling to me personally. No decision is more frightening than seeking the death penalty. We owe ourselves certainty on it.' Unfortunately, he says, Ruben Cantu was very likely innocent. Miriam Ward, forewoman of the jury that convicted Cantu has said, 'We did the best we could with the information we had, but with a little extra work, a little extra effort, maybe we'd have gotten the right information. The bottom line is, an innocent person was put to death for it. We all have our finger in that.'

At the time of Ruben Cantu's execution in 1993, Juan Moreno has said, someone from Cantu's family tried to phone him, but he was not at home.

JOHN WAYNE GACY

As a child, John Wayne Gacy Jr seemed happy
enough. Born in 1942 in Chicago, the second of
three children, he grew up in a middle class area, a
normal kid with a newspaper round as well as some
weekend work in a local grocery store. The only
cloud on the horizon was his relationship with his
father, John Wayne Gacy Sr. The problems with
his father arose from John Sr's alcoholism and his
antipathy to the boy whom he frequently called a
'sissy'. He would beat his wife and verbally abused
all of his children.

John Jr was also victim of a serious accident when
he was hit on the head by a swing when he was
eleven years old. A blood clot on the brain caused
by this accident was not discovered until he was
sixteen, but at last the worrying blackouts from
which he had suffered for five years were treated.

Gacy attended four different high schools before
eventually dropping out and leaving for Las Vegas
to start a new life. The new life was not really as

he had hoped, however, and he ended up working as a janitor in a funeral parlour. It took him three months to earn enough money to be able to buy a ticket back to Chicago.

Enrolling at a business college shortly after his return, he at last found his purpose in life; he was a born salesman. He put his new-found talent to work in his first proper job, working for a shoe company. Starting as a management trainee, he was soon fast-tracked into managing a men's clothing outlet in Springfield, Illinois. In Springfield, Gacy became involved in a number of community and civic organisations, rising to senior positions in several. He was obsessively committed to them and the Jaycees, for instance, named him as their 'Man of the Year'. He gave so much of his spare time to these activities that at one time was hospitalised for nervous exhaustion. His health was not great anyway. He had gained a good deal of weight and his heart which would give him problems throughout his life was troubling him.

In September 1964, he married a woman he met at work. Marlynn Myers' parents owned a string of Kentucky Fried Chicken franchises in Waterloo, Iowa and his new father-in-law offered him a job at one. Gacy and Marlynn moved to Iowa where they began a family, a son being born not long after their arrival. Again, he threw himself into voluntary work, especially with the Jaycees.

But a problem soon began to arise. Nasty rumours spread around town about Gacy. People thought it funny that he was always surrounded by young boys and some said he must be homosexual, especially when stories also emerged of him flirting with some of the kids who worked with him at the restaurant. In May 1968, some substance was added to the rumours when Gacy was arrested for committing sodomy on a teenager named Mark Miller, who claimed that while visiting Gacy's home Gacy had tied him up and raped him. Gacy denied everything, claiming, somewhat ridiculously, that he was being set up by opponents in the Jaycees who did not want him to be president of a new chapter. However, a boy he paid to beat up his accuser was arrested and confessed that Gacy had paid him to carry out the beating. Gacy was arrested, convicted and sent to the Iowa State Penitentiary for 10 years. Marlynn understandably divorced him not long after and he never saw his children again.

He was paroled for good behaviour on 18 June 1970, after serving just eighteen months, and, his father now dead, moved back home to live with his mother and found work as a chef. Four months later, he and his mother and sisters moved into a house at 8213 West Summerdale Avenue in the Norwood Park Township, where he lived in one half of the building and they had the other half. The building had a four-foot deep crawl space under the floor that would, in time, become very useful to John Gacy.

Much as his mother was convinced he had learned his lesson and was trying to make a fresh start, he was still into young boys. In February 1971, he was charged with disorderly conduct after a teenage boy claimed that Gacy had tried to force him to have sex with him. The boy failed to turn up for court, however and luckily for Gacy, the Iowa Parole Board was not informed. Eight months later he was discharged from parole. Just as well really, as in June 1972 he was again arrested and charged with battery. He had shown a young man a sheriff's badge to get him into his car and then forced him to have sex. Again he walked free when the boy dropped the charges.

He remarried in 1972, his new wife, Carole Hoff, a childhood friend who already had two daughters. They moved into his half of the Summerdale house. Three years later, he started his own business, a construction company, PDM Contractors. He hired teenage boys to work for him, claiming that they were cheap. This, of course, was not the only reason.

The marriage, however, was beginning to fall

apart. Gacy began to stay out all night and she found wallets with IDs belonging to young men lying around the house. When he began bringing gay pornography home, she divorced him.

By the time Gacy was engaged to Carole Hoff, he had already killed his first victim. He picked up Timothy McCoy at Chicago's Greyhound Bus terminal and took him home with him. The next morning he stabbed him to death and buried him in the crawl space beneath the house. He later claimed it was an accident; he had thought McCoy was going to attack him with a knife.

In 1975, Gacy had created a clown character he called Pogo the Clown, teaching himself how to apply the make-up and performing at children's parties. He also continued with his civic duties, becoming active in the Democratic Party in Chicago and serving on the Norwood Park Township Street Lighting Committee. But rumours began to circulate once again about his relationships with young boys. One boy, sixteen-year-old Tony Antoniucci, accused him of making inappropriate advances to him. Next month, at his home, Gacy tricked Antonucci into putting on a pair of handcuffs and began to undress him. The boy fought free of the cuffs and overpowered Gacy, forcing him to the floor and putting the handcuffs on him. Gacy promised to leave him alone and, amazingly, Antonucci carried on working for him.

His second victim, another PDM employee, Johnny Butkovich, loved cars, especially his 1986 Dodge. As he frequently did with his employees, Gacy tried to con him out of a couple of weeks' pay. Butkovich drove to Gacy's house with a couple of friends to collect what he was owed, but after an argument Johnny realised he was getting nowhere and drove off. After he had dropped off his friends, he was never seen again.

Another employee, Michael Bonnin disappeared en route to the train station in June 1976. Billy Carroll Jr, a kid with a nose for trouble, vanished on 13 June. Carroll Jr, who at the age of sixteen made money pimping teenage boys to male adults left home and never returned. PDM employee, Gregory Godzik dropped his girlfriend off at her house on 12 December 1976. The next day the seventeen-year-old's car was found, but he was nowhere to be seen.

They continued to vanish – nineteen-year-old John Szyc on 20 January 1977. Szyc, who did not work for PDM but knew both of Gacy's last two victims, had driven off in his 1971 Plymouth Satellite and was never seen again. Not long after, however, the Plymouth was stopped leaving a gas station without paying. The young driver said that the man he lived with could explain everything. Police visited Gacy who explained that Szyc had sold the car to him. If police had checked, however, they would have learned that the car was made over to Gacy eighteen days after Szyc's disappearance. Furthermore, the signature was forged.

Young men were disappearing sometimes at the rate of two a month. In 1976, he killed in April, May (twice), June (twice), August, October (twice) and December. In 1977, he killed in January, March, July, September (twice), October, November (twice) and December. The year 1978 saw the crawl space being filled up by teenage boys murdered in February, June, November (twice) and December.

The last boy he killed was Robert Piest, a fifteen-year-old who vanished on 11 December 1978 from outside the pharmacy where he worked. His mother was waiting inside the store for Robert who had said he had to talk to a contractor about some work, but he failed to return. Three hours later, she called the police.

Robert had told her the name of the contractor and within a short space of time, Lieutenant Joseph Kozenak was knocking at John Wayne Gacy's door. Kozenak asked him to accompany him to the station to answer some questions but Gacy apologised, telling him he was unable to go with him as there had been a death in the family and he had to make some telephone calls to relatives. He finally arrived at the police station a few hours later but told them he knew nothing about Robert Piest's disappearance.

Kozenak did not end the matter there, however. When he ran a check on Gacy he found his conviction for sodomy on a teenager a number of years previously. He immediately obtained a search warrant and returned to Summerdale. What they found was fascinating. Amongst the items confiscated were drugs, a 6mm Italian pistol, police badges, handcuffs, and hidden in the attic beneath the insulation was an 18-inch rubber dildo. There was a hypodermic syringe and a small brown bottle filled with an unknown liquid, and clothing that was too small for John Gacy's ample frame.

His three vehicles were confiscated and in one, a 1979 Oldsmobile Delta 88, were found strands of hair that matched Robert Piest's.

Crawling into the space beneath the house, investigators were almost knocked out by the stench. The earth had been sprinkled with lime but appeared untouched. They called him in and read him his rights, but eventually, having nothing to go on, they had to let him go. They decided, however, to charge him with possession of marijuana and Valium. At least they had him for something.

Work on the materials taken from his house continued and at last they came up with something – a ring that belonged to John Szyc who had disappeared a year before. Gradually, they began to assemble the facts that another three employees of PDM had also mysteriously vanished. Critically, a receipt they had taken away turned out to have belonged to a co-worker of Robert Piest who had given it to the missing boy on the day he disappeared. Kozenak began to realise that this was going to be the case of his life.

They returned to Summerdale and Gacy finally cracked, confessing that he did kill someone but that it had been in self-defence. He told them the body was buried beneath the garage. They were more interested in the crawl space, however, and when the County Cook Medical Examiner, Dr Robert Stein had a look, he recognised the unmistakable odour of human decomposition. They started digging.

On 22 December, Gacy confessed to the murders of more than thirty people, tricking them first into putting on handcuffs and then sexually assaulting them, a sock stuffed into their mouth to silence them. He killed his victims by pulling a board against their throats as he raped them. They were then buried in the space under the house.

A total of twenty-seven bodies were removed

from beneath the house and another two had been found in the Des Plaines River. The crawl space had been full. Another body was found under the patio while yet another was discovered under his recreation room. Robert Piest was found in the Illinois River. Thirty-two bodies and all but nine of them had been identified by the start of his trial on 6 February 1980.

John Wayne Gacy was found guilty on 13 March and sentenced to death. For the next fourteen years, he studied law in prison and watched as appeal after appeal was rejected.

On 10 May 1994, as Gacy was executed by lethal injection at Stateville Correctional Centre in Illinois, rowdy crowds outside the prison walls threw execution parties. Merchandise was on sale and when it was announced that Gacy was dead there were loud cheers.

At no point did Gacy express any remorse for his crimes.

His last words were 'Kiss my ass'.

TIMOTHY MCVEIGH

It was all so cold and calculated, not unlike Timothy McVeigh.

He had decided he was going to blow up the nine-storey Alfred P. Murrah Federal Building in Oklahoma City. Named after a federal judge, the building had been opened in 1977 and housed around five hundred and fifty employees working in the regional offices of the Social Security Administration, the Federal Bureau of Investigation (FBI), the Drug Enforcement Administration (DEA) and the Bureau of Alcohol, Firearms and Tobacco (ATF). There was also a day-care centre for children of employees on the building's ground floor. It was perfect for the kind of hell McVeigh wanted to unleash.

He had bought three 54-gallon drums of nitro-methane in October 1994, dressed as a biker and claiming that he and his friends wanted to use it to race their motorcycles. Gradually, he bought the other components of the huge bomb that he and his associate Terry Nichols planned to explode. Nichols had taught him how to make a bomb out of simple, innocuous household materials and now they rented storage space in which to store it all until the big day. They had stolen blasting caps and other useful equipment from a quarry in Marion, Texas and to reassure themselves that they were on the right track, they built a prototype bomb which they exploded successfully in a remote corner of the desert.

On 14 April, McVeigh checked into a room in the Dreamland Motel in Junction City, Kansas, before renting a truck from the Ryder Car Rental Company. He signed the name Robert D. Kling, an incongruously humorous reference to the Klingon warriors from his favourite television show *Star Trek*.

Two days later, with Nichols in the passenger seat, he drove the truck two hundred and forty-seven miles from Junction City to Oklahoma City. They had bought a yellow 1977 Mercury Marquis which was to be used as the getaway car and parked it a few blocks away from the Alfred P. Murrah Building, removing the licence plates and taping a note to the windscreen saying it had broken down and requesting that it should not be towed away as it would be moved by 23 April. They drove back to

Kansas where they began to assemble the bomb.

It was ready by 18 April and they loaded it carefully onto the truck – one hundred and eight 50 pound bags of ammonium-nitrate fertiliser, three 55-gallon drums of liquid nitromethane, crates of an explosive called Tovex that was safer to transport and store than ordinary dynamite, seventeen bags of the explosive ANFO, mostly used in mining and quarrying, and shock tubes and cannon fuse to set off the explosion.

At Lake Geary County State Lake, they nailed boards to the floor of the back of the truck to hold the barrels in place. They mixed the deadly chemicals that made up the bomb and poured the liquid into the drums. They next arranged the barrels in the way that they hoped would lead to the most damage being done.

Holes drilled in the back wall of the truck's cab would allow McVeigh to ignite the fuses but nothing was left to chance – a failsafe second fuse was provided in case the first failed. They changed one element of their plan. Originally, they were both going to drive the truck and position and ignite the bomb, but now they reasoned, it would be simpler if just one of them did it. McVeigh volunteered. Terry Nichols returned to Kansas, leaving McVeigh to drive back to Junction City where he decided on one more slight amendment to the plan, bringing forward the time at which the bomb would go off from 11 a.m. to 9 a.m. He believed it would be more effective as people arrived for work.

At 8.50 a.m. on 19 April – the anniversary of the 1993 siege at Waco in which David Koresh and seventy-four members of his Branch Davidian cult died, as well as the two hundred and twentieth anniversary of the Battle of Lexington and Concord, Timothy McVeigh drove the Ryder truck into Oklahoma City. At around 8.57 a.m., as the truck approached the Alfred P. Murrah Building, he lit the five-minute fuse. Three minutes later, at 9 a.m., he lit the two-minute fuse. He parked the truck in the building's drop-off zone, unaware that it was directly below the building's day centre that at that time was filled with children and employees arriving for the day. Not that he would have really cared, however. He switched off the engine, leapt from the cab and walked hurriedly away, making for the yellow Mercury. He had a couple of minutes to get out of range.

At 9.02 a.m., the truck exploded creating a huge crater 30-feet wide and 8-feet deep. The massive explosion had the desired effect, destroying a third of the concrete and glass structure and damaging or destroying three hundred and twenty-four nearby buildings. One hundred and sixty-eight people died in that dreadful moment – many of them killed by flying glass – and four hundred and fifty were injured. Among the dead were nineteen children who died as the bomb went off directly beneath them, 'collateral damage' to McVeigh, although he did later say that had he known the day centre was there, he might have changed the target.

McVeigh himself felt the power of the explosion as he ran towards the getaway car, being lifted off his feet by the blast. He jumped into the Mercury and drove out of the city, heading north, knowing that the emergency services were preoccupied with the mayhem back there and not interested in his car. However, as he headed north on Interstate 35, close to the town of Perry, an alert trooper noticed that the Mercury was missing its licence plates and stopped the car. McVeigh immediately informed the officer that he was in possession of a gun that was not licensed in Oklahoma – the officer could not fail to notice a bulge beneath his jacket – and he was arrested and charged with being in possession of a concealed weapon as well as for driving without licence plates.

Three days later, while in custody, he was identified by a clerk at the Dreamland Motel as Robert Kling, from a sketch created by the FBI from the description provided by workers at the Ryder agency. The truck had already been traced back there. They knew he was the Oklahoma City bomber.

Several days later, while desperate rescue efforts continued in Oklahoma City, Terry Nichols handed himself in. Incriminating material was found throughout his house when a search was carried out.

It was the largest crime task force assembled in the United States since the assassination of President John F. Kennedy. No fewer than nine hundred federal, state and local law enforcement officers participated, conducting 28,000 interviews and amassing an almost unmanageable 3.5 tons of evidence.

Timothy McVeigh, Terry Nichols and a man called Michael Fortier and his wife Lori were charged with the bombing.

It should have come as no surprise that Timothy McVeigh would end up in prison charged with perpetrating a vile act of revenge on authority. He had been fighting it all his life, a life dominated by guns and an obsessive sense of being constantly wronged and personally let down by the US Government.

The love of guns had been passed on to him by his

grandfather, but to McVeigh guns were important. He believed in having one for every occasion, every purpose. He even thought as a kid that he might own a gunshop when he grew up. Although he might not have owned one, he certainly owned enough guns to open one. Essentially, however, he believed guns to be a tool of freedom, the means of overcoming adversity when societal breakdown finally arrived. With guns you could defend your supplies and destroy enemies. His views were so extreme that he resigned from the right-wing National Rifle Association which he believed to be too liberal.

McVeigh had been bullied at school, although he felt a certain sense of power when he would take a gun in to show off to the other kids. Ultimately, however, he was an introverted loner who found it hard to make friends. The only thing he excelled at was computing and he was already hacking into government computers at an early age.

Born into an Irish Catholic family in Pendleton, New York, his parents divorced when he was 10, while his sisters moved to Florida with their mother, he remained with his father, graduating from high school and working as a security guard before enlisting in the US Army. He was posted to Fort Riley in Kansas and when the first Gulf War broke out, was awarded a bronze star, serving as a gunner on a Bradley Fighting Vehicle with the 1st Infantry Division. It was his dream to join the Special Forces when he returned from Iraq, but his application was rejected on the grounds that he was not fit enough. He was disappointed and angry with the military. He left the Army, seething with indignation.

He found work as a security guard, but soon quit and hit the road, claiming that the Buffalo area was too liberal. He visited former Army colleagues and wrote numerous letters to newspapers, ranting about the amount of tax for which United States citizens were liable. In one he wrote about the inevitability of civil war in America and asked whether Americans were going to have to shed blood to reform the system. The level of violence he was anticipating began to escalate. To his mind only the shedding of blood would bring about the type of change he longed for.

His feelings of alienation and downright loneliness were exacerbated by his difficulties with women. He had only had one proper relationship in his life mainly because he found it almost impossible to communicate with the opposite sex. He became increasingly angry and dangerously frustrated. He took to gambling heavily but was not much good at that either, running up crippling debts on credit cards. To cap it all, he received a letter from the Army informing him that he had been overpaid $1,058 during his service and they wanted it back. He was incandescent with rage. 'Go ahead,' he wrote back to them, 'take everything I own; take my dignity. Feel good as you grow fat and rich at my expense; sucking my tax dollars and property.' He was furious with the injustice of it all.

When religious nut and cult leader, David Koresh holed up with his followers in a compound at Waco in 1993, and remained besieged by the FBI for fifty-one days, McVeigh was fascinated. He was so pleased that someone was at last making a stand against the system that he travelled to Waco to hand out pro-gun leaflets and bumper stickers outside the compound. He was later horrified when federal agents stormed the building and Koresh and his followers were all killed in the ensuing fire.

Meanwhile, he spent his life travelling the country, working at gun shows. His new obsession was an FBI marksman, Lon Horiuchi who had shot dead a woman, Vicki Weaver, at a siege at Ruby Ridge, Idaho in 1992. When Horiuchi was acquitted of the manslaughter of Weaver, McVeigh wrote him hate mail. He handed out cards and leaflets about the incident at the gun shows he attended and when he was planning his major act of defiance, he wondered if it might be more satisfying to go after Horiuchi.

He lived in Arizona for a while, with Michael Fortier and his wife Lori, experimenting with drugs, before heading for the farm where his friend and future conspirator, Terry Nichols lived.

Meanwhile, his views were becoming increasingly extreme and his letters angrier. He wrote to the Bureau of Alcohol, Firearms and Tobacco:

ATF, all you tyrannical motherfuckers will swing in the wind one day for your treasonous actions against the Constitution of the United States. Remember the Nuremberg War Trials. But…but… but…I only followed orders…Die, you spineless cowardice bastards.

He was getting close to making it happen.

Terry Nichols, found guilty of conspiring to build a weapon of mass destruction and eight counts of involuntary manslaughter of federal officers, was sentenced to life imprisonment without possibility of parole. In 2004, he was found guilty of one hundred and sixty-one counts of first-degree murder. The jury could not agree to give him a death sentence and he received instead a life sentence for each murder. He is seeing out the rest of his life in the maximum-security Florence Federal Prison in Colorado where he alleges that others were involved who have never been charged.

Michael Fortier who helped McVeigh and Nichols to raise funds for the bombing by selling guns and who had also participated in surveying the doomed Alfred P. Murrah Building, made a plea bargain to testify against the others. He was sentenced to twelve years and on his release entered the US Government's Witness Protection Programme, living under an assumed identity somewhere in the United States. His wife Lori was granted immunity from prosecution.

Timothy McVeigh was found guilty on eleven federal counts, including conspiracy to use a weapon of mass destruction, use of a weapon of mass destruction, destruction by explosives and eight counts of first-degree murder. He was sentenced to death. McVeigh's request for a nationally televised execution was denied, but to the end he remained upbeat, claiming callously that even after his execution the score would remain '168 to 1' and that he would, therefore, have won.

He suddenly dropped all his appeals, without giving any reason, and an execution date was fixed for 16 May 2001. On 10 May, however, the FBI handed over to his attorneys thousands of documents that had previously been withheld. The execution was postponed for one month, the new date being 11 June.

On the eve of his execution, he invited a Californian composer, David Woodard to perform a pre-requiem, a Mass for those about to die and requested the presence of a Roman Catholic priest. His last meal consisted of two pints of mint chocolate chip ice cream and his final statement was Ernest Henley's poem *Invictus* which ends:

> *It matters not how strait the gate*
> *How charged with punishments the scroll*
> *I am the master of my fate*
> *I am the captain of my soul.*

Timothy McVeigh died by lethal injection at 7.14 a.m. on 11 June 2001, the first convicted criminal to be executed by the federal government since 1963. A witness described him at the end as having a 'totally expressionless, blank stare. He had a look of defiance and that if he could, he'd do it all over again.'

PART THREE

DEATH ROW
USA

RAY KRONE

Ray Krone was the one hundredth American to be exonerated from death row since the 1973 decision by the United States Supreme Court that the moratorium on executions could end. Sentenced to death in 1992, he was found guilty again at a retrial in 1994 and sentenced to forty-six years in prison. Then, in 2002, his innocence was proved by DNA testing and he was free to walk out of prison. His story is remarkable, especially as throughout he maintained an astonishing amount of dignity even when he had lost all trust in the justice system that had let him down so abominably. He was an innocent man who could well have been executed.

On the morning of 29 December 1991 the bloody, nude body of thirty-six-year-old Kimberly Ancona was found in the washroom of the CBS Lounge and Restaurant on 16th Street and Camelback Road in Phoenix of which she was the manager. She had been sexually molested and stabbed in the back several times. She had been viciously stabbed from behind and raped as her assailant held the knife to her throat to keep her quiet. It is likely that as the sexual assault was being carried out, she bled to death. There were fourteen size nine-and-a-half bloody shoe prints in the kitchen area leading to and from the place where her killer had found the knife. Apart from a drop of blood on Kimberly's underwear, the blood all belonged to the victim and saliva found on her body suggested the perpetrator had the most common blood type. Investigators found no semen but, crucially, no DNA tests were performed. Kimberly had been bitten on the breast and the neck and it was on these bite-marks that police concentrated their efforts.

It emerged that Kimberly had told a friend that a man called Ray Krone, a regular at the bar who was a member of its darts and volleyball teams was going to help her close up that night. Officers visited Krone, an employee of the US Postal Service who had been born in 1974 and was a former US Air Force sergeant. He told them he had been at home in bed at the time of the murder, but they asked him to make an impression with his teeth on a piece of styrofoam so that they could compare his bite with the distinctive bite-marks on Kimberly Ancona's body. He did as they asked and went home, expecting that to be the last he heard about it. But he had been injured in a car accident when younger and had undergone extensive jaw and dental surgery. Now one of his top front teeth protruded a little. He had a distinctive bite-mark and, according to the police, it was a match for the ones of Kimberly Ancona's body.

They also found his telephone number in Ancona's address book and it emerged that Krone had given her a lift to a party the previous Christmas. Ray Krone insisted, however, that there was nothing between them.

He was arrested and, to his stunned disbelief, charged with first-degree murder, in spite of the facts that his roommate told police that Krone was at home during the time the murder was committed; his shoe size was ten-and-a-half while bloody footprints in the bar were a size smaller; fingerprints found at the crime scene did not belong to him and body hair found on Kimberly Ancona was not his.

Unable to afford a private defence team, Krone relied on the public prosecutor. Consequently awarded $5,000 for his defence, their case, when it came to court early in 1992, was hurried and unprepared. Experts testified that the bite-marks were a perfect match for Ray Krone's and just three-and-a-half days into the proceedings, the man the press had dubbed the 'Snaggletooth Killer' was found guilty of murder and kidnapping. Standing before the judge, he showed no remorse, as he said, 'How can you show remorse for something you're not guilty of?' This lack of remorse contributed to him being sentenced to death, even though the trial judge noted there were lingering doubts about his guilt.

After three years on death row, watching fellow inmates being led away to their executions, Krone was granted a new trial on the grounds that some of the evidence about the bite-marks had only been disclosed to the defence by the prosecution a day before the trial started, breaching the rules regarding disclosure. The court should have granted a continuance or should have excluded the evidence.

Krone had learned his lesson first time round and this time his family remortgaged their house and cashed in their retirement funds while friends and family raised money in any way they could in order to enable him to hire a good private attorney and put up a proper defence. They found a man who believed in the case and took it on merely for expenses.

In February, 1996, the trial started. It lasted six-and-a-half weeks, introduced more than five hundred exhibits, and heard the testimony of more than thirty expert witnesses. Each day Ray felt more confident that his attorney was doing a good job and each day he felt he was a day closer to freedom. Finally, as the jury was sent out, he felt sure justice was going to be done. Three-and-a-half days later they filed back in and delivered a shocking verdict. They had found him guilty again. Ray Krone was outraged and broken-hearted. He had still retained his faith in the system until that point but as he heard sobs coming from his mother and sister behind him in the courtroom and watched as the prosecution pumped the air and jumped up and down, 'like they just won the big game,' as he put it, his belief in justice oozed out of him.

His attorney spent the next three hours arguing for mitigation, bringing forward every single dubious element of the prosecution case and afterwards the judge did admit there remained residual and lingering doubt about Ray Krone's guilt. Nonetheless, he had been found guilty and was sentenced to twenty-five years to life for the murder of Kimberly Ancona and twenty-one years to run consecutively for kidnap. It was a sentence of forty-six years in total, which meant Ray Krone would be eighty-one years old by the time he was released; it was as good as a death sentence. Few lived that long in America's increasingly violent and harsh prison system.

In 2001, the Arizona State Legislature passed a new law making it easier for prisoners to request DNA testing if there were appropriate materials available, if it had never been tested before and could have a bearing on a case. In Krone's case

Kimberly Ancona's trousers and underwear had never been tested and they were still available. The judge overruled objections by the prosecution and gave permission for DNA testing to be carried out.

It had also been learned that prior to the second trial, two of the country's leading dental forensic experts had told the prosecuting attorney that there was no way that the teeth marks on the victim's body had been made by Ray Krone. The attorney neglected to inform the defence about this and continued in spite of such evidence to seek the death penalty.

The DNA found on Kimberly Ancona's clothing was entered into the national DNA database that contained the DNA of everyone who had been found guilty of a crime in the United States. It came up with the name of Kenneth Phillips, a man in prison at the time for sexual assault. It emerged that when Kimberly Ancona was murdered, he was out of prison on parole. He had the same blood type as that found at the crime scene.

That night, Kenneth Phillips, a Native American had got very drunk and Ancona had exercised her right to refuse to serve him any more alcohol. Later when the bar emptied, he wanted to use the men's toilets, but Ancona was cleaning it and she told him he should go home. He lost his temper, took a knife from behind the bar and viciously stabbed her to death and raped her. He then replaced the knife back after washing it. He later said that he was subject to blackouts and could remember nothing of the incident; the first he knew of it was when he woke up the following morning covered in blood. No one ever linked him with the murder and just three weeks later, he was arrested for sexually assaulting and attempting to strangle a seven-year-old girl.

On 8 April 2002, Ray Krone at last walked through the gates of Arizona State Prison at Yuma, a free man. Sixteen days later the District Attorney's office officially dismissed all charges against him.

He had served 3,769 days in prison for a crime he did not commit. Unsurprisingly he now campaigns for the abolition of the death penalty in the United States, saying, 'There is a serious problem with the death penalty and there are serious mistakes made. The punishment is irreversible, irrevocable. We can't bring back someone when we execute them; it is no longer right for a punishment like that to be in a society like ours.'

NICK YARRIS

His is a story of astonishing deceit, double cross and obfuscation, a Kafkaesque legal maze in which was trapped for twenty-one years, being let down by his lawyers and treated with disdain and downright dishonesty by the United States justice system.

It began early in December 1981 when thirty-seven-year-old Linda Mae Craig mentioned to her fellow workers at the Tri-State Mall in Delaware that she thought a man had been watching her. Tragically, she did nothing about it, because on 15 December she left work and never completed her ten-minute drive home. Her husband phoned the police whose search located her shoes in the car park at the mall and at 7 pm her car, a 1977 Chrysler Cordoba, was found abandoned a mile and a half from a church in Chichester Township, Delaware County, Pennsylvania.

Next morning, they found Linda Craig's body in a car park at the church. She had been raped before being murdered.

Nick Yarris entered the story on 20 December when he was stopped in the city of Chester,

Pennsylvania by patrolman Benjamin Wright. Yarris was no angel, a methamphetamine addict, an escapee from prison, a car thief, a drug dealer and an armed robber. As Yarris himself puts it, he was a criminal, but was no murderer. Therefore, when Officer Wright placed a restraining hand on his shoulder as Yarris tried to get out of his car, he did not take kindly to it. When the officer grabbed him by the arm, a scuffle followed. The officer's revolver went off accidentally, firing a bullet into the ground. Yarris was subdued and taken into custody where he was charged with attempted murder and the kidnapping of a police officer. It would later take a jury less than an hour to find him innocent of all charges, but for the moment it looked bad to the frightened twenty-year-old.

As a drug-user, he was placed in solitary confinement while he underwent 'cold turkey' from his methamphetamine habit. While there, he read about Linda Craig's murder and devised a plan that he hoped would obtain his release. He decided to tell the police that he knew the identity of her murderer and would tell them everything he knew in return for his release. He gave them the name of a friend that he thought had recently died of a drug overdose. When it transpired, however, that the friend was alive and that he had a rock-solid alibi for the night in question, Yarris was really in trouble, especially as the police now believed that he knew so much about the murder that he must have done it. They threw him back into solitary, at the same time letting it be known to other prisoners that he was a snitch who had tried to inform on a friend. After being constantly attacked for a week, he could stand no more and tried to hang himself.

After a stay in hospital, he was returned to a cell, allowed to wear only boxer shorts, even though it was a freezing cold January. Further attacks by fellow inmates followed – urine was thrown over him and he was subjected to verbal attacks. Yarris spoke to a prison guard, hoping to at least be given some clothing if he seemed to be helping. He asked him what would happen if he admitted that he had been part of the crime but had not committed the murder. The story was taken to the officers investigating Linda Craig's murder and Yarris was arrested. He received clothes and a blanket and, having now achieved the status of a murderer, the attacks from other inmates stopped.

One inmate, however, Charles Cataleno – serving time for burglary – offered the District Attorney handling the Yarris case a deal. In exchange for a dismissal of the twenty-year sentence he expected to receive, he would share a cell with Yarris and try to get a confession from him. Ironically, around this time, on 17 April 1982, Nick Yarris would have walked free after the jury in the case for which he had originally been arrested reached a verdict of not guilty. Instead, a couple of months later, on 5 June 1982, proceedings began on the murder charges. Yarris learned that District Attorney Barry Goss who had taken over the case, was seeking the death penalty, instead of a charge of second-degree murder. Yarris was horrified, but his descent into hell had only just begun.

At the trial, it did not look good for Yarris from the outset when the judge opened by saying, 'In light of the 4th of July Holiday coming on Friday, I intend to make sure you all get to go home and enjoy yourselves in time.' He was not going to waste much time on this trial, it seemed.

The prosecution presented its only evidence – semen left by the killer both in and on the victim. The tests that had been run on it, however, were incomplete and it could even have belonged to Linda Craig's husband who said they had sex the night before the attack. When he learned, however, that there was a suspect he had said that he had worn a condom. No one thought it strange that the couple were unable to have children. Wearing a condom was, therefore, a pretty pointless exercise.

The real deceitfulness began almost immediately when the prosecution refused to hand over to the defence team more than twenty pages of homicide files. In those that were handed over, paragraphs had been deleted, as if they wanted to hide certain elements of the investigation. What they were hiding were conflicting witness statements and inaccurate identifications. They also hid the fact that the murderer wore gloves. Charles Cataleno testified against Yarris, claiming that he had confessed to him and denying that he had been offered a deal for his evidence.

After one of the briefest murder trials in US legal history – three days – Nick Yarris, a totally innocent man, was found guilty of the murder of Linda Mae Craig. On 24 January 1983, he was sentenced to death as well as being sentenced to an additional thirty to sixty years in prison. He was sent to one of the most notorious prisons in the United States – Huntington Prison, high in the mountains of Pennsylvania.

Needless to say, Yarris sacked his defence team and hired a new one, which launched an appeal on the basis of the files that had been withheld by the prosecution and evidence that had been destroyed. At one point before the appeal, Yarris was offered a commutation to a life sentence, but he declined. He was after justice, not compromise.

In February 1985, when he was being taken to his appeal hearing, Nick Yarris did a second stupid thing – he escaped from custody, becoming the most hunted man in the USA. It enabled the prosecution to dismiss his appeal on the destruction of files. twenty-five days after the escape, Yarris handed himself in to the authorities in Florida. A few days later, his conviction and sentence were upheld.

In 1988, Yarris read about DNA testing in a newspaper and when he asked his lawyer to investigate whether it would be possible in his case, he became the first death row prisoner in America to seek DNA testing to prove his innocence. To their dismay, however, they learned that the evidence in the case had been disposed of. All that remained were two slides of material that were in no condition to provide accurate test results. Yarris found out, however, that some material had been sent to another laboratory and had never been returned. He ordered his attorney not to tell the prosecutors about it, fearful it would be lost or tampered with, but the lawyer ignored him. The material was collected by two detectives and never arrived at the testing facility. One of the detectives transporting it refused to hand it over, keeping it for two years in unsuitable conditions while the court refused to force him to hand it over.

Once again, Yarris fired his counsel.

In 1989, Yarris tried to get a retrial on the basis of the gloves about which the prosecution had kept him in the dark at his trial. He was refused and protested about the judge making the denial, Justice Toal, to the Judicial Review Board. He got nowhere again.

Between 1989 and 1991, the authorities did everything they could to prevent DNA testing but finally they allowed it, on the condition that it was carried out in a police lab in Alabama, a lab that had never before carried out the type of testing necessary. They came back with inconclusive results, but with no detail about how they had tested or what the results actually were. It had been a sham.

In 1994, he was once again, after a review of the evidence in court, denied a new trial. He was denied again in 1999.

The legal quagmire in which he had floundered for so many years took its toll, and in 1993 he had been struck by hepatitis C and by 2000 he was very ill. Staff at Greene County Prison where he was now being held, made his condition worse by giving him the wrong doses of the drugs being used to treat him.

As he lost the will to live, his latest attorney asked

a lab in California to make one last effort to prove Nick Yarris's innocence by testing some untested DNA evidence from the pair of men's gloves found in Linda Craig's car. Yarris agreed to accept his verdict once and for all if this evidence did not exonerate him.

Two samples of DNA were found, but sensationally, neither of them was a match for Yarris's DNA. Although they made every effort to block the proceedings, the prosecution had no alternative but to drop the case against Nick Yarris and he walked out of prison a free man, having had his sentence reduced to the time he had already served. He was the 140th US prisoner to be exonerated by DNA testing, the thirteenth to be exonerated on death row.

Even then, however, they would not leave him alone. The case had been dropped in such a way that if new evidence was found of his involvement, Yarris could be thrown back in prison. His family were hounded for DNA samples as late as June 2004, as they pursued him. Yarris responded by going public. For weeks he protested outside Delaware County Courthouse, addressing people entering and leaving the building through a megaphone and distributing thousands of leaflets. He was protesting about the fact that the authorities were refusing to put the DNA found on the gloves onto the FBI national DNA database.

Eventually, for Nick Yarris, incarcerated for more than half his life for a crime he did not commit, everything turned out fine. He was aware he could still be in serious trouble in the United States due to the 'three strikes' law – if he committed the slightest misdemeanour, he stood a chance of returning to prison for the rest of his life. He moved to Britain, the land of his forefathers, married and started a new life.

He had been in prison for twenty-one years. Admittedly, at the start of it all he had been stupid, but you cannot execute a man for stupidity.

RICHARD
ALLEN DAVIS

Richard Allen Davis has languished for the last ten years on death row in California's San Quentin State Prison, a pariah to his fellow inmates. Not only is he the lowest of the low in criminal circles, a child-killer, he is also the reason that the California State Government introduced its 'three strikes and you're out' legislation that enables courts to impose lengthy periods of incarceration on criminals who have committed serious offences three times.

In 1996, he was convicted of the first-degree murder of twelve-year-old Polly Klaas who he had abducted from her bedroom on 1 October 1993.

That night, Polly Klaas was fearful of the dark as ever, terrified that a mysterious bogeyman was going to come into her bedroom and kidnap her. Tragically, that is exactly what happened.

On that first day of October, Polly was having a sleepover at her house with her two best friends, Kate McLean and Gillian Pelham. As they did the usual things little girls do when together, playing with make-up and putting on funny clothes, a thick-set man with a beard and bushy grey hair was hanging about on the pavement outside the house which was situated in Petaluma, a quiet, affluent town about forty miles from San Francisco. Polly lived there with her mother, Eve, who was at the time separated from her second husband, and her younger sister, Annie. A number of people recall seeing the figure outside the house, but Petaluma was a town unfamiliar with crime and they surmised that he was just a local resident out for a walk.

As it was getting late, Polly decided to fetch the girls' sleeping bags from the living room. When she opened the door, however, her heart was almost stopped by the sight of a middle-aged man she had never set eyes on before. In his hand was a knife. He hissed at her, 'Don't scream or I'll cut your throats!' The terrified girls' chatter stopped at once. 'Who lives here?' he asked. 'I do,' Polly answered, her voice trembling with terror. 'I'm just doing this for money,' the man added. Polly immediately fetched a box with $50 in it. But he refused it, ordering the three girls to lie on the floor. He tied their hands behind their backs and covered their heads. 'I'm not going to hurt you. I'm just doing this for the money,' he reiterated, as if trying to convince himself. As he tied Polly up, she pleaded with him not to hurt her mum and sister. He picked Polly up and snarled at her friends to count to a thousand before they did anything. He then carried the little girl out of her house.

As soon as he was gone, Gillian and Kate began to tug at their bonds and succeeded in freeing themselves. They ran to Polly's mother's bedroom and blurted out what had happened. It was around 10.45 p.m. when she called 911.

As soon as the officers arrived, a description of the abductor was broadcast to patrol cars throughout Sonoma County but they failed, critically, to send it to every station which would probably prove fatal for Polly Klaas. This was because the abductor's truck had broken down around midnight, twenty-five miles from the Klaas house. Dana Jaffe phoned the police to report a trespasser on her property. Her nineteen-year-old babysitter, Shannon Lynch, had seen a stranger standing by a Ford Pinto that had become stuck in a ditch. When she stopped and lowered her window a few inches, the man had told her he was stuck and needed a rope. Lynch did not like the look of him, however, and sped off. At the first payphone she found she phoned Dana Jaffe to warn her.

Jaffe became frightened, piled her child into her Toyota and drove away from her house, passing the stricken Pinto. She called the police from a petrol station.

Two police officers in a patrol car pulled up behind the Pinto. When they asked the man what he was doing in the area, he calmly told them he was 'sightseeing'. He then pulled out a can of beer from his car and began drinking it. When one of the officers told him he should not be doing that, he tossed the can into nearby bushes. They ordered him to pick it up.

Meanwhile, a check was being run for outstanding warrants on him after he told them his name was Richard Allen Davis. Sadly, if they had checked further, they would have found that Davis had a an extensive and worrying rap sheet that included robbery, burglary, assault and kidnapping, and numerous convictions for violence against women. At that time, he was on parole and was in violation of it.

The officers told him to leave the property and helped him to get the Pinto out of the ditch. He drove off, Polly Klaas possibly in the boot of the car and, it has been speculated, still alive at that time.

The following morning Davis was identified as the abductor from a palm print in Polly's room, but the information was not yet made public. A citizens' group was assembled by a local printer, Bill Rhodes, who also printed thousands of leaflets carrying Polly's photograph and a description of her. He organised the Polly Klaas Centre which coordinated search efforts. The case was feature on the television show, America's Most Wanted, and Polly's face and a sketch of her abductor's face, stared out from posters in malls and supermarkets.

A massive search was launched with bloodhounds, hundreds of police officers and local people. Thousands of tips were received by telephone and the movie star Winona Ryder, who grew up in Petaluma, donated a $200,000 reward. A benefit concert featuring stars of the San Francisco music scene and hosted by the comedian and actor Robin Williams, raised $12,000 to help in the search. As the days turned into weeks, however, she had still not been found. There was a sad, but growing certainty that she was dead.

The police had another chance to catch Davis on 19 October when he was picked up for driving under the influence of alcohol. None of the officers involved spotted his resemblance to the sketches of Polly's abductor, nor did they connect his white Pinto with that night as he drove off in it five hours later after sobering up.

Strangely, stories about Bill Rhodes who had organised so much to help the search, began to emerge. It transpired that he was in fact a registered sex-offender, convicted of masturbating in front of a group of children in 1967. In 1968, he had forced four young girls to undress at knife-point. He resigned, but many began to wonder just how involved he was. Was he the abductor? The police thought not. He was eliminated as a suspect.

On 28 November, while out walking on her property, Dana Jaffe discovered some strange items – a dark sweatshirt, knotted red tights, a condom wrapper and an unwrapped condom. There were also strips of tape and a hood-like piece of white cloth. Police immediately made the link to the trespasser in the Pinto who had been allowed to leave that night.

Two days later, they arrested Richard Allen Davies and Polly's two friends immediately picked him out in an identity parade. On 4 December, he confessed to the kidnapping and murder of Polly Klaas and led investigators to the body.

But who was Richard Allen Davis and how did he become a child-killer?

He had been born in 1954 to parents who were both alcoholics and who divorced when he was eleven. His father Bob won custody of Richard and his four siblings because of what was described in a probation report as his mother's alleged immoral conduct in front of her children. Davis developed a pathological hatred of women from the three stepmothers his father inflicted on him and his brothers and sisters. But his home life was generally unstable. Bob Davis suffered from hallucinations and was known to take a gun outside and shoot at things only he could see.

Richard Davis was torturing and killing animals from an early age and by his early teens he was carrying a knife and was already settling into a life of crime. He dropped out of high school in his second year, but at seventeen was told by a judge as he appeared in court yet again, that he had a choice – either join the army or be locked up. He chose the army and was posted to Germany where he worked as a driver. He was unable to resist stealing, however, and after just thirteen months, was dishonorably discharged.

Back in California, there were suspicions that he killed eighteen-year-old Marlene Voris in October 1973. He was at a party celebrating her acceptance into the US Navy and at the end of the evening, as he was leaving, Davis told some friends he had to go back into the house. Shortly after, a shot rang out. Marlene was found dead with no fewer than seven suicide notes around her. Many believed Davis had become jealous of her success, where he had failed, had forced her to write the notes and had then killed her. He claimed she had shot herself and the authorities belived him.

For the next couple of years he was in and out of prison for petty crimes, but in September 1976, he attacked a twenty-six-year-old secretary, Frances Mays in a car park. He bundled her into her car at knife-point and drove off. When they stopped and Davis was preparing to rape her, she managed to escape and flag down a car that happened to be driven by an off-duty policeman. He arrested Davis who claimed that he had heard Frances Mays' voice telling him to rape her. He was transferred to a psychiatric hospital for evaluation, but on 16 December, he escaped.

That night he broke into the home of a nurse. Thirty-two-year-old Marjorie Arlington was beaten with a poker. He kidnapped a bartender, Hazel Frost, as she got into her car. She grabbed a gun she kept under the seat, however, and fired at Davis as he ran off into the night. Finally, he was apprehended and in June 1977, was sentenced to one to twenty-five years in prison for the kidnapping of Frances Mays.

Paroled in 1982, Davis continued to offend, robbing banks with his new girlfriend, Sue Edwards. Arrested again in 1985, he went to prison until 1993, serving half of a sixteen-year sentence.

He went to Petaluma, he claimed, to visit his mother who was living there. Unfortunately, he was unable to find her. He recalled nothing about going to the Klaas house, saying that he had smoked a joint that he thought must have been spiked with PCP. He found himself driving around, wondering what to do with Polly and said he had arrived at the conclusion that he had no option but to kill her. He insisted, however, that he did not rape or molest her. However, when Polly's body was at last found two months after her murder, her skirt was up around her waist and her legs were spread open. He had strangled her from behind with a piece of cloth.

Richard Allen Davis was found guilty and sentenced to death. Defiantly evil to the end, he raised two fingers to the court after the verdict was announced.

He remains on death row in San Quentin State Prison, hated by everyone.

KENNY RICHEY

Amnesty International, the organization that fights for human rights and justice around the world, described the case of Kenny Richey as 'one of the most compelling cases of apparent innocence that human rights campaigners have ever seen'. Richey, himself, resolutely insisted on his innocence throughout his incarceration, declining a plea bargain before his trial that would send him to prison for eleven years and four months in return for pleading guilty to involuntary manslaughter. In the late 1990s, he also turned down the opportunity to be transferred to a Scottish prison from which he would eventually be released under the Scottish probation law. Instead he spent twenty-one years on death row and, on one occasion, in 1994, was just one hour away from being executed when a stay of execution was phoned through.

Richey came from a chaotic and troubled background and by the age of thirteen had been subjected to his first mental health evaluation, being treated in various mental institutions. He had an obsessive fascination with death and violence and his acts of self-harming and attempts at suicide had resulted in his body being covered with more than six-hundred scars. He was a severely maladjusted and dangerously anti-social young man.

Was he, however, an arsonist whose acts led to the murder of a young girl, or a victim of an incompetent and vengeful justice system?

At about 4.15 a.m., 30 June 1986, a fire broke out in a second floor apartment at the Old Farm Village apartment complex in Columbus Grove, Ohio. It was the home of Hope Collins and her two-year-old daughter, Cynthia and Cynthia was, at the time, the only one in the apartment. Hope had gone to spend the night with a boyfriend following a party in a neighbouring apartment, having invited Kenny Richey to sleep in the apartment in return for babysitting her daughter. When firefighters finally fought their way into the apartment, they found Cynthia dead from smoke inhalation.

The fire was initially believed to have been started by a faulty electric fan but when further investigations were carried out, it was concluded that it had been caused by arson and the chief suspect was Kenny Richey. It was alleged that Richey was furious with a former girlfriend, Candy Barchet, who had dumped him for a new man. Her apartment was directly below Hope Collins' and it was alleged that Richey had set the fire in the apartment above hoping it would burn through the floor and into Candy's. He was accused of stealing petrol and paint thinner from a nearby greenhouse, which he splashed throughout the apartment, setting fire to it before escaping, taking the empty containers with him. Very quickly the apartment turned into an inferno.

Numerous witnesses were found to support this series of events. Many knew that Richey had lost his temper when Candy had started sleeping with John Butler. He had threatened Butler with a knife one night and Butler and he had fought. Richey later broke his hand when he punched a door violently in frustration.

By 29 June, Candy had a new boyfriend and she took him to the party, kissing him and making Richey very jealous. However, he was calmed by Candy and she went home with her new man. Richey remained angry, however, and was also very drunk, telling anyone who would listen that if he could not have her, no one could. Some witnesses also said that he had threatened to start a fire. According to Peggy Price, in whose apartment the party was taking place, he said to her, 'Before the night is over, part of A Building is going to burn.'

Around 2 a.m. as the party was winding down, he had made his arrangement with Hope Collins and she had driven off with her boyfriend.

As the fire raged, Richey arrived on the scene, becoming aggressive and argumentative when he was restrained from going into the apartment by the police. Later, as he looked at the wreckage of the apartment, he drank a beer and is alleged to have laughed, saying, 'Looks like I did a helluva good job, don't it?'

He admitted he had broken into the greenhouse across the street and had stolen two plants, which he had offered to get for Peggy Price. She had told him she did not want them and they were found outside Candy's apartment. The owner of the greenhouse told police that he also kept thinners and petrol in there, but he could not confirm whether any was missing.

A good deal of the fire-damaged contents of the apartment had been disposed of by the time investigators decided that they were evidence. Six pieces of material were retrieved, some of them pieces of carpet that had been thrown on a rubbish dump. They were brought back two days after the fire and left outside on the sheriff's car park – not the best way to store vital evidence. They remained there for three weeks before being taken away for testing. The spot in which they lay was about forty feet away from petrol pumps and the risk of contamination was huge. Other samples, such as chips of wood were removed from the apartment weeks after the fire, also providing ample scope for contamination.

Nonetheless, the samples provided conclusive evidence, to the prosecution's mind, at any rate, that an accelerant had been used to start the fire.

Kenny Richey was arrested on July 1 after being interviewed and making a statement in which he admitted being drunk on the night of the fire and unable to recall very much. However, he denied any involvement in the fire and also denied that Hope had asked him to babysit Cynthia. His alibi was that he had been at his father's apartment when the fire broke out.

A dangerously aggressive individual, Richey did not help his case by claiming that he would cut the prosecutor's throat. He also added threatening comments directed at anyone who testified against him. Neither did a letter he wrote to a friend in Scotland while in custody help his cause. 'If they just give me prison time' he wrote, 'they better hope to hell I die in there, cause when I get out I won't stop hunting them all down until everyone who is involved in this case is dead!'

Psychological examinations highlighted the problems he had been found to have when he was younger. One doctor attributed to him the emotional level of a ten or eleven-year-old. Another pointed to his troubled family, his early history of drug abuse and violence and diagnosed him as suffering from antisocial personality disorder. Nonetheless, he was declared able to understand the difference between right and wrong as well as the consequences of his actions and, therefore, fit to stand trial.

Richey's defence was that there never was any arson; therefore, no crime had taken place. Cynthia Collins' death was no more than a tragic accident. But tragically for him, his defence team proved not to be up to the job. One of their expert witnesses gave evidence that supported the prosecution case and the man was, in fact, called to give evidence for the prosecution later in the trial.

The waters were clouded by witnesses recanting their original testimonies. One of the neighbours who claimed to have heard Richie threaten to burn down the apartment block withdrew the testimony she gave during the trial. She also revealed that the dead little girl, Cynthia Collins like to play with matches and had twice set fire to her bed. This never came up during the trial. Nor did the fact that firefighters had been called to the flat on three occasions in the weeks before the fire when smoke had been found.

Those campaigning for Kenny Richey's release pointed out that there was no trace of flammable materials on his clothing or his boots, even though the accelerants were said to have been liberally splashed around the apartment.

One witness reported, in addition, that Richey had been so drunk that he had collapsed in bushes on the night in question. This coupled with a broken hand would have made it difficult for him to climb noiselessly up into the second-floor apartment, carrying cans of petrol and thinners.

A fire alarm in the apartment had been disconnected, but there was absolutely no evidence that Richey had done this, even though the judge used it as one of the reasons he should be subjected to the death penalty. If Richey's defence attorney had been on the ball, he would have learned that those who lived in the apartments regularly disconnected their alarms.

In 1992, an appeal lodged with the Ohio Supreme Court, was defeated by four votes to three. Another appeal, in 1997, to the judge who had originally sentenced him to death was inevitably rejected. The following year another appeal to the Ohio Supreme Court was similarly dismissed. Meanwhile, Richey constantly requested that what appeared to be unsafe forensic evidence, be reexamined, but the prosecution constantly objected to this.

In June 1998, his thirteenth execution date was stayed and the case was moved to the federal courts.

In the meantime, the clamour for Kenny Richey's release had reached astonishing proportions from international figures and celebrities such as Irvine Welsh, Robbie Coltrane, members of the Scottish Parliament, Pope John Paul II, Jack Straw, Tony Blair, actress Susan Sarandon, the European Parliament and, of course, Amnesty International.

It was taking its toll on forty-three-year-old Richey, however. In August 2006, he suffered a series of heart attacks in his cell – not his first – and was operated on, making a full recovery.

On 10 August 2007, the United States Court of Appeals for the Sixth Circuit upheld its 2005 overturning of Kenny Richey's conviction and death penalty due to ineffective counsel. They ordered that he be retried within ninety days or released. The retrial was set for 2 October. It was announced, however, that Richey had agreed to a plea bargain. The arson and murder charges were dropped and he pleaded 'no contest' to involuntary manslaughter, child endangering and breaking and entering. He was sentenced to the amount of time he had already served and was released on condition that he leave the United States immediately.

Many were disappointed that he did not remain in the United States to fight the retrial, a trial that his defence team were confident he would win. However, one leader of the 'Kenny Richey Campaign' wisely counseled, 'What Kenny always said was that he would never plead to starting the fire or trying to kill anyone. And he hasn't. The State has caved in and dropped those claims because it can't prove them. What he is pleading 'no contest' to is failure to babysit and stealing a plant. After twenty-one years in prison for an unconstitutional conviction on charges the State has now dropped, what sense did it make to spend six more months in prison to fight about a failure to babysit and stealing a plant?'

On 19 January 2010, Kenny Richey, back in the USA, appeared in court in Minnesota charged with beating his son Sean with a baseball bat. He could be sentenced to seventeen years in prison.

MICHAEL MORALES

It is a fascinating legal conundrum. In 2006, a California court declared that intravenous lethal injections can only be carried out by a licensed medical professional. The lethal injection, if administered incorrectly by an insufficiently trained person could lead to suffering of the condemned person, constituting cruel and unusual punishment. As medical professionals are, of course, prevented by the ethics of their profession from taking or contributing to the taking of life, that presented a problem.

In 2006, as Michael Angelo Morales, convicted in 1981 of murdering seventeen-year-old Terri Lynn Winchell, waited to walk to San Quentin State Prison's death chamber where he would be strapped onto a gurney on which he would receive a lethal injection, two anaesthesiologists refused to participate in the execution due to the ethical issues that had been raised. The anaesthesiologists issued a statement through the prison saying that they were concerned about a requirement that they intervene in the event that Morales woke up or seemed to be in pain during the execution process. Such an intervention, they claimed, would be unethical. The American Medical Association, the American Society of Anaesthesiologists and the California Medical Association agreed.

The execution was rescheduled – the third re-scheduling – for 21 February 2006. They said they would use a different method, a fatal overdose of barbiturates, rather than the three-drug cocktail that was normally used in lethal injection executions. It was this latter method that Morales's attorneys had claimed provided a risk of excruciating pain, if the condemned man were not properly sedated.

Still, no medical professional would agree to take part and at 11.59 p.m. on that Tuesday, Michael Morales' death warrant ran out. California's six hundred and fifty condemned men, including Michael Morales, woke up on Wednesday 22 February to what amounted to a moratorium on capital punishment and the impasse continues to this day.

Morales has never denied the murder for which he was sentenced to death, but says that he was high on the drug PCP when he committed it. He was already a felon, having been convicted of burglary on 4 October 1979 and sent to prison. Shortly after killing Terri Winchell, he was convicted on two counts of robbery for which he was sentenced to a term of imprisonment. He had gone into a store to buy beer but when the assistant refused to serve him, he left, returning later with two companions. They grabbed the assistant, put a knife to his face, hit him with a milk crate and kicked him. Another shop assistant, a pregnant woman, was viciously knocked to the ground, suffering cuts to her head and face.

It began in early 1980, when twenty-one-year-old Michael Morales's nineteen-year-old cousin, Rick Ortega, had a homosexual relationship with seventeen-year-old Randy Blythe. At the same time as he was seeing Ortega, however, Blythe was also dating Terri Winchell. Terri had no idea about her boyfriend's relationship with Ortega but, to her cost, Ortega found out that she was seeing his boyfriend and became insanely jealous.

When Randy Blythe tried to end what was an already stormy relationship with Rick Ortega, Ortega reacted violently, becoming openly hostile towards Terri whenever he was in her company. With his cousin, Michael Morales, he concocted a plan to murder Terri.

On the day of the murder, 8 January 1981, Morales told his girlfriend he was going to strangle and 'hurt someone'. That day, Ortega tricked Terri into travelling with him in his car to a remote area close to the city of Lodi, California. When they arrived at the designated spot Morales leapt out from his hiding place in the back of the car, attacking Terri from behind. He tried to strangle her with his belt but the belt snapped as Terri struggled to break free. He began smashing her on the head with a hammer and she screamed for Ortega to help her, not realizing that the attack was happening at his instigation. As she tried to escape, her hair was ripped from her scalp in the struggle. He continued to beat her with the hammer, leaving her with twenty-three wounds and her skull smashed. As she lay unconscious and near death, Morales dragged her face-down across the road and into a vineyard where he raped her. He started to leave, but returning moments later to make sure she was dead, stabbed her viciously four times in the chest. She was left in the vineyard, naked from the waist down, her sweater and bra pulled up above her exposed breasts.

The following day, Rick Ortega was brought in for questioning about her disappearance. His open hostility towards her in the weeks before her disappearance made him a prime suspect. Morales was also brought in and while in a cell, confessed his part in Terri's disappearance and murder to a police informant, Bruce Samuelson, who was also in custody. Morales had already confessed to Raquel Cardenas, his girlfriend, and his housemate, Patricia Flores, but had threatened them not to testify against him at his trial.

When Morales was arrested on 10 January, police found the broken belt, covered in Terri's blood, concealed under a mattress. They also found three knives, and hidden in his refrigerator, a hammer on which analysis revealed were traces of blood. In the dustbin were found the blood-stained floor mats from Ortega's car. They also found Terri Winchell's purse and credit cards.

At Morales' trial, the story of the love triangle emerged. His defence was based on a claim that the murder was not premeditated, although this was hard to believe as Morales had already told Ortega that he would help him and had informed his girlfriend on the day of the murder that he was going to 'hurt someone'. The prosecution leapt on the fact that Morales had put together the tools he was going to use on the day, the belt, the hammer and the knife. Damningly, it emerged that he had actually practiced for the murder, trying out his strangulation method on two women friends.

Michael Morales was sentenced to death and the appeal process was launched immediately, one of his lawyers being Kenneth Starr, later known for his tenure as independent counsel while Bill Clinton was president of the United States. His Starr Report into the Monica Lewinsky affair led the way to the attempt to impeach President Clinton. In February 2006, towards the end of the process, the defence team filed papers that claimed that five out of the twelve jurors had doubts about sentencing Michael Morales to death. Prosecutors, however, alleged that these documents were false and the case was damaged when one juror appeared on a radio show expressing surprise that she had been named in this context. Starr and his team withdrew the documents a week later. Eventually one of the defence investigators, Kathleen Culhane, would be sentenced to five years in prison for forging the documents.

Clemency for Michael Morales was, unsurprisingly, denied and the execution date was set for 21 February.

That night, as Morales prepared to walk to the death chamber and be strapped down on the gurney on which he would die, the court made its decision and the lack of a medical professional willing to carry out the execution meant that the execution could not take place. The state of California had no option but to allow the death warrant to lapse.

Interestingly, if they ever find a way to make the death penalty work again, the new death warrant may only be issued by the original trial judge. That judge, Charles McGrath, has since announced that he has reservations about the testimony of the police informant Bruce Samuelson in the case. No wonder – the informant testified that Morales confessed to him in Spanish. Although of Hispanic origin, Michael Morales does not speak a word of Spanish. As a result, McGrath has asked California Governor Arnold Schwarzenegger to grant clemency to Morales.

Meanwhile, Michael Morales, now fifty-one years old, claims to have found God in prison and has expressed remorse for his terrible crime.

RICHARD RAMIREZ
THE 'NIGHT STALKER'

The bride was elegant in a white wedding dress with lacey chiffon sleeves. The groom was less elegant, dressed in ill-fitting standard-issue starched prison blues. The ceremony was simple and tasteful (they removed the groom's restraints) and took place in main visiting room of San Quentin Prison. Present were two attorneys, Ramirez's brother, sister and seventeen-year-old niece.

It was 3 October 1996, and forty-one-year-old Doreen Lioy, a freelance editor who worked part-time for teenage magazines and lived on a houseboat, was the bride. The groom was thirty-six-year-old serial killer, Richard Ramirez, known as the 'Night Stalker', the murderer of thirteen people, the man who struck terror into the hearts of the inhabitants of Los Angeles between 28 June 1984 and 24 August 1985.

He had been born Ricardo Leyva in El Paso, Texas in 1960, youngest of a family of five. Outwardly, his family seemed decent and hard-working but behind closed doors, they lived in fear of their father's terrible temper. When he blew it usually meant a beating for one of them. The young Ricardo would often spend the night in the local cemetery in order to avoid one of those explosions and the inevitable beating that followed. At school, things were not much better and he was set apart by epileptic seizures from which he suffered. He was a loner who found it hard to make friends.

The person he liked best and looked up to most was his cousin Mike, a Vietnam vet who could talk about what it was like to kill and torture. He had gruesome photographs that were a testimony to his wicked acts during that conflict. He explained to Ricardo as they sat smoking weed and drinking beer that killing made you feel good, it gave you power, made you feel like a god. Ricardo drank it all in, listening wide-eyed to his cousin's stories.

Mike also had a bad temper and it got the better of him one day when, tired of his wife's nagging about getting a job, he pulled a gun and shot her in the face, killing her. Ricardo watched him do it and was sprayed with blood from the dead woman's wounds. Mike was found to be insane and was consigned to a secure hospital.

Ramirez was already getting out of control. He dropped out of school at fourteen, smoked too much marijuana and stole to pay for his habit. His diet of junk food rotted his teeth and left him with dreadful halitosis; it would be recalled with horror by many of the women he later attacked and raped. He also had an unhealthy fascination with Satanism, which his father blamed on too much dope. Satanic rock music was his preference as personified by Australian rock band AC/DC's anthem *Night Prowler*.

Was that a noise outside your window?
What's that shadow on the blind?
As you lie there naked like a body in a tomb
Suspended animation as I slip into your room…

It was like a blueprint for his future life.

In 1978, aged eighteen, Ricardo, now calling himself Richard Ramirez, moved to Los Angeles where in his first few years he came into contact with the law a few times, mostly for car theft and drug possession. He began to burgle houses, stealing valuables and sometimes, it is claimed, hanging around a little longer than was necessary, perhaps even photographing their sleeping owners.

He graduated to murder on 28 June 1984, following a night spent doing cocaine. After removing a screen from a window of an apartment in Glassel Park, he clambered in and found seventy-nine-year-old

Jennie Vincow. He slashed her throat so viciously that he almost decapitated her. He then stabbed her repeatedly before rampaging through the apartment searching for valuables. Her son discovered her body the following day and investigators discovered signs of sexual assault. They also found fingerprints on the window screen.

Eight months later, twenty-two-year-old Angela Barrios arrived home at the condominium she shared with thirty-four-year-old Dayle Okazaki in Rosemead, to the north of Los Angeles. As she got out of her car, she thought she heard a man behind her. She turned to find Ramirez, dressed entirely in black, a baseball cap pulled down low over his face. In his hand was a gun that he fired at her face. She raised her hands in self-defence and remarkably the bullet ricocheted off her key ring. She fell to the ground and pretended to be dead while he went into the condo. As soon as he had gone, she left the garage and went round to the front door, but she encountered her attacker on his way out. As she ducked down behind a car, he again levelled his gun at her. When she begged him not to shoot, he suddenly lowered the weapon and ran away. She ran inside to find her housemate dead on the kitchen floor with her blouse pulled up and a bullet through her forehead. Police found a baseball cap outside with the AC/DC logo on it. He was not finished yet, however. A patrolling police officer came upon a car near Monterey Park in which he found thirty-year-old Tsian-Lian Yu, shot several times. She died at the scene.

He returned to Monterey Park on the night of 26 March, breaking into the home of Vincent and Maxine Zazzara. Sixty-four-year-old Vincent, who owned a pizzeria, was found shot in the left temple on the sofa in his den. Forty-four-year-old Maxine was lying in bed naked. Horrifically, her eyes were gouged out and she was subjected to a frenzied knife attack, although she had also been shot in the head and it is probable that she died instantly before he started stabbing and mutilating her. He had pillaged the house for valuables afterwards.

Two weeks later, he broke into the house owned by sixty-six-year-old William and sixty-three-year-old Lillian Doi. Mr Doi was shot in the mouth and then savagely beaten. Mrs Doi was warned not to scream, tied and, after he had searched for valuables, raped. Mr Doi, however, was still alive and managed to crawl to a phone and dial 911. He died in hospital, but Lillian Doi lived and was able to provide the first description of the killer.

On 29 May, eighty-three-year-old Malvia Keller and her invalid eighty-year-old sister, Blancha Wolfe were found in their Monrovia home, both having been beaten viciously with a hammer. An inverted pentagram was found scrawled in lipstick on Ms Keller's inner thigh and a second pentagram was drawn on the bedroom wall above Ms Wolfe's bed. They had been there for two days when they were found and only Blancha Wolfe survived.

Eight people had now been killed and Los Angeles was in a panic. Sales of handguns and alarms went through the roof as Los Angelenos sought to protect themselves against the killer the press were now calling the Night Stalker. The attacks were unprecedented. It seemed that the man just liked breaking in and exercising control. He did not seem to be interested in robbery or murder although valuables were being taken and people were dying. Gender and age seemed to be irrelevant to him; his victims were male and female, old and young. He was described as a thin Hispanic male, with black greasy hair and very bad breath as a result of his seriously decayed teeth. Police stopped anyone who looked remotely like him, but he continued to kill.

On 30 May, forty-one-year-old Ruth Wilson was awakened by a flashlight being shone in her face in the bedroom of her Burbank home. Holding a gun to her head, Ramirez ordered her to the bedroom of her twelve-year-old son, who he handcuffed and locked in a cupboard. She gave him all the valuables she could find and he took her back to the bedroom where he raped and sodomised her. But he did not kill her and the boy managed to escape from the locked cupboard and call 911. By the time they got there, however, he had fled.

On 27 June, he raped a six-year-old girl in Arcadia and the following day, in the same area, the body of thirty-two-year-old Patty Higgins was found with her throat brutally cut. The 2 July was the day they found seventy-five-year-old Mary Louise Cannon in Arcadia, beaten and with her throat slit. On 5 July, Whitney Bennett, also of Arcadia, was savagely beaten with a crowbar. She needed four hundred and seventy-eight stitches but survived. Two days later, Joyce Nelson did not. She was beaten to death with a blunt object at home in Monterey Park. The same night he turned up in the house of sixty-three-year-old registered nurse, Sophie Dickman. Pointing a gun at her, he ordered her into the bathroom while he ransacked the house. He tried to rape her, but was unable to maintain an erection. Frustrated and humiliated, he grabbed the valuables he had found, shouting angrily at her as he fled.

On 20 July, he broke into the home of Lela and Max Kneiding, both aged sixty-six and shot and killed them before butchering their bodies with his new toy, a machete. That same day, he entered the house of thirty-two-year-old Chitat Assawahem whom he shot dead before raping his wife Sakima and forcing her to perform oral sex on him. He then horrifically sodomised their eight-year-old son before leaving with $30,000 of jewellery. On 6 August, he shot a couple, thirty-eight-year-old Christopher and twenty-seven-year-old Virginia Petersen in Northridge. She was hit under the left eye and he was shot in the temple, although, amazingly, the bullet failed to pierce his skull. As Christopher leapt up at Ramirez, he was shot at two more times but both bullets missed The two men wrestled on the floor before Ramirez fled through the sliding doors through which he had initially gained entry. The Petersens both survived.

Thirty-five-year-old Elyas Abowath was not so lucky. Ramirez shot him in the head while he slept and he then raped and sodomised his thirty-five-year-old wife Sakina before forcing her to perform oral sex on him.

He was killing increasingly frequently and the violence appeared to be escalating, but as Los Angeles awaited the next horrific attack he headed north to San Francisco where he killed Peter and Barbara Pan in Lake Merced. Sixty-four-year-old Mrs Pan survived but would be an invalid for the remainder of her life. Scrawled on a wall in their house was an inverted pentagram and the words 'Jack the Knife'. A bullet found at the scene provided a perfect match for one fired by the Night Stalker in Los Angeles. The San Francisco Police Department's worst nightmare had happened. The Night Stalker had relocated.

A man who ran a boarding-house in San Francisco came forward to tell police about a young Hispanic man with halitosis and bad body odour who had stayed at his place several times in the past year and a half. In the room he used, a pentagram had been scrawled on the bathroom door. He had vacated the room the day the Pans were attacked.

Ramirez returned to Los Angeles and attacked a couple in Mission Viejo, fifty miles south of the city, shooting and seriously wounding the man before dragging his fiancé into the next room where he informed her that he was the Night Stalker. He raped her twice but was furious that there was nothing of value in the house. He made her say over and over that she loved Satan and then made her perform oral sex on him before he stepped back, laughed at her and left.

She crawled to the window and watched as he drove off in an old orange Toyota. Coincidentally, a teenager had earlier become suspicious when he saw the vehicle in the neighbourhood and had scribbled down its licence number. He called the police with it the next morning when he heard about the attack. The car which had been stolen from Chinatown, was found in the Rampart area. Although he never returned to it, there was a fingerprint in it which matched up with one Ricardo 'Richard' Leyva Ramirez. Now, at last, they knew who they were looking for.

They got him seven days later. Looking for another car to steal, he climbed into an unlocked Mustang owned by fifty-six-year-old Faustino Pinon. Unfortunately for Ramirez, he failed to notice that Pinon was actually under the car at the time, working on it. When Ramirez turned the key, Faustino leapt up from beneath the vehicle, reached inside and grabbed him by the throat. Ramirez put his foot down in an attempt to speed away but lost control of the vehicle and crashed into a fence. Pinon dragged him out of the car and threw him to the ground but Ramirez clambered up and took to his heels, trying to steal another car along the road. Angelina Torres, the car's owner screamed for help and her husband Manuel came out to see what the fuss was. He picked up a metal post and went after Ramirez. By now there was a posse after him and when one said that he looked like the description of the Night Stalker, the cry went up. Eventually, Manuel caught up with him, poleaxing him with the metal post. The Night Stalker had at last been brought to the ground.

It took four years to finally get Richard Ramirez into court and when he did finall arrive, the gallery was filled by his groupies, a bunch of women who had become ghoulish fans of the Night Stalker. He played to them in the same way that Charles Manson had done decades previously to members of his Family. Ramirez unfailingly dressed in black and sunglasses and occasionally shouted out 'Hail to Satan!' during court proceedings. He had tattooed a pentagram on his palm.

Needless to say, the bad-breathed, malodorous murderer was found guilty of all of the forty-three charges he faced and was given nineteen death sentences.

Richard Ramirez remains on death row in San Quentin to this day. He is held in the prison's Adjustment Centre where the so-called 'worst of the worst' are kept under heavy guard and always in isolation. His appeals are almost exhausted but he doesn't care.

'Dying doesn't scare me,' he said. 'I'll be in hell, with Satan'

KRISHNA MAHARAJ

In 2001, an astonishing array of thirty British politicians, of every political persuasion, wrote a letter to Governor Jeb Bush of Florida. Martin Bell, Sir Menzies Campbell, former Attorney General Lord Goldsmith, Ken Livingstone, Charles Kennedy and twenty-four others pointed out to Governor Bush that there were 'astonishing flaws' in the murder conviction of Trinidadian born British businessman Krishna Maharaj. They insisted that the governor should call for a retrial. So far, however, it has not been forthcoming.

It is a strange case.

At 7 a.m. on Thursday 16 October 1986, security guard Jorge Aparicio arrived at the DuPont Plaza Hotel in downtown Miami. It was still dark outside and inside all seemed quiet.

On the twelfth floor, a maid was doing her cleaning round, wheeling a trolley from room to room, changing linen, making beds and tidying up. She went into room 1215 and saw nothing untoward. The curtains were pulled shut but the twin beds at the top of the suite's wooden staircase were undisturbed and had not been slept in. The towels had not been used and the soap remained in its wrapper, unused beside the sink.

Throughout that morning no one can remember anyone entering or leaving that room and there were no unusual noises or bangs. Just after noon, however, a passing maid noticed a red stain appeared on the carpet outside the door to 1215. She could not help feeling it looked like blood and, hoping there was some other explanation, immediately contacted hotel security.

Jorge Aparicio, halfway through his day's work, came upstairs and knocked on the door to the suite, calling out to ask if there was a problem. A voice from the other side of the door replied that there was no problem. 'Everything is fine,' he assured the security guard. Aparicio went away but, still curious, returned to the door ten minutes later. When he knocked this time, there was no reply. He took out his pass key, slipped it into the lock and slowly pushed the door open.

The room was a mess. The tiled floor was streaked with blood and on the floor lay a body, that of fifty-three-year-old Derek Moo Young. He lay on his back, his feet facing the door. There were six bullet holes in him. In the upstairs bedroom,

Aparicio discovered another body. Derek Moo Young's twenty-three-year-old son Duane lay at the foot of one of the beds, killed by a single bullet, fired into his head at close range, execution style.

That morning, forty-seven-year-old Krishna Maharaj had awakened at the Broward County home he had shared with his wife since moving to Florida from Britain the previous year. Maharaj who had been born into a family of thirteen in Trinidad in 1939, had risen from earning his living as a truck driver to becoming a successful importer of bananas and West Indian goods into Britain. He became a millionaire, and with a stable of one hundred racing horses and twenty-four Rolls Royces, he became something of a fixture in British high society.

He and his wife, Marita spent a few months in Florida every year, primarily to escape the vagaries of the British winter, but never one to do nothing, Maharaj had started a new career in publishing. With a business partner, he had launched a weekly newspaper, the *Caribbean Times*, targeted at Florida's tight-knit Caribbean community. The first issue was published on 4 July 1986.

That October morning, Maharaj climbed into his blue Chevrolet Caprice and drove off to a meeting with a Bahamian businessman with whom he wanted to discuss overseas distribution of the newspaper.

It was a meeting that he later came to believe was a trap. He had been set up and had unknowingly walked straight into it.

The meeting was for 8.30 a.m. at the DuPont Plaza. It had been arranged by Neville Butler, a writer he'd hired as a freelancer several weeks previously. Maharaj parked at the hotel and Butler was there to meet him. They took the lift up to room 1215 to wait for their appointment to arrive. Maharaj opened a bottle of soda and watched some television as he waited but no one arrived and at 10.20 a.m. he said he gave up and left for another meeting at midday with an estate agent in Margate, around thirty miles away. He was going to check out a little shopping mall that he was interested in buying. Before that, at around 11 a.m., he drew up at the printing press he owned at Fort Lauderdale. There he bumped into Tino Geddes, a writer for the newspaper. Geddes was heading for a nearby cafe for a coffee and Maharaj joined him there, ordering a beer. He spent some time chatting with Geddes before paying for their drinks and leaving. He eventually met the estate agent and his accountant, George Bell, at around 1 p.m. and after looking at the property, treated the two men to lunch at Tark's seafood restaurant in Dania Beach. They finally went their separate ways at 3.30 p.m that afternoon.

On the evening of 16 October. Neville Bauer, a City of Miami homicide detective took a call from a man claiming to have seen two people shot dead in a Miami hotel room that day. He named the murderer as Krishna Maharaj, added that he could be found at a Denny's close to Miami International Airport and hung up. Butler found another officer, Lieutenant John Buhrmeister and the two men headed for the diner, situated at LeJeune Road and NW 25th Street. They walked into the restaurant, and Buhrmeister slid into the booth next to Krishna Maharaj. He stuck a gun into Maharaj's side and told him to get up slowly from the table.

Three months later, Krishna Maharaj was charged with the murders of Derek Moo Young and his son.

At his trial, the prosecution based its case largely on the testimony of the only eyewitness, Neville Butler and it emerged that it had been Butler who had phoned the police later that day. Maharaj had known Derek Moo Young for more than twenty years and the two had been business partners since 1984, even at one point living next door to one another in Broward County. There had been a very public falling-out, however, a dispute over a property deal and only a month before the murders, Maharaj had filed a civil suit against the other man for the recovery of $424,000 he claimed he owed him. Butler claimed that Maharaj had insisted on settling matters face to face and for that reason he had been asked to set up the meeting.

Butler said that when Moo Young arrived, Maharaj was hiding behind the bathroom door with a gun. He leapt out and an argument ensued in the course of which he pumped half a dozen bullets into the Jamaican. Maharaj then ordered Butler to tie up Duane Moo Young, but the young man escaped and ran upstairs. Maharaj ran after him and shot him, even though he had known him since he had been a toddler and Duane called him 'Uncle'. According to Butler, he was marched at gunpoint to Maharaj's car and the two sat there for the next three hours awaiting the arrival of the police at the hotel.

Of course, Maharaj had never denied being in the room and it was littered with his fingerprints. The bullets and casings that were found on the floor came from a 9mm Smith and Wesson Model 39 gun. Maharaj owned just that make and model of weapon.

It seemed pretty clear, but there were numerous inconsistencies. Butler initially said that he had booked the room, but later told police that Maharaj had done it. He admitted lying about when Maharaj actually appeared in the room. At first he said he arrived after the Moo Youngs and then he gave them the version where Maharaj was waiting for them behind the bathroom door. Critically, he failed a polygraph and a lie detector test, while Maharaj passed several.

Police also fell down on the investigation. For instance, they failed to run a simple test to check whether Butler had fired a gun that morning and his clothing was never checked even though it was claimed that he had been wearing blood-soaked clothes and had changed them before making a statement.

The entire story did not add up. Why would Krishna Maharaj commit a double murder, spare the life of the only witness to it and then hold him at gunpoint for hours afterwards, only a short distance from the murder scene, before letting him walk away to inform the authorities?

Tino Geddes was the state's other main witness. He had initially provided an alibi for Maharaj, but not long before the trial had changed his story, claiming that Maharaj had been talking about his plan to murder Derek Moo Young. He said that on that day Maharaj told him to tell anyone who asked that he had been with him that morning. He became frightened when he realised what Maharaj was asking him to do.

Interestingly, Geddes was, at the time, facing

charges for illegally bringing ammunition into Jamaica from the United States. The prosecution attorneys in the Maharaj case flew to Jamaica and testified on his behalf at his trial and helped him to escape jail time.

Maharaj was let down by his counsel who for some reason failed to call witnesses who were able to place him in Fort Lauderdale at the time of the murders. Many of them have since died or cannot be located. To the astonished delight of the prosecution team, the defence part of the trial consisted simply of the words 'the defence rests.'

The Moo Youngs were presented as ordinary hard-working Jamaicans living off a modest income. Documents discovered since the trial suggest otherwise, however. Million dollar life insurance policies and loans of $1.5 billion have led to speculation that they were involved in money-laundering or drug trafficking. It has been noted that there were a large number of people in South Florida at the time who had reasons to want to kill them, amongst whom is Adam Hosein, a Trinidadian who at the time owned a garage in Broward County. He closely resembled Maharaj and had even used this resemblance on occasion to gain access to horse races. He was an associate of Derek Moo Young and owed him a considerable sum of money. He placed a call to room 1215 on the day of the murders. Adam Hosein was never even questioned by police about the murders.

Colombian importer/exporter Jaime Maijas, who originated from Medellin, the drug capital of South America, was renting room 1214 at the DuPont Plaza that day. He was linked to Hosein but was questioned only cursorily and ruled out as a suspect. There is little doubt, however, that Derek Moo Young and his son were the victims of an assassination by a Medellin drug cartel

In his trial, the jury took just three hours to convict Krishna Maharaj. He was sentenced to death and spent fifteen years on death row exhausting the appeals process before his sentence was commuted to life in 2002 due to violations in due process at his trial.

In his six-by-nine-foot cell at Martin Correctional Institution in Indiantown, Florida, Krishna Maharaj, now seventy, his fortune long gone on legal fees, continues to protest his innocence.

KARL CHAMBERLAIN

Karl Chamberlain's last meal request was extraordinary and easily the biggest of any that had been ordered up to that time by any of the four hundred and five inmates executed in Texas since the state recommenced carrying out the death penalty in 1982. He ordered a fresh fruit tray, fresh orange slices, apples, sliced watermelon, honeydew melon, cantaloupe, peaches, plums, grapes, strawberries; a fresh vegetable tray with carrot sticks, celery, two sliced tomatoes, lettuce, cucumber slices, olives, sweet pickles and any other fresh vegetables; slices of cheese and lunchmeat, served with a bowl of ranch dressing, two deviled eggs; six jalapenos stuffed with cheese, breaded and fried; a chef salad, ranch dressing on the side; a plate of onion rings, ketchup and hot sauce on the side; one half-pound of French fries, covered with melted, shredded cheese, salsa, jalapenos and ranch dressing on the side; a bacon double cheeseburger, smothered with grilled onions, three to four slices of cheese and mayonnaise with garlic and onion powder mixed in; two pieces of fried chicken, breasts preferred, or substitute two thighs and two legs; one bean and cheese quesadilla, salsa and jalapeno to the side with sour cream or guacamole if possible; a three-egg omelet with grilled onions, mushrooms, ham and lots of cheese. Ketchup to the side; two barbecue pork rolls; pitcher of orange juice (only a little ice) and a pitcher of milk to wash his enormous meal down.

Chamberlain, thirty-seven, was executed by Texas's preferred method, lethal injection, on 11 June 2008 in Huntsville, Texas for raping and murdering thirty-year-old Felecia Prechtl in her apartment.

That day, 2 August 1991, Felecia had arranged for her brother and his girlfriend to babysit her five-year-old son so that she could go out with friends in the evening. At about six in the evening they had taken the boy to go to the grocery store while she got ready to go out. Returning to the apartment shortly after, they noticed that the bathroom door was closed and her clothes were still in the hallway. They thought she must be still getting ready but when they had heard nothing for a while and she had not emerged, her brother opened the bathroom door and went in. He found his sister lying face down, her jeans and underwear pulled down around her knees and her ankles and hands bound by duct tape. She wore nothing on the top half of her body and around her head was a pool of blood.

An autopsy revealed that the cause of death was a gunshot wound to the head. The trajectory of the bullet as it entered her head suggested that when she was shot she must have been seated on the toilet or possibly kneeling on the floor, indicating an execution-style killing. A .30 calibre bullet was found and when they checked her to establish whether she had been raped, they discovered sperm in her anal cavity. There was a roll of duct tape at the scene and from the duct tape that had been used to tie her up, they were able to lift fingerprints. Unfortunately, when these were submitted to the police criminal database, there were no matches.

As part of their door-to-door enquiries, a neighbour, Karl Chamberlain, was questioned but he denied knowing anything about the murder and neither he nor anyone else was arrested.

For five years, the case remained unsolved but in 1996, someone diligently decided to run another check on the prints from the duct tape. Karl Chamberlain's name popped up as a potential match. His fingerprints had been taken after he was involved in an attempted robbery in Houston on 17 July 1996. He was subsequently arrested for the murder of Felecia Prechtl.

Chamberlain confessed. He claimed to have been drinking heavily on the day of the murder and had gone to her apartment to borrow some sugar but when she answered the door, he noticed that she wasn't wearing much. She gave him the sugar and asked him to leave. He took the sugar back to his apartment but as he was preparing to take his dogs out for a walk, decided to go back down to hers again. This time he took with him the roll of duct tape and his .30 calibre rifle. He claimed that she had consented to have anal intercourse with him but an argument ensued when she threatened to tell his wife. He lost his temper, he said, and shot her. Afterwards, he took his dogs for a walk. The rifle, he told them, was at his father's house. He gave a sample of his DNA and it matched the sperm that they had discovered that night back in 1991.

It was an open and shut case and Chamberlain was found guilty in June 1997 and sentenced to death. The sentence was confirmed by the Texas Court of Criminal Appeals in June 1999. Subsequent appeals were all denied.

While wishing that his lawyers and the jury had paid a little more attention to the fact that in the five years following the murder he had managed to stay out of trouble, he did show regret for what he did that night. 'My greatest regret,' he said, 'is going down there and not killing myself. I had kind of like a slip into delusion. It makes absolutely no sense… It was like I lost all control.'

There had been a hiatus in executions from September 2007 when the Supreme Court had questioned the legality of lethal injection as a method of execution. Chamberlain gained a brief stay while the point was argued once again, claiming that this method violated his rights under the Eighth Amendment of the Constitution of the United States because it represented cruel and unjust punishment. The appeal on this basis was overturned, however, and the execution was scheduled for 11 June.

On the day of his execution, after twelve years on Death Row, Chamberlain was permitted to spend four hours with his family and friends before being transported to Huntsville Prison where Texas's execution chamber is situated. He then spent the afternoon in a holding cell from which he was able to make phone calls, speak with a spiritual advisor and eat as much of that enormous last meal as he could.

The last words of the now thirty-seven-year-old killer, Karl Chamberlain, were as dignified as they were poignant. 'I want you all to know I love you with all my heart,' he said. 'I want to thank you for being here. We are here to honour the life of Felicia Prechtl, a woman I didn't even know, and celebrate my death. I am so terribly sorry. I wish I could die more than once.' As the drugs were pumped into his veins, he said, 'I love you. God have mercy on us all.' He was smiling and with that smile still on his face, he started to add, 'Please do not hate anybody because…' He slipped into unconsciousness and nine minutes later he was pronounced dead.

PART FOUR

WOMEN ON DEATH ROW

RUTH SNYDER

They called her 'Ruthless Ruth' and Barbara Stanwyck would smoulder through her story in the 1944 Oscar-nominated Hollywood blockbuster, *Double Indemnity*. But it was a grim photograph that would commit her to posterity, the photograph of the decade that was the 1920s. It depicted Ruth Snyder, seated on the electric chair at Sing Sing Prison in New York on 12 January 1928, at the moment the current was switched on, the first woman to be executed in this way since Martha M. Place in 1899.

The photograph was cunningly snapped by photographer Tom Howard who was posing as a writer for the *New York Daily News* but had a miniature camera strapped to his left ankle, the shutter release button concealed inside his jacket. At the critical moment, Howard simply hoisted his trouser leg up and pushed the button. Later that day, the front page trumpeted the execution with the word 'DEAD!' and beneath it the stark black and white photograph of the condemned woman with a hood over her head and the electrodes ready to pulse 2,000 volts of electricity through her body. It is one of the most memorable images of the twentieth century.

It was a sordid murder, one that was described by one crime writer as a 'cheap crime involving cheap people.' Celebrated newspaper reporter and author, Damon Runyon called it the 'Dum-Bell' murder, because it was so dumb.

In 1925, thirty-two-year-old Ruth Snyder was a bored Long Island housewife whose husband Albert was art editor of the magazine *Boating*. When Albert was at work, Ruth began to enjoy the attentions of a thirty-four-year-old corset salesman, Judd Gray. The two did not, at first sight, seem that well suited. Ruth was tall, blonde and good-looking while Gray was short and insignificant, with a cleft chin and thick glasses. The two had first met when they were having lunch in the same restaurant in New York and soon they were involved in a torrid affair, often rendezvousing at the Snyder home while Ruth and Albert's nine-year-old daughter, Lorraine, was at school. On other occasions, they would book a room in a hotel and the little girl would be told to wait in the lobby while they made love upstairs.

Ruth was bored with her husband and whatever passion there had once been between them was long gone. She wanted out of the marriage but realised there was only one way to do that and enjoy life to the full. They would have to get rid of Albert. She started to feed her lover with bits of information about her husband abusing her and suggested to him that he would have to be killed. Gray was against the idea, but Ruth was persistent, cajoling, begging and teasing him toward the point where he would agree. Finally, he capitulated and they decided to go through with it on Saturday 19 March 1927.

Gray had been drinking for much of that day – in fact, he had been drinking for much of the past few months. Today, however, he was drinking to build up enough Dutch courage to kill a man. He travelled by train to New York from Syracuse and then took a bus to Long Island. Arriving at Queen's Village where Ruth and Albert lived, he spent an hour just walking around, stopping every now and then to take a swig from a hip flask. Finally, he summoned up enough courage to go into Ruth's house through the back door.

The house was empty, the Snyders having left earlier to go to a party and not expected to be back until late. He hid, as arranged, in a spare room where Ruth had left a pair of rubber gloves, a bottle of chloroform and a heavy window weight.

At around two the following morning the family returned and while the others prepared for bed,

Ruth opened the door to the spare room to make sure he was there. A little later, she came back in her nightdress and the two of them had sex while her husband slept just down the corridor. Ruth then led Gray to the master bedroom where Albert was asleep. He took with him the weight, the gloves and the chloroform. they went into the room and he stood on one side of the bed while she stood on the other. Raising the weight high above his head, he brought it down on Albert's head. It was a hesitant, ineffective blow, however, and Albert let out a roar and sat up attempting to grab hold of his assailant. Gray shouted to Ruth for help, using his pet name for her, 'Momsie'.

Ruth Snyder remained cool, however. Grabbing the weight from Gray's trembling hands, she smashed it down on her husband's skull, killing him instantly.

They went downstairs and talked through the rest of their plan while they had a drink to steady their nerves. Gray pushed over a few chairs to make it look like there had been a scuffle, tied Ruth's hands and feet and put a gag around her mouth. After he left, Ruth waited for a while before banging on her daughter Lorraine's bedroom door. Lorraine hurriedly removed the gag from Ruth's mouth and Ruth shouted to her to run next door and get help. The police were called.

The investigating officers were immediately suspicious. Ruth listed items that the burglar had taken but all of them were found to be hidden in the house. They noted that the burglar had left little evidence of actually having had to break into the house and they did not think Mrs Snyder behaved like a woman who had just been terrorised by a killer. Foolishly, when a detective showed her a piece of paper with the letters 'JG' on it, she asked him what Judd Gray had to do with it. It emerged that the letters were actually the initials of Jessie Guischard, a young woman that Albert had dated who had died before he met Ruth. Police immediately became interested in this Judd Gray and when they began to question her, she immediately caved in, blaming Gray for everything.

They found him hours later, hiding in a Syracuse hotel room. He screamed that he was innocent and that he had not been to New York. That was fine until they presented him with the train ticket that he had earlier tossed into the room's waste paper basket. He confessed and like Ruth, blamed it all on his partner in crime. The carping continued all the way to the trial, as each threw accusations at the other.

When it finally arrived, the trial was a circus. Celebrities such as film director D.W. Griffith, author Will Durant and, of course, Damon Runyan, sneering at the stupidity of the two main players in the drama, turned out in droves.

Ruth's attorney launched the defence by saying that her husband had driven her out of the house by pining for Jessie Guischard even though she was long dead. She claimed also that Judd Gray had persuaded her to take out a $50,000 double indemnity insurance policy on Albert Snyder. He put Ruth on the stand and she acted like a wronged woman, describing how Albert had paid no attention to her most of the time, only taking her out occasionally. The affair with Gray was, of course, barely mentioned. When she did talk about him it was disparagingly. She spoke of how he drank too much while she rarely touched a drop and did not smoke. She even suggested that Gray had once sent her poison with instructions to give it to Albert.

Judd Gray took the stand and his attorney described how he had been duped by a, 'designing, deadly conscienceless, abnormal woman, a human serpent, a human fiend in the disguise of a woman.' He added that he had been 'drawn into this hopeless chasm when reason was gone, mind was gone, manhood was gone and when his mind was weakened by lust and passion.'

Gray testified that Ruth had tried to murder Albert several times previously, giving him poison when he had hiccups, trying to gas him and putting sleeping powders in his drinks. He claimed that she alone had taken out the insurance policy and that it had nothing to do with him. He described how it had been Ruth who had dealt the fatal blow that night. As he talked, Ruth's sobs echoed noisily in the courtroom.

The jury took a mere ninety-eight minutes to come up with a verdict of guilty for each of them. They were sentenced to death.

On 12 January 1928, Judd Gray was the first to be strapped into the electric chair. The warden described how he had found him smiling in his cell when he had arrived to escort him to the execution chamber. His wife had written a letter to him in which she told him she forgave him. He told the warden that he was ready to go, that he had 'nothing to fear.'

Ruth followed him down the corridor minutes later. She had earlier watched the prison lights flicker as the current had coursed into the body of her former lover. She said as she was being led to the electric chair she said that God had forgiven her; now she hoped the world would.

She sat down, was strapped in and was frozen for eternity in Tom Howard's photograph.

RUTH ELLIS

Hangman Albert Pierrepoint had done a good job. She had a fracture-dislocation of the spine and a two-inch gap and transverse separation of the spinal cord. For good measure, both wings of her hyoid, the horseshoe-shaped bone between the chin and the thyroid cartilage, were broken and her larynx was fractured. It was what was supposed to happen to a person who has been the victim of a hanging.

Her execution, however, would linger over the English legal system for decades to come, long after capital punishment had been banned and it would continue to resonate in the lives of those who had known her. Two of them would commit suicide and another would die of a broken heart.

She was born Ruth Hornby in Rhyl, North Wales on 9 October 1926, the third of six children of Arthur Hornby and his Belgian wife Elisaberta. Arthur, a musician on cruise liners, struggled to make ends meet and was forced to take a job as a porter at a mental hospital. His musical career over, he sought solace in alcohol and became abusive to his wife and two daughters. He would not be the last angry, drunk man to enter Ruth Ellis's life.

By 1941, Ruth was working as a waitress in Reading where her father was now employed as a caretaker. He moved to London later that year, finding employment as a chauffeur in Southwark. Ruth moved in with him and found some menial work. Now sixteen, she had begun to bleach her hair blonde and was a pretty girl, brimming with confidence. She spent her nights dancing and frequenting London's drinking clubs. Just after Christmas 1944, however, she met a French-Canadian airman and got pregnant. Unfortunately, he already had a wife and family in Canada and he returned to them leaving Ruth and her unborn child behind. The baby, a boy, born in September 1945, was christened Clare – his father's surname – but was always known as Andy.

In order to keep herself and her baby, she found work as a model at a camera club. It was around this time that she met a wealthy club owner, Morris Conley, and he offered her a job as a hostess in his clubs. She earned good money, met a better class of people and she was soon managing a number of his clubs across the West End. She worked with Conley for nine years, living the good life while leaving her sister, Muriel, to look after Andy.

In 1950, she was pregnant again, the father being one of her regular customers. She had an abortion and was back at work soon after. Later that year, however, she met the man she would marry.

George Ellis was a Mancunian who had trained to be a dentist. Married once before, it had ended in a haze of boozy arguments with his wife. He got over it by spending all his spare time drinking in West End clubs and bars. Ruth and George enjoyed a whirlwind courtship and he showered her with gifts and treated her like a queen. Slowly she began to fall for him and could see a life of respectability and financial stability stretching ahead for her and six-year-old Andy. She moved in with him.

The one cloud on the horizon, however, was his excessive drinking, but after she finally persuaded him to be treated for alcoholism at a clinic in Surrey, they were married on 8 November 1950. In early 1951, George found work in a dental practice in Southampton and they moved to the Hampshire village of Warash. He started drinking again, however, and they began to fight both at home and in public. She was also worried that he was having relationships with other women. In May 1951, George was fired from the dental practice and as they separated and came back together again countless times, she discovered she was pregnant.

On 2 October 1951, she gave birth to a girl, Georgina. But the marriage was over, Ellis divorcing her on the grounds of cruelty. The fiery marriage had lasted less than a year and, aged twenty-five, Ruth found herself with two children and no means of support. She contacted Morris Conley and was soon back working for him. She moved into one of his properties and the good times returned.

In the hot summer of 1953, she began making new acquaintances. They were a group of racing drivers, exuberant young men who risked their lives on the track every weekend. Led By Mike Hawthorne, they were based at the Steering Wheel Club, located opposite the Hyde Park Hotel. It was there, amongst this crowd of drivers, socialites and groupies that she first set eyes on David Blakely.

At first sight, she thought him 'a pompous little ass' and the two of them argued when first introduced. He was the product of a good public school, Shrewsbury, and came from a wealthy background. Ruth's daughter, Georgina, would later describe him as a 'sponger and a ponce' who rarely bought anyone else a drink, but was content to benefit from other people's hospitality. A racing driver friend described him as a 'supercilious shit' but added that he was likable. The only things that interested him, however, were cars and, eventually,

Ruth. She fell head over heels in love with him but all he would give her would be heartache.

In October that year, Conley appointed Ruth manager of the Little Club on Brompton Road in Knightsbridge. The best thing about it was that she got to live in the two-bedroomed flat above the club, rent free.

The first customer she served at her new club was Blakely who was a member there, and soon they were sharing the space upstairs, too. But just a month later, he became engaged to a woman called Linda Dawson. It did not stop him spending week nights with Ruth, however.

But matters became even more complex when Ruth met a man named Desmond Cussen, referred to at her trial as 'her alternative lover'. She began seeing him, she claimed later, as a way of getting back at the diffident and unfaithful Blakely, who had gone to drive in the twenty-four hour race at Le Mans and weeks later had still not returned. Cussen had been a bomber pilot in World War Two, after which he had trained to be an accountant. When Ruth met him, he was a director of the family business, a chain of wholesale and retail tobacconists in London and South Wales. A habitué of the Steering Wheel Club, he and Blakely disliked each other intensely.

Cussen fell deeply in love with Ruth, but was

frustrated by the fact that she was falling ever deeper in love with Blakely, even as he treated her badly. Coupled with that was the fact that Blakely was ten years younger than him. It was hard to see how he could win.

Meanwhile, in 1954, George and Ruth decided it would be best if their daughter Georgina was put up for adoption. The environment in which Ruth lived was not suitable for bringing up a young girl.

Early that year, Ruth met the Findlaters for the first time, Anthony 'Ant' Findlater, who worked for an engineering company, and his wife Carole, a journalist. They lived in Hammersmith and soon David Blakely was spending a lot of time with them, mainly because he had fallen for Carole. By the autumn of 1954, he was begging her, at twenty-seven – six years older than him – to run away with him. She almost did, but Ant succeeded in persuading her to stay.

When Blakely returned from France, he broke off his engagement to Linda Dawson and asked Ruth to marry him. She had been fighting George Ellis's divorce suit because she wanted to continue to receive the maintenance she had been receiving, but now decided to let it go ahead. Meanwhile, her son Andy went off to boarding school, all paid for by Desmond Cussen. Blakely, spending all his time building a racing car and earning nothing, persuaded Ruth to let him move in with her, but they began to become more jealous of each other's relationships. Their arguments were also increasing in violence and Blakely was regularly beating Ruth.

Eventually, she began to neglect her work at the Little Club and the takings plummeted. In December 1954, she either resigned or was sacked by Morris Conley. She moved into Desmond Cussen's flat at Goodwood Court. Blakely was furious, of course, that she was living in Cussen's flat, although she assured him she was not sleeping with him. But the rows continued and the pattern of violent confrontations followed by passionate reconciliations persisted.

On 9 February, using money borrowed from Cussen, Ruth moved into 44 Egerton Gardens which at least meant she was not sharing with Cussen any more. It did not prevent their increasingly violent arguments, however. At the end of March she learned she was pregnant again, and the father could have been any one of a number of men. But she miscarried after another terrible fight with David during which he punched her in the face and in the stomach.

In the second week of April everything came to a head. Ruth was feeling awful, suffering from a cold and the after-effects of her miscarriage. On Friday 8 April when David failed to return home, she phoned the Findlaters. Although they said he was not there, she was certain he was. She was exhausted by it all, by two years of struggling to make it work and now she thought it truly was over.

She kept phoning the Findlaters until they left the phone off the hook. She called Cussen and got him to drive her to their house in Hampstead but no one would answer her knocks at the door. Outside she found David's green Vanguard car and smashed its windows. It was 2 a.m. and the police were called. They found her screaming in the street and Ant in pyjamas trying to calm her down. David Blakely, no doubt would be hiding inside, as usual. The police left without taking any action and Cussen drove Ruth home.

Over the weekend, she returned to Hampstead several times, now irrationally convinced that David was having an affair with the Findlaters' nanny. She was losing her grip on reality and spent the weekend fuelled by drugs and alcohol.

It was Easter Sunday and around 9 a.m. she rang the Findlaters' number again, telling Ant, 'I hope you are having an enjoyable holiday, because you have ruined mine.' He hung up.

At 8.45 p.m., Carole ran out of cigarettes and David offered to drive down to the Magdala pub to buy some. Meanwhile, Ruth was driving north through London to Hampstead with Desmond Cussen to confront her lover for the final time. At the Findlaters' house there was no sign of the Vanguard and she surmised that he would probably be at the Magdala. When they arrived there, sure enough the green car was parked outside. After kissing Cussen on the cheek, she got out and walked across the road while he drove off. She peered into the pub and spotted David, drinking with his friend, Clive Gunnell. She moved along the front of the pub, slipping into the shadowy doorway of a newsagent next door.

A short while later, Blakely and Gunnell emerged and as David bent to put his key in the Vanguard's lock, she stepped from the shadows and shouted 'David!' Either he did not hear her or chose to ignore her, but he continued without looking round. She shouted his name again, taking a .38 Smith and Wesson revolver from her handbag.

Blakely looked up and took fright. He ran around to the back of the car where Gunnell was standing, but she pulled the trigger, firing twice. He screamed 'Clive!' as the bullets ripped into him. Blood sprayed from his wounds onto the shiny metal of his beloved Vanguard. She followed him round the vehicle, ordering Gunnell to get out of the way. As Blakely tried to run, she shot him again and he fell to the ground. As he lay on the ground, face down, she pumped another shot into him at point-blank range. As she stood above him, she raised the gun to her head but there was just a dull click when she squeezed the trigger. She then pulled the trigger again and the bullet fired this time, ricocheting off the pavement and hitting a woman nearby in the hand. Her bullets exhausted, she told Clive Gunnell to go and call the police. However, there was an off-duty police officer in the pub who came out, took the gun from her and arrested her.

It took the jury less than twenty-three minutes on Tuesday 21 June, only the second day of the trial, to find Ruth Ellis guilty. She was given the only sentence possible – death.

On the morning of 13 July 1955, a crowd of hundreds gathered outside Holloway Prison. Appeals had been denied and petitions signed by tens of thousands of people had failed to change the rigid process of the law. Ruth's son Andy was told his mother had gone to Italy to model swimwear.

She was led into the execution chamber by Pierrepoint, the hangman who had hanged more than four hundred men and women in the past twenty-five years. Her wrists were strapped behind her back and her ankles shackled. A white hood was placed over her head and Pierrepoint made his final adjustments before pulling the lever that opened the trapdoor. Ruth Ellis was dead less than ten seconds after entering the execution chamber.

In the decades since, there has been much speculation about the murder of David Blakely. Many questions have been asked about the role of Desmond Cussen. Ruth's son Andy recalled seeing Cussen clean the gun and give it to Ruth and some suggest that he had taught her how to use it, even taking her for target practice. Ruth, however, had told police that she had acquired the weapon three years earlier in settlement of a drinks bill at the Little Club. No one recalls this, however, or remembers ever having seen the gun before.

She said that she had taken a taxi to Tara Road on the night of the murder, but the police never followed up on this. However, shortly before her execution she made a statement that did implicate Cussen in the murder, but Cussen had disappeared and could not be questioned. The delay of the execution her lawyers had asked for was not granted.

Meanwhile, around the world, news of the execution was greeted with horror. One French newspaper, criticising the failure to recognise a crime of passion, said, 'Passion in England, except for cricket and betting, is always regarded as a shameful disease.'

The tragedy did not end with her death. Her

youngest sister, Elizabeth died a few months after her, of a broken heart, according to Ruth's daughter, Georgina. Leo Simmons, one of her lawyers was so disgusted with her treatment the he gave up a promising law career. Ruth's former husband George Ellis hanged himself in 1958.

Her son, Andy, who had shared all those flats above clubs with her grew increasingly mentally unbalanced and ended it all around twenty-five years after his mother's death, with a cocktail of drugs and alcohol.

In 1977, Desmond Cussen was tracked down in Australia. He denied supplying Ruth Ellis with the gun or driving her to the Magdala pub on that fateful night in 1955.

VELMA BARFIELD

People had a habit of dying around shy, rosy-cheeked, Velma Barfield. So much, in fact, that she was like a walking virus. Marry her, start a relationship with her, or just be a family member – before long you were suffering from stomach pains, feeling dizzy and throwing up. A little while later, you were dead and Velma, thoughtful, caring Velma, who looks more like a granny than a serial killer, was collecting a nice fat insurance cheque from that policy she told you she recently happened to have taken out on you.

Times were hard in rural South Carolina in the early 1930s. The economy had gone to hell and farms and businesses were falling foul of the banks who were engaged in an orgy of repossession. Velma Margie Bullard screamed her way into such a world on 23 October 1932. Her father, Murphy, owned a small farm on which he cultivated tobacco and cotton. Unfortunately, what he failed to cultivate were profits and not long after Velma was born, he was forced to hand the farm back to the bank and the family moved in with his parents in Fayetteville. Soon, however, the house was his and his wife Lillie's when his parents died. It should be pointed out that even murderous Velma could not have been responsible for their deaths. She was a little too young.

From an early age, however, she was in conflict with her father, a strict disciplinarian who did not shrink from the use of a leather strap to beat his daughter. Her only respite from the casual violence of her home life was school, even if there she was looked down upon by her school friends because of her poverty, which was plain to see from the ragged clothes she had to wear and the plain food in her lunchbox every day.

To try to improve her social standing at school, she began to steal money, from both her father and an elderly neighbour. The beatings merely intensified and her workload at home increased. She would later accuse her father of sexually molesting her when she was a child, a charge that was resolutely denied by her family.

Around high school age, the Barfields moved to Red Springs in Southern California where Murphy had found work in a textile factory. As she had shown at her previous school, Velma was poor academically, but excelled at sport. She had played in a baseball team her father had organised and at high school she became a good basketball player. She also found a boyfriend, Thomas Burke, a year ahead of her in school, whom she dated according to strict rules imposed by Murphy.

At the age of seventeen, however, Velma and Burke decided to quit school and get married. What Murphy thought of this decision can only be imagined, but Velma was too big for beatings now. She was strong, single-minded young woman.

Their first son, Ronald Thomas was born in December 1951 and in September 1953, a daughter, Kim, followed. Velma stopped work to stay home and look after the house and the kids, while her husband moved from job to job. They were poor but happy and well-respected by friends and neighbours.

When the children were old enough to go to school, Velma became bored. She went back to work to occupy her time and they saved enough to move into a bigger house in Parkton, South Carolina.

Everything seemed to change in 1963 when Velma underwent a hysterectomy. She began to suffer from severe mood swings and was easily angered. She felt less attractive as a woman because she was no longer able to have children and this feeling was exacerbated when Thomas started going out more and drinking late into the night with friends.

In 1965, the family suffered another trauma

when Thomas was involved in a car crash, suffering serious head injuries. In the same way that Velma's hysterectomy had radically changed her, he too, began to change. He suffered from blinding headaches and began to use alcohol as a painkiller, drinking heavily and getting involved in endless arguments with Velma. The Barfield house became a powder keg that could explode at any moment and Velma, ill with stress, was sent to hospital where they treated her with sedatives and vitamins. Back home again, she became addicted to Valium, and devised strategies to ensure she maintained her supply, using numerous different doctors and pharmacies.

Thomas had to go. His drinking was driving Velma mad and the house was a dysfunctional disaster. One day, after she had sent the kids off to school, she went to the laundromat for a short while to wash some clothes. On her return she found her house on fire. Inside they found her husband Thomas, dead from smoke inhalation.

That was one problem dealt with.

Another fire a few months later drove the newly widowed Velma to go and live with her children at her parents' house for a while. The pain of leaving the family home was mitigated somewhat by the arrival of a cheque from the insurance company.

Jennings Barfield was a widower. He was also a sick man, suffering from diabetes, emphysema and heart disease. Not long after being widowed, Velma started seeing Barfield and shortly after they were married. It was doomed from the start, however, mostly by Velma's escalating drug habit. Barfield, unable to stand it any longer walked out and the two filed for divorce. But if Velma was going to walk away from the marriage with something to show for it, she was going to have to do something. Sure enough, before the case got to the courts Jennings' weak heart finally gave out – with a little help from a liberal sprinkling of arsenic. A widow – and a killer – for a second time, Velma seemed to be devastated. She sank into a pill-enhanced oblivion and took to her bed. She pulled herself together again and found a job in a department store, but her depression returned with a vengeance when her beloved son, Ronald enlisted in the US Army to go and fight in Vietnam. Things just got worse. Her father was diagnosed with lung cancer and, unbelievably, her home burned down for a third time. The insurance company was becoming familiar with her name.

She moved back in with her parents just in time for her father to die. She also had trouble with the law around this time, receiving a fine and a suspended sentence for forging a prescription. It was an unhappy time, or rather a slightly unhappier time than previous ones. Ronnie announced he was getting married and Velma became unnaturally jealous of her son's future bride. She was also arguing furiously with her mother. Lillie was demanding and railed against Velma because of her pill habit. Suddenly, in the summer of 1974, Lillie was felled by what appeared to be a bad stomach virus. In hospital, the doctors could not get to the bottom of it. Just as quickly as she became ill, however, she got better and was sent home.

Velma's mood was improved a little by the arrival of an insurance cheque for $5,000. She had taken out a policy on a man she had been dating who had been killed in a car accident. This one had been nothing to do with her, however.

The following Christmas, Lillie asked one question too many for Velma's liking, enquiring of one of her sons why she would have received a final demand for an overdue payment on a car when she had already paid for it. A few days later, Lillie was vomiting and suffering from stomach pains again. She died in hospital shortly after. Another problem dealt with, thought Velma.

In 1975, she went to prison for six months for passing dud cheques. On her release she found a much easier scam, however. Caring for the elderly could be extremely lucrative and by 1976, she was a live-in carer for ninety-four-year-old Montgomery Edwards and his eighty-four-year-old wife Dollie at their well-appointed brick ranch house. Dollie was a difficult employer, however, constantly telling Velma off about her work. Nevertheless, when Montgomery died in January 1977, Velma carried on working for Dollie. It was not for long, of course. Next month, Dollie died suffering the same stomach pains that seemed to have done in her husband.

Velma Barfield had now murdered five people and no one suspected a thing. Not only were the authorities not looking for a serial killer, they were not even aware that there was one out there.

Victim number six was eighty-year-old John Henry Lee, another victim of the stomach virus for which Velma seemed to be the carrier.

Fifty-six-year-old Stuart Taylor was a widower and a tobacco farmer and he and Velma were soon living together, although to the shame of Velma's family, he was not interested in marrying her. He was fully aware of her criminal past of drug use and prescription forgery but he believed she was, like him, a devout Christian. One night, after dinner, the two jumped in his pickup to go and see the famous preacher Rex Hubbard who was holding a revival meeting in Fayetteville. At the interval, however,

Stuart began to feel ill with painful stomach cramps. He was unable to return to watch the second half, instead lying down in the truck and moaning in pain. A few days later, he was dead and even Rex Hubbard would have been unable to revive him.

This time, it was not quite so simple, however. A worried Velma was informed by Stuart's baffled doctors that they had no idea what had killed him and they were going to perform an autopsy. They were certain, they added, that she would also want to know. She already did – a sprinkling of arsenic on his dinner.

Before reports were received back on the results of the autopsy, Detective Benson Phillips at Lumberton police headquarters received what began as a mysterious anonymous telephone call, but was soon discovered to be from Velma's sister. She was distraught and claimed that her sister had murdered Stuart Taylor and that he was not the only one.

One of Taylor's doctors called the chief medical examiner of North Carolina, Page Hudson, and explained the details of how the dead man had expired. Hudson had no hesitation whatsoever in telling him that it sounded like arsenic poisoning to him. He also suggested Velma Barfield as the person most likely to have administered it. Police began to check back through the death certificates of everyone who had died around Velma. They found that they had all died of gastro-enteritis and at no time had anyone tested them for poison. It had happened too often to be a coincidence. At last they realised that the tragedy-laden, God-fearing woman that everyone had been feeling sorry for was actually a psychopathic, cold-blooded serial killer.

They brought her in for questioning, ostensibly about dud cheques but surprised her by telling her they knew that Stuart had died of arsenic poisoning. She denied any involvement, reminding them that she and Stuart were going to be married, that she loved him. Why would she kill him?

The next day, however, she began to realise that it was only a matter of time before they charged her with Stuart's murder. She confessed to her son Ronnie, but told him that she had only intended to make him sick, not to kill him.

At her trial, her attorney tried to persuade the court that Velma had merely wanted to incapacitate Stuart Taylor so that she could return money she had stolen from him without him knowing. Her judgement had not been good, however, due to her long-term drug habit. Soon, the judge gave permission for information about her other victims – John Henry Lee, Dottie and Montgomery Edwards,

her own mother, Lillie, Jennings Barfield and
Ronnie's father Thomas Burke – to be introduced
in court.

The verdict was never in doubt and sure enough
Velma Barfield was pronounced guilty of murder in
the first-degree. She was sentenced to die by lethal
injection and would be the first women in the United
States to be executed using this method.

In prison Velma became a born-again Christian
and had high profile opponents to her death
sentence, including the famous evangelist, Billy
Graham. She even wrote an autobiography during
the six years in which her appeals were heard.

Approaching the date of her execution, she
confessed to each of the murders, apart from those
of Stuart Taylor and Jennings Barfield.

On 2 November 1984, Velma Barfield was led
to the execution chamber dressed in pink pyjamas
and wearing an adult nappy. She lay down on the
gurney without struggling and the two intravenous
drips were inserted in her arms. None of the three
volunteers selected to administer the drugs would
ever know which of them administered the single
lethal one.

When asked if she had any last words, Velma said
in a voice that did not waver, 'I want to say that I
am sorry for all the hurt that I have caused. I know

that everybody has gone through a lot of pain – all the families connected – and I am sorry, and I want to thank everybody who has been supporting me all these six years. I want to thank my family for standing with me through all this and my attorneys and all the support to me, everybody, the people with the prison department. I appreciate everything – their kindness and everything that they have shown me during these six years.'

Shortly after, she died.

BLANCHE TAYLOR MOORE

The residents of North Carolina were horrified to find they had another 'black widow' in their midst so soon after the execution of Velma Barfield. It was hard to believe that Blanche Moore, a pillar of the local society, would stoop so low as to murder for money. It was even harder to believe, due to the fact that she came from a highly religious background, the daughter of a Baptist minister.

Blanche Kiser was born on 17 February 1933. On the outside her father was an upstanding citizen, but beneath the façade was an alcoholic who was addicted to gambling. Blanche was frequently abused by her father and was often made to prostitute herself to pay off some of his debts. She was desperate to escape the life she had always known, and resorted to marrying James N. Taylor when she was just eighteen years old. James was five years older than Blanche and her ticket to freedom. Little did Blanche know that her husband was cut from the same cloth as her father, another hardened drinker and gambler who disappeared for days on end spending whatever money they had. Their daughter, Vanessa, was born in 1953, the same year that Blanche started a job as a cashier at a local supermarket. She was a popular member of staff and within a few years received a promotion to head cashier. Another daughter, Cindi, was born in 1959, but all was not well in the Taylor household. Blanche was fed up with her husband gambling away all their money and she got her own back by having affairs with several of her work associates. When her husband got wind of her behaviour, it sparked off violent rows and she received several severe beatings.

In 1962, Blanche turned her attentions to the new manager at the supermarket, twenty-seven-year-old Raymond Reid. Like Blanche, Reid was married with two young children, and it took all her womanly ways to persuade him into having an affair with her. It was a passionate affair which lasted many years.

In September 1966, Blanche decided to try and reconcile the relationship with her father. Shortly after her arrival he became ill and Blanche, the loving daughter that she had become, nursed him until the bitter end. On the death certificate the cause of death was put down as a 'heart attack triggered by chronic emphysema' – somehow the violent stomach cramps, diarrhoea, vomiting and blue face were dismissed by the attending doctor! These symptoms would normally indicate acute poisoning.

In 1968, following a heart attack, Blanche's husband turned over a new leaf. He stopped drinking and gambling and became a model husband and father – perhaps a little too late for Blanche. She continued her affair with Reid, a romance she was not prepared to walk away from. When her mother-in-law, Isla Taylor, became bedridden in 1970, Blanche was the devoted daughter-in-law and nursed her constantly. She died of 'natural causes' on 25 November that same year, despite the fact that there were large quantities of undigested arsenic in her stomach.

Reid eventually left his wife in 1971 and rented a small apartment so that Blanche could join him and make their relationship permanent. He filed for divorce, expecting Blanche to do the same. As news of their affair became more public, Blanche's husband went down with a mysterious illness. Shortly after Blanche fed him some ice cream, James was hospitalised and died a few hours later.

James had left a modest estate, but Blanche bought a new house and kept delaying the offers of marriage from her lover, Reid. In fact Reid was starting to get in her way. She had set her sights on a new handsome divorcee by the name of Rev Dwight Moore.

Still anticipating marriage, Reid was diagnosed with a skin condition called shingles in 1986. By April of that year he was submitted to hospital suffering from violent stomach cramps, vomiting, diarrhoea and a loss of feeling in his hands. The attending doctor ordered special tests for 'heavy metals intoxication', which proved that he had six times the normal amount of arsenic in his system. Somehow these results got mislaid and never reached the doctor.

When Reid died a couple of months later, Blanche managed to dodge any requests for an autopsy. She had convinced Reid to change his will on his deathbed, leaving his entire estate to her.

Dwight Moore accompanied Blanche to Reid's funeral, supporting her on his arm as she displayed all the signs of a grieving widow. Her grief assuaged somewhat by the $75,000 left to her by her former lover.

Moore and Blanche left a decent period of mourning before getting married. The wedding was delayed though until 21 April 1989, while Blanche recovered from a mastectomy after being diagnosed with breast cancer. Her husband of just two weeks was taken ill while they were still on honeymoon in New

Jersey – the symptoms were violent stomach cramps, diarrhoea, vomiting and loss of feeling in his limbs. The conclusion – too much arsenic in his body. Moore survived, but Blanche's run of luck had quite simply come to an end. Despite the fact that her husband refused to believe that Blanche had had anything to do with his illness, the police were not so convinced and she was arrested on 18 July 1989 and charged with the first-degree murder of Raymond Reid.

The trial opened on 21 October 1990. Blanche was adamant that she was innocent and denied ever giving Reid any contaminated food. However, there were just too many witnesses to say that she regularly brought food to the hospital and the jury was convinced of her guilt.

Blanche was found guilty of Reid's murder on 14 November 1990. The presiding judge announced to Blanche that she was to die by lethal injection.

Blanche Moore is currently under the jurisdiction of the North Carolina Correctional Institute for Women – prisoner number 0288088. Because of the automatic appeals system, she has been able to delay her execution for nearly twenty years, while charges are still pending in the deaths of several other of her suspected victims.

KARLA FAYE TUCKER

As a gospel singer sang *Amazing Grace*, her voice was drowned out by the crowd outside Mountain View Prison in Gatesvill, Texas, chanting 'Kill the bitch!' It was 3 February 1998 and Karla Faye Tucker had just been killed by lethal injection, the first woman to be executed in the state of Texas since 1863.

The young Karla Faye had struggled with self-esteem. For a start, her two older sisters, Kathi and Kari, were far better looking than her. They were blonde, blue-eyed and fair of skin. She, on the other hand was a small brunette with dimpled cheeks, hideously self-conscious about a large birthmark on her arm. She was a loner, finding it difficult to make friends or communicate with the other kids at school and in her neighbourhood. The Tuckers were a couple who could not live with each other and could not live without each other. They married and divorced several times before finally calling it a day when Karla was ten. Larry, her father, was given custody and it all began to go downhill, especially when, during the divorce proceedings, Karla learned why she looked so different to her sisters. Larry was not her father. Karla suddenly felt like she did not belong to anyone. She was devastated.

Her older sisters were into drugs and Karla, hanging around with them and their older friends, was already smoking marijuana by the age of ten. But, it was never enough for her and at eleven she began mainlining heroin. She first had sex at the age of twelve when she went to the house of a friend of her sister's, a member of the Bandidos biker gang. She got high with this considerably older man who then took her out on his bike and the two had sex in the countryside.

Karla Faye was out of control. Her father rarely saw her as he worked until late in the evening. She dropped out of school around the age of thirteen, but no one really noticed. A year later, she was back living with her mother, Carolyn, now working as a prostitute. Carolyn took Karla Faye to work with her one night and Karla also began to earn her living that way. She would later say she did it simply because she was so anxious to please her mother. They had some good times. Carolyn was a groupie and the two toured with a number of bands, including the Allman Brothers, the Eagles and the Marshall Tucker Band. It was exciting and all was experienced in a haze of sex, drugs and rock and roll.

In 1975, aged sixteen, Karla Faye got married to Stephen Griffith, a mechanic. It was good at first, even though the two fought like a cat and dog, sometimes with their fists. But Karla Faye was not one to be tied down. She moved on.

In 1981, she befriended Shawn Dean who introduced her to her next boyfriend, Danny Garrett, a drug dealer and part-time barman. One weekend in June 1981, there was a three-day party at the house in Houston, Texas where Karla Faye was now living with Danny. It was for her sister Kari's birthday and there was a copious supply of pills and other drugs. Before long, the whole thing had developed into an orgy with everyone high or drunk or both. Karla was especially trashed as she had been doing coke and speed, a drug that she usually stayed away from because of the effect it had on her, making her 'go crazy', as she described it. This night she was injecting it.

There was some bad feeling at the party because Shawn Dean's biker husband Jerry Lynn, had recently beaten her up, not for the first time, and she had walked out on him. Karla Faye had not got on with Jerry Lynn, ever since he had wheeled his motorbike into her house, and wanted to go round to his house to have it out with him. The group of friends spent the evening seething about Jerry

Lynn and discussing revenge. Danny had gone to work at a local bar and Karla Faye and a friend Jimmy Leibrant drove over to pick him up when he finished at 2 a.m. He had been thinking about the Jerry Lynn situation all evening and had concocted a plan. They would go over to his house and steal his Harley Davidson. As Jerry Lynn was a member of a biker gang, it was the most hurtful thing they could do to him. The others loved it.

They went back to their house and changed into dark clothing, also arming themselves, Jimmy grabbing Danny's shotgun and Danny slipping a .38 down inside one of his boots. Karla Faye later claimed they were more for protection in the rough neighbourhood where Jerry Lynn lived, rather than to use against him.

They parked outside his house and easily got inside. By the light of a torch, they saw Jerry Lynn's precious hog in the hallway. He had obviously been working on it as it was partially dismantled and tools and engine parts were spread out around it. Karla Faye though that it might be better to steal some parts of the bike rather than the whole thing. Suddenly, however, a light came on off the hallway. Jerry Lynn had heard them. He growled, 'Who the hell's out there?' Karla Faye froze, but Danny grabbed a hammer from the toolbox on the floor and ran into the room, swinging it hard at Jerry Lynn's head. The sickening blow threw the biker backwards onto his pillow, blood seeping from his nostrils and the corner of his mouth. Danny did not stop there, however. He continued to smash the hammer down on him.

Watching, Karla Faye suddenly saw movement beside Jerry Lynn. There was a girl in bed with him. Jerry Lynn had met Debbie Thornton earlier that day at a party and had brought her back to his place that evening. Karla Faye saw red. She was furious that he had been with a girl while his wife's cuts and bruises had not yet healed. She picked up a pickaxe that for some reason Jerry Lynn had brought indoors, raised it high above her head and brought its point down on Thornton. Thornton screamed and a gurgling sound emerged from deep inside her. The noise enraged Karla Faye even more and she brought the pickaxe down on the helpless girl's blood-soaked body again and again. Blood sprayed over the walls and over Karla Faye as the girl's body was reduced to a pulpy mess. She told friends later that she experienced a triple orgasm during those horrific moments.

Finished with Thornton, she brought the pickaxe down on Jerry Lynn a few times, venting the hatred she had always felt for him.

The bodies were discovered the next day by the landlord of the building, but it did not take long for the investigating police officers to learn that Karla Faye and Danny had been threatening to do something to Jerry Lynn and had then bragged about killing him. Everybody talked, even Jimmy Leibrant who told them he had remained outside during the murders. He would eventually turn state's evidence and be allowed to walk free after the trial.

Karla Faye and Danny were indicted in September 1983 and tried separately. She pleaded not-guilty. While awaiting trial, however, she borrowed a Bible and began reading it in her prison cell. She claimed that she had been reading it when suddenly she found herself on her knees in the middle of her cell, pleading with God to forgive her. She was born again.

In capital cases, the death penalty was rarely sought for women, but in late 1984, Karla Faye was sentenced to death, as was Danny Garrett. He would die of liver disease nine years later during the appeals process, but Karla Faye's appeals continued and were rebuffed. She tried to mitigate her acts by saying she was high on drugs when she carried them out, but again she was turned down.

Amazingly though, her story began to draw support, from often unexpected quarters. Television evangelist, Pat Robertson and Newt Gingrich, the

Republican Speaker of the United States House of Representatives, both argued for her sentence to be commuted. They were joined by voices from around the world such as Pope John Paul II and the World Council of Churches. Most surprising of all was Ron Carlson, brother of the murdered girl, Debbie Thornton, who became a frequent visitor to her in Gatesville Prison.

Her last appeal, after fourteen years on death row, was turned down on 28 January 1998. With the execution looking inevitable, she was asked by a reporter what she would be thinking about when she was lying on the gurney. She replied, 'I'm certainly going to be thinking about what it's like in heaven.'

On February 2, she was flown to Huntsville Prison where the state's execution chamber was situated. She was described as 'upbeat' and ate a last meal of a banana, a peach and some salad. With her was the man she had married while in prison, Dana Brown, a member of the prison ministry group that visited Christian inmates, as well as some family and friends. Also there was Debbie's brother, Ron Carlson.

The news that Texas Governor George W. Bush had rejected her appeal for clemency was relayed to her at 5.25 p.m. and she made her farewells to everyone. An hour later, she was escorted to the execution chamber with its one-way glass for spectators to view the proceedings. Present, apart from her own family, were the victims' families.

She sat back on the gurney and was strapped down. Her last words contained apologies to the victims' relatives for what she had done and thanks to her husband and the prison warden for their kindness. She closed her eyes, coughed, groaned and then went silent as the drugs entered her veins.

Karla Faye was going to see heaven at last.

JUDI BUENOANO

She spent thirteen years on death row at the Broward Correctional Center at Pembroke Pines in Florida, writing letters, crocheting blankets and baby clothes and teaching the Bible to other inmates when she was not tied up with appeals and receiving death warrants. Her cell was six-feet wide by nine-feet long and she ate at strictly regulated times. Breakfast was at 5 a.m., lunch could be eaten between 10.30 a.m. and 11 a.m. and the last meal of the day was served between 4 p.m. and 4.30 p.m. Meals were eaten in her cell, distributed from a trolley and she was permitted a plate and spoons with which to eat. Visitors were allowed at the weekend, between 9 a.m. and 3 p.m. and she was allowed to receive mail any time except weekends and holidays. In her cell she could enjoy cigarettes, snacks, radios and black and white televisions. There was no air conditioning and she was not allowed to associate with other inmates. She wore an orange t-shirt and blue trousers and was counted at least once an hour. Out of her cell, she was always escorted, wearing handcuffs, even when she showered or went into the exercise yard. At all other times, she was confined to her cell. Only if she had a medical appointment, visit from her lawyer or an interview with the media could she leave it.

This was Judi Buenoano's world as she waited to die for the murder of her husband, her fiancé and her son. They were the murders for which they called her the 'Black Widow'.

Judias Welty was born at Quanah in Texas on 4 April 1943, her father was an itinerant farm worker. She claimed her mother was a native American, but she never really got to know her as she died of tuberculosis before Judias was two years old. Judi, as she was known, and her brother, Robert, went to live with their grandparents while two older siblings were put up for adoption. It was not the best of starts and it really did not get any better.

Her father remarried and settled in Roswell, New Mexico, where Judi joined him and his new wife. They were abusive parents, however, and Judi was beaten, burned with cigarettes and made to work like a slave around the house. Rarely did she get enough to eat. Finally, at the age of fourteen, she snapped, scalding two of her stepbrothers with hot grease and flying at her father and stepmother, striking out with anything she could get her hands on. They called the police and Judi went to jail for sixty days, sharing her cell with grown-up prostitutes. When they asked her if she wanted to go home she opted for reform school instead. At least she would get enough to eat there.

Foothills High School was a girls' reformatory in Albuquerque where she remained until she graduated in 1959, aged sixteen. Returning to Roswell, she worked as a nurse's aide, using the name Anna Schultz. She had a son, Michael Schultz, but never divulged the name of his father who was rumoured to be a pilot from a nearby US Air Force base.

On 21 January 1962, she looked like she had found happiness when she married an air force officer, James Goodyear. Four years later they had a son, James Jr. At the same time, James Goodyear adopted her son, Michael Schultz. A year later, in 1967, a daughter, Kimberly, was born. By this time, the family had moved to Orlando in Florida, where Judi opened the Conway Acres Child Care Centre. Her husband was listed as joint owner in the enterprise but he remained in the air force and would soon be sent to do a tour of duty in Vietnam.

Three months after his return from Vietnam, James was admitted to the US Naval hospital in Orlando suffering from an unknown illness. He deteriorated and finally died on 15 September 1971.

Doctors could not find out what had killed him. Five days after his death, Judi cashed in three insurance policies she had taken out on his life. Before the year was out, she was on to the insurance company again after her house burned down, picking up $90,000.

It had been a difficult year, but at least she wasn't short of cash.

In 1972, she relocated to Pensacola, moving in with a man called Bobby Joe Morris. Meanwhile, she managed to get her son Michael into a residential facility for military dependents. He had become disruptive in school and suffered from learning difficulties.

When Morris moved to Trinidad in Colorado in 1977, Judi and the family, including Michael, followed, but not before she had collected the insurance on another house that had burned down in Pensacola.

Soon after arriving in Trinidad, Morris began to complain of feeling unwell and went into hospital in early January 1978. On 21 January, he came home but two days later, he collapsed as they ate dinner and was rushed back into hospital. He died on 28 January, of cardiac arrest and metabolic acidosis, according to his death certificate. A few weeks later three insurance policies paid out substantial sums to Judi.

Morris's family were suspicious, however, and believed that Judi had poisoned him. Furthermore, they were convinced he was not the first man she had killed. In 1974, when Judi and Morris were visiting his family in Brewton, Alabama, a man was found dead in one of the town's hotels, shot with a .22 calibre weapon and with his throat slashed. Morris's mother had overheard a chilling conversation between Judi and her son in which Judi had been heard to tell him, 'The son of a bitch shouldn't have come up here in the first place. He knew if he came up here he was gonna die.' Further confirmation that they had killed the man came in the night when Morris shouted out in his sleep, 'Judi, we should never have done that terrible thing'. The murder remained unsolved, however. Police could find no fingerprints or evidence of any kind.

On 3 May 1978, Judi legally changed her name and those of her children to Buenoano; Spanish for Goodyear, the name of her first husband. They moved back to Pensacola where she bought a house in the Gulf Breeze suburb. Her son, Michael, was still trouble, however. He had dropped out of school and in June 1979, enlisted in the army, being posted to Fort Benning in Georgia. He stopped off to visit his mother en route to Georgia but by the time he arrived at the military base, he was complaining of feeling unwell. When he was checked out, he was discovered to have seven times the normal level of arsenic in his body. There was nothing they could do as he horrifically lost the use of his arms and his legs. He eventually left hospital wearing braces on his legs and with a prosthetic device on one arm. He went back to be cared for by his mother.

On 13 May 1980, Judi took Michael and his younger brother out canoeing on the East River, near Milton, Florida. Suddenly, their boat capsised and although she and her younger son made it to the shore, Michael with his heavy braces and prosthetic arm, drowned. It seemed like a simple but tragic accident, but Military investigators persisted in their search for evidence as to what really happened. When, in September, Judi cashed in a $20,000 insurance policy she had taken out on Michael's life, the police renewed their interest in the case. There were two insurance policies and when handwriting experts examined Michael's signature on them, they concluded it had been forged both times.

Judi, meanwhile, had opened a beauty parlour in Gulf Breeze and had a new man in her life, Pensacola businessman, John Gentry. She told him she had been at nursing school, had been head of nursing at West Florida Hospital and had PhDs in biochemistry and psychology from the University of

Alabama. Her lies paid dividends as Gentry lavished gifts and Caribbean cruises on her.

In October 1982, Judi and John Gentry took out life insurance policies on one another and later, Judi increased the coverage on John from $50,000 to $500,000 without his knowledge. A couple of months later, Gentry was suffering from dizzy spells and constantly throwing up. It might just have had something to do with the 'vitamin' pills that she had been giving him. He spent twelve days in hospital in mid-December, noticing that his symptoms disappeared when he stopped taking the pills. Strangely, however, he took his suspicions no further and continued his relationship with Judi.

On 25 June 1983, John Gentry left a dinner party early, going out to buy some champagne to drink later with Judi. They planned to celebrate as she had just told him she was going to have his child. He climbed into his car, turned the key in the ignition and the car exploded. He was pulled from the burning wreckage still alive, but only just. Surgeons succeeded in saving his life, however.

Four days later Judi was brought in for questioning by the police. Immediately, they began to untangle 'Dr' Buenoano's web of lies and to delve into her insurance situation. A distressed Gentry was told that she had lied about being pregnant. She had, after all, been sterilised in 1975. They also discovered that she had been telling friends for months that Gentry was dying of an incurable disease and that she had booked tickets for a world cruise. She had not booked one for him, not expecting him to be around long enough to enjoy it. Gentry passed some of the vitamin pills she had been giving him to police officers and they were found to contain paraformaldehyde, a poison with no medical application. The authorities still did not have enough evidence to prosecute her for attempted murder but a search of her home revealed wire and tape that was a match to materials found in the bombed car, and she was finally arrested and charged with attempted murder. They traced the dynamite used in the car bomb back to her.

On 11 January 1984, they charged her with the murder of her son Michael and grand theft for the insurance fiddle. The bodies of Bobby Joe Morris and James Goodyear were exhumed and found to contain high levels of arsenic.

On 6 June 1984, she was sentenced to life imprisonment with no parole for the first twenty-five years.

On 15 October, she was given twelve years to run consecutively with her life term for the attempted murder of James Gentry. Then on 16 November she was sentenced to death for the murder of her first husband, James Goodyear.

At 7 a.m. on 30 March 1998, aged fifty-four, she became the first woman to be executed in the state of Florida since 1848 and only the second, after Karla Faye Tucker, in the whole of the United States. She insisted she was innocent to the bitter end.

CHRISTINA
MARIE RIGGS

She described it as 'an act of love'. On the evening of 4 November 1997, at her small duplex home in Sherwood, Arkansas, Christina Riggs crushed a small quantity of the antidepressant Elavil into some water and called her kids, five-year-old son, Justin and two-year-old daughter, Shelby. She told them to drink the mixture. The drug did its job and the kids went to sleep. She placed them in their beds and at about 10 p.m., she injected a large dose of potassium chloride into Jason's neck. Being a nurse, she was very aware that, taken in large doses, potasssium chloride causes cardiac arrest and rapid death. Ironically, it is the third drug to be delivered in the process of execution by lethal injection. Taken undiluted, potassium chloride can cause burning and pain and Justin woke up, writhing in agony and moaning with the pain. Christina quickly injected the boy with morphine to dull the pain, but it did not seem to work. She wrapped her arms around him and gently rocked him, desperately trying to soothe his pain. Eventually, tears rolling down her cheeks, she placed his head back on the bed, picked up a pillow and pushed it down on his face. She held it there until she was sure he was finally dead. She then lifted the pillow from the dead boy's face and went over to Shelby. Not wanting to subject the toddler to the pain that Justin had suffered, she placed the pillow on her face and held it there. Within a few minutes, she was dead. She picked up Shelby's tiny two-year-old body and carried it over to where Justin lay, placing her by his brother's side. She pulled a blanket over them.

Christine next composed a suicide note, trying to explain her dreadful actions. 'I hope one day you will forgive me for taking my life and the life of my children,' she wrote. 'But I can't live like this anymore, and I couldn't bear to leave my children behind to be a burden on you or to be separated and raised apart from their fathers and live knowing their mother killed herself.'

She picked up the syringe, plunged its point into the top of the bottle of potassium chloride, got rid of the air bubbles it by flicking her fingers against it and then injected herself with a dose sufficient to kill five people. She took the bottle of Elavil and began swallowing the pills, washing them down frequently with gulps of water. By the time the bottle was empty, she had swallowed twenty-eight tablets, again more than enough to kill her. As she lay there, the undiluted potassium chloride burned a large hole in her arm.

The following day, she did not arrive for work at the local hospital where she put in twelve-hour shifts for $17,000 a year. When she failed to call in to say there was a problem, her mother Carole Thomas was informed and she went round to the house to find out what was wrong. She walked in on a horrific scene. 'My daughter and her babies are dead,' she said when she called police in a distressed state. They were rushed to hospital where it was found that the children had been dead for between twelve and fourteen hours. Christina was barely alive when she arrived, but they managed to stabilise her and she was moved to intensive care where she was kept under police guard.

They had kept her alive just so that they could kill her all over again.

When she was well enough, she was interviewed by investigating police officers and made a full confession. She explained how her life seemed to be collapsing under financial pressures. She told them she was having difficulty obtaining the child support monies from her children's fathers and even her long shifts at the hospital were not enough to cover daycare for the children while she was at work or her day-to-day expenses. She even told them how she had to pawn her television and VCR just to be able to throw a small birthday party for her son Justin. To make matters worse, she had recently been arrested for passing bad cheques and had the threat of going to jail hanging over her if she did it again. She was severely depressed and, at two hundred and eighty pounds, seriously overweight.

Her childhood had been a car crash and as she got older, it did not really get any better.

Born in Lawton, Oklahoma in 1971, she claimed that between the age of seven and thirteen she had been sexually abused by her stepbrother and at thirteen by a neighbour. By fourteen she was already drinking, smoking and indulging in marijuana. She was also grossly overweight, which depressed her and gave her low self-esteem. Convinced that because of her weight there was little chance of any boy liking her, she became sexually promiscuous. She hoped it might make boys like her, if she was easy. The inevitable happened, however; she was pregnant at the age of sixteen. In January 1988, the baby was born and given up for adoption.

At least she graduated from high school and trained for a career, becoming a licensed practical nurse. She started to work part-time at a Veterans

Administration hospital, dating several men, including a sailor and a man who worked as a bouncer at a bar. Then she met Timothy Thompson who was stationed at Tinker Air Force Base.

In October 1991, she discovered she was pregnant again. She told Thompson the day before he was to be discharged from the Air Force but he would not accept that he was the father and moved back to his home in Minnesota, leaving Christina behind, devastated.

She resumed her relationship with the sailor she had previously dated, Jon Riggs, and he said he would marry her and accept the baby as his. A boy, Justin was born in June 1992 and in July 1993, she and Riggs were married. On her wedding day, she was pregnant with Riggs' baby, but tragedy struck that night when she suffered a miscarriage.

The marriage was soon in trouble and Christina became depressed and even suicidal, partly, she claimed, because of the birth control medication she was using. She was put on the antidepressant Prozac, but when she began to feel better she stopped taking it. In December 1994, a daughter, Shelby, was born and the couple moved to Sherwood, Arkansas, to be closer to her mother who would be able to help with childcare while Christina and Jon were at work. The children were a handful, however;

Shelby suffered from ear infections while Justin had attention deficit disorder and was hyperactive. The marriage was crumbling and was finally over when Jon Riggs punched Justin in the stomach so hard that the boy had to go to hospital. Riggs moved to Oklahoma and Christina filed for divorce.

She was now left on her own to care for two small children on an inadequate income. Soon, it all became too much for her and she stole the potassium chloride, morphine and syringes from the hospital where she worked and planned to end it all.

At her trial, she pleaded not-guilty by reason of mental disease or defect. The prosecution, however, tried to paint her as a self-centred, selfish, premeditated killer. There was a suggestion that the children were an encumbrance and were getting in the way of Christina having a good time. The prosecutor coldly opined, 'I think the jury just saw her as the manipulative, self-centered person she really and truly is. She claims she was horribly depressed, she was overweight, she was a single mom, and she didn't have enough money. My response to that is welcome to America. Plenty of folks are in far worst situations than she was.' He even said that her desire to be executed so that she could be with her children in death at last, was no more than a sign of her capacity for manipulating people.

The jury of seven women and five men took just fifty-five minutes to find her guilty of two counts of first-degree murder and as the verdict was read out, Christina collapsed.

At the sentencing phase she delivered a short statement to the jury. 'I want to die,' she said. 'I want to be with my babies. I want you to give me the death penalty.'

They did.

She waited for death at the McPherson Unit at Newport Prison, the only resident of the three-cell death row that was housed there. She said she was well looked after, complaining that the food was so good that she had put on thirty pounds since she had been there. She spent her time watching television and reading books and could exercise in an outdoor yard next to her cell. She looked forward to her execution. I'll be with my children and with God, she said. 'I'll be where there's no more pain. Maybe I'll find some peace.'

The date was set for Tuesday 3 May, to be carried out between the hours of 8 p.m. and 9 p.m. in the Cummins Unit, outside Pine Bluff, Arkansas where she was flown three days before. When they lay her down on the gurney on which she would receive the injection that would end her life, there was a delay. They were unable to find a vein to which to attach the catheters. She gave them permission to insert them in her wrists.

Strapped to the gurney, her last words were as expected, 'Now I can be with my babies, as I always intended. I love you, my babies.'

Nine minutes later, Christine Marie Riggs was pronounced dead.

AILEEN CAROL
WUORNOS

It was an incongruous but powerful double act. Arlene Pralle, a born-again Christian who bred horses near Ocala in Marion County, Florida and the thirty-five-year-old serial-killer prostitute, Aileen Carol Wuornos, languishing in prison in Florida awaiting trial for the murder of seven men.

Pralle had entered Wuornos's life out of the blue, writing her a letter in which she said, 'My name is Arlene Pralle. I'm born-again. You're going to think I'm crazy, but Jesus told me to write you.' Pralle would become her advisor and her defender, appearing on talk shows and giving interviews to newspapers throughout 1991, in all of which she talked about 'the real Aileen Wuornos' and what she perceived to be the goodness of the serial killer's nature. Time and time again she rolled out the story of Wuornos's horrific upbringing, a story of violence, incest, alcoholism and possibly murder.

To cap it all, on 22 November she and her husband legally adopted Aileen Wuornos, claiming they did it on God's instructions. They were thirty-five years too late to save her, however.

She was born Aileen Carol Pittman on 29 February 1956, although she was always known as Lee. Her mother Diane Wuornos had married Leo Dale Pittman at the age of fifteen and had two children by him, Aileen and her brother Keith, born the year before her. Pittman was a psychopathic child molester and, fortunately, Aileen never met him – he was in prison when she was born, for the rape and the attempted murder of an eight-year-old boy. He hanged himself in prison in 1969.

Bringing up two young children on her own proved too much for Lee's mother. In 1960, she abandoned them and they were adopted by her parents, Lauri and Britta Wuornos who raised them as their own. In fact, it would not be until the age of twelve that Lee would learn that Lauri and Britta were actually her grandparents. Life was strict in the Wuornos household. Lauri dished out regular beatings to both kids, Lee sometimes receiving these lying face-down on the bed, spread-eagled and naked as he whipped her with a belt. Lee was sexually precocious and claims to have first had sex with her brother Keith at a young age. At fourteen she got pregnant and the Wuornoses sent her to a home for unmarried mothers. The child, a boy, was adopted.

In July, 1970, Britta Wuornos died of liver failure. She had been drinking heavily under the stress of having a violent husband and kids who were clearly out of control. The family now went into meltdown and tragedy stalked them at every turn. Lauri committed suicide and Lee's beloved brother Keith would die of throat cancer aged only twenty-one.

Lee, meanwhile, hit the road, earning her keep through prostitution. She did have one unlikely chance at the good life which, of course, she characteristically blew. In 1976, she was hitch-hiking in Florida when she was picked up by sixty-nine-year-old Lewis Fell. Fell, a well-off yacht club president, fell in love with her almost at first sight and they married. Lee was unable to change, however. She abused Fell and went out drinking, getting into fights and generally causing trouble. A month or two of marriage was all Fell could take. He threw her out and had the marriage annulled.

Lee returned to her old habits. She spent the next ten years in one failed relationship after another, taking drugs, drinking heavily and getting involved in forgery and even armed robbery. She could not get much lower and on one occasion attempted suicide. She could not even do that properly.

In 1986, however, she fell head-over-heels in love with a twenty-four-year-old motel maid she met in a gay bar in Daytona. Tyria Moore seemed like the best thing that had ever happened to Lee. They moved in together and Moore quit her job, Lee supporting her from her earning as a prostitute. But these were rarely enough and they were sometimes reduced to sleeping rough. Lee's looks were beginning to fade, making it increasingly difficult to earn enough and she was terrified of losing Moore. There had to be another way to get her hands on some money.

Middle-aged owner of an electronics repair business, Richard Mallory, liked to party. He often disappeared for days at a time, engaged in a sex and booze binge and so no one was particularly concerned when the door to his shop was closed one day in early December 1989. They knew that as soon as he ran out of cash he would be back. When his car was found abandoned outside Daytona, however, people began to worry. A few days later, his naked body was found wrapped in a carpet on a back road not far from Interstate 95. He had been killed by three shots from a .22 calibre pistol.

Six months later on 1 June 1990, they found another naked male corpse who had also been dispatched by shots from a .22. Forty-three-year-old David Spears, a heavy equipment operator, was found in a wooded area, 40 miles north of Tampa, a used condom next to his body. He had last made contact with his boss on 19 May telling him he was en route for Orlando. The truck was located on Interstate 75.

Five days later, a third naked male body was found close to Interstate 75. Charles Carskaddon had been shot nine times with a .22.

On 4 July, near Orange Springs in Florida, a 1988 Pontiac Sunbird crashed off State Road 315. Two women, later confirmed to have been Lee and Moore, clambered out of the vehicle, obviously drunk and swearing at each other. When someone asked if they needed any help, Lee begged him not to inform the police. She said her father lived nearby and would sort them out. They walked off.

The Pontiac was discovered to belong to a sixty-five-year-old retired merchant seaman, Peter Siems who had not been seen since 7 June, having set out to visit family in Arkansas but never having arrived. Delivery man Troy Burress also failed to arrive at his destination, the depot of a sausage manufacturer, on 30 July. Next morning, his truck was found twenty miles east of Ocala. Five days later his badly decomposed body was found by a family picnicking in the Ocala National Forest close to Highway 19. He had in him two slugs from a .22.

Police were baffled. They picked up a drifter seen hitch-hiking on Highway 19 on the day that Burress had disappeared but he was soon eliminated from their enquiries. These appeared to be random killings carried out in different places. The only things in common were the fact that the victims were all men who had been driving and were likely to have picked up a hitch-hiker who was a murderer and of course, all the bullets came from a .22.

On 11 September, a day after celebrating his thirty-fifth wedding anniversary, former police chief Dick Humphries disappeared. Next day he was found, shot seven times with a .22. A month later, trucker and security guard Walter Gino Antonio's body was found on a logging road in Dixie County. He had been shot four times.

It became obvious to investigators that the perpetrator was probably a woman and the two women who had crashed Peter Siems' Pontiac Sunbird looked like the best prospects. Sketches were made from descriptions provided by witnesses to the crash and when these were circulated, the identities of the two women soon became known – Tyria Moore and a woman called Lee. Tracing some of the items taken from the victims and pawned, it soon emerged that Lee was Aileen Carol Wuornos.

A couple of undercover officers found her in a bar at Port Orange on 8 January 1991 and arrested her on an outstanding warrant issued against one of her many aliases, Lori Grody. The murders were not mentioned. Next day, they picked up Tyria Moore who had been visiting her sister in Pennsylvania. She started to talk about the killings, describing how Lee had driven home one night in Richard Mallory's Cadillac and bragged about killing him. Meanwhile, they tried to trick Lee into confessing in phone calls she made to Tyria from prison. They reasoned that if Moore told her that the police were trying to implicate her in the murders, Lee would confess to everything rather than see her lover go to jail. Wuornos realised what they were up to, however, and watched her words carefully.

On 16 January, however, she confessed, emphasising that Moore had nothing to do with the murders. She insisted that in each case she had killed in self defence, that all her victims had tried to rape her or were threatening violence to her. But every time she told her story she changed it, embellishing it and making it even more sensational than it already was. She was certain there was a lot of money to be made in book and movie deals and, indeed, there was a firestorm in the media as her story began to emerge. Even the investigating officers were being besieged in their homes by the media. However, she was to be frustrated in her efforts to at last earn some serious money. The state of Florida does not permit felons to profit from their crimes. Throughout 1991, Arlene Pralle worked her way around the media and Wuornos herself gave interviews to the media. Attorneys came up with a plea bargain, in which she would plead guilty to six charges and receive six consecutive life terms. One state attorney, however, was adamant that she should receive the death penalty and on 14 January 1992, she went to trial for the murder of Richard Mallory.

There was little chance of any other verdict except guilty, especially after she took the stand. It took the jury only two hours on 27 January to reach a verdict of guilty of first-degree murder and as they filed out of the courtroom, Lee Wuornos exploded with rage, screaming, 'I'm innocent! I was raped! I hope you get raped! Scumbags of America!' On 31 January, she was sentenced to die in the electric chair.

In March, she pleaded no contest to the murders of Dick Humphreys, Troy Burress and David Spears, claiming she wished to 'get right with God'. She made a statement to the court in which she said, 'I wanted to confess to you that Richard Mallory did violently rape me as I've told you. But these others did not. [They] only began to start to.' She then turned to Assistant State Attorney Ric Ridgeway and snarled, 'I hope your wife and children get raped in the ass!' Another three death sentences were handed down.

In the next year she received death sentences for the murders of Charles Carskaddon and Walter Antonio, but as Peter Siems' body was never found, no charges were brought on that case.

When it emerged that Richard Mallory had done time for sexual violence, it was thought that a retrial might be ordered but it failed to happen and all six death sentences were confirmed by the Florida Supreme Court. In April, she stopped all her appeals and also chose to die by lethal injection rather than in the electric chair.

Aileen Carol Wuornos was executed on Wednesday 9 October 2002, a decade after she had terrorised the byways of Florida. She had more or less volunteered for execution as she could easily have continued to appeal for years to come. It was also a time when there were doubts about the ethics of capital punishment and Florida Governor, Jeb Bush, had issued stays on a number of executions. But she could not conceive of continuing to live in her six-by-nine foot prison cell, starved of human contact.

By the end, the relationship with Arlene Pralle had soured and Pralle, her adoptive mother, did not even know the date of the execution.

Aileen Wuornos died pretty much as she lived, alone and unloved. 'I'd just like to say I'm sailing with the Rock,' she said after they had strapped her into the electric chair, 'and I'll be back like Independence Day with Jesus, June 6, like the movie, big mothership and all. I'll be back.'

LYNDA CHERYL LYON BLOCK

In 1927, when Alabama legislators decided to switch from hanging to electrocution as their method of execution, there was only one thing missing – an electric chair. They turned for help to a man called Edward Mason, a British-born cabinet-maker in prison for a series of burglaries in Mobile, asking him to build the chair that would become famous as Yellow Mama. As Mason told a reporter at the time, he hoped to get a chance at parole in exchange for the chair. 'Every stroke of the saw meant liberty to me,' he said 'and the fact that it would aid in bringing death to others just didn't occur to me.' Unfortunately for Mason, he did not get that parole. He completed his sentence and disappeared from history.

The 178th and last person to experience Mason's craftsmanship, Lynda Lyon Block, who was executed on 10 May 2002, the first woman to be executed in the state of Alabama since 1957. Her crime was the murder of a police officer, Sergeant Roger Motley on 4 October 1993.

Born in Orlando, Florida in 1948, Lynda had always been a bit strange, even as a kid. She is remembered as being different to her peers, preferring to read a good book to watching television and opting for Ravel over rock. Her mother thinks that Lynda was badly affected by the death of her father when she was young and that she spent her life trying to replace him. With her first husband she certainly got the age right. Moving back to Orlando in 1983, at the age of thirty-five, she married Karl Block, a man twice her age.

Undoubtedly, Block enjoyed the attention of a woman so much younger than him, but he was also desperate for a son, having lost his only son in a car accident in 1974. He wanted someone to carry on the family name and hoped that Lynda would provide that. His family was horrified, of course, especially his daughter, Marie, who had actually been in the same class at high school as her future stepmother. The Lynda Block she encountered now, a noisy woman with clattering jewellery, long, manicured fingernails and dyed black hair, was very different to the quiet, studious girl she remembered from twenty years previously. She thought that Lynda was a gold-digger and that the marriage would be over in a short time. Lynda surprised her, however, by hanging around for eight years and giving Karl Block the son he so badly wanted. She swapped her husband for politics, becoming interested in the Libertarian Party, a small patriotic militia group whose members believe that governmental functions and things such as driving licences, income tax and birth certificates are illegal. They argue that the government has been taken over by power-hungry bureaucracies that do not remain faithful to the Constitution of the United States of America and have betrayed the ideals of the founding fathers. The individuals holding these views have, as it were, seceded from the United States and in support of their extreme stance they cite obscure legal precedents, forgotten constitutional amendments and quote liberally from the founding fathers.

Lynda Block attended rallies and lectures and began to publish a magazine, Liberatus for which she wrote articles with titles such as 'The Day Our Country Was Stolen.' Many in the movement took a huge interest in the 1993 siege at Waco, where Branch Davidian cult leader, David Koresh, engaged in a stand-off with government agents. When the compound was destroyed and Koresh and most of his group were killed, party members accepted it as proof that the federal government was out of control.

By August 1993, there was a new love in Lynda Block's life, George Sibley, also a member of the

Libertarian Party. Block, however, was not yet free of Karl and their divorce was mired in disputes about money. One evening in the summer of 1993, she and Sibley visited his apartment to discuss the money, but there was an argument and then a scuffle in which Karl received a knife wound to the chest.

Sibley and Lynda were charged with assault and battery but prosecution attorneys were keen not to waste too much time on what was merely a minor domestic dispute to their minds. They decided that they would be happy if the accused would accept six years' probation. Lynda Block and George Sibley brought their Libertarian principles to the case, however. They saw the criminal justice system as an enemy and decided to take it on. Rejecting the plea bargain, they sacked the lawyer appointed for them by the court and put together their own defence, interlacing it with the paranoia of the outsider. Sibley, for instance, believed that the judge in the case was using hand gestures to transmit secret signals to the court reporter to omit from the court record certain statements that were being made.

Eventually, they refused to appear at the final sentencing hearing, barricading themselves instead inside what they hoped would be their own version of Waco – Sibley's Pine Hills home, complete with guns and a copious supply of ammunition. A dramatic fax was delivered to newspapers saying that they would 'rather die than live as slaves'. But the police ignored them, keeping the house under routine surveillance, but refusing to do much more. Finally, an officer arrived to serve them with some papers only to find they had loaded their arsenal – three handguns, two semi-automatic rifles and an M-14 rifle – and belongings, including Lynda's nine-year-old son, into Sibley's Ford Mustang and fled in the direction of Mobile, Alabama.

At Opelika, just off Interstate 85 between Atlanta and Montgomery, they stopped in a Wal-Mart car park so that Lynda could make a phone call. That need to make a call led them to their own Waco at last, in the shape of a thirty-nine-year-old police sergeant, Roger Motley, who had never fired a shot in anger.

Motley was shopping for supplies for the town jail which he was in charge of. He had just finished having lunch with his wife when a woman approached him. In a car in the car park she said she had seen a little boy who looked like he needed help. The car was filled with bedding and it looked like the family were actually living in it. She urged him to go and investigate. It was an act of kindness she and Roger Motley would live to regret. Motley climbed into his patrol car and started to cruise along the lines of cars, finally pulling up behind the Mustang the woman had described. Inside the car, Sibley was alone with the boy, Lynda having gone to the phone booth to make her call. The officer approached the car and asked Sibley to show him his driving licence. Sibley replied that he didn't need one and began to explain why, citing his Libertarian beliefs, when he noticed Motley's hand on his gun holster. Sibley reached down and pulled out a gun.

Motley cursed but acted quickly on seeing the weapon, spinning away from the Mustang back to his car and crouching down behind it out of sight as Sibley fired his weapon. There were screams as people loading their shopping into their cars fell to the ground or ran back into the store. Motley failed to see Lynda Block who had dropped the phone on which she had been speaking to a friend and started to run toward the scene, a 9mm Glock pistol that she had pulled from her bag in her hand. She kept firing as Motley seemed to reach into his vehicle. She thought, she claimed later, that he was reaching for a shotgun, but he was actually reaching for his radio, calling in 'Double zero' which was the code for an officer in trouble. At that moment, a bullet from Lynda Block's Glock thudded into his chest. He was not wearing a bulletproof vest because they were in short supply and he had loaned his to a rookie cop.

He clambered into the patrol car and tried to get away but lost consciousness as it started to move. It crashed into a parked car. Sergeant Motley was rushed to hospital but died later that afternoon. Meanwhile, Sibley and Lynda tore out of the car park, trying to get out of town. They were stopped by a roadblock outside Opelika. Fearing that there would be another shoot-out, Lynda shouted to a negotiator, 'Let's not have another Waco happen here.' The puzzled officer replied, 'What's Waco?'

Lynda and Sibley were found guilty and sentenced to death. The murder of a police officer could bring nothing less.

On 10 May 2002, Lynda Block, wearing prison whites with her head shaved and her face covered by a black veil, was strapped into Yellow Mama and at 12.01 a.m. 2,050 volts of electricity were deivered into her body for a period of 100 seconds. She had no last meal request and made no final statement.

George Sibley followed her two years later.

At last they had found their Waco.

BETTY LOU BEETS

She was a grandmother with five children, nine grandchildren and six great-grandchildren. She was also the murderer of three of her five husbands and the fourth woman to be executed in the United States since the Supreme Court had lifted its ban on capital punishment in 1976.

On 6 August 1983, forty-six-year-old Betty Lou Beets reported her husband of just under a year, Jimmy Don Beets, a retired Dallas firefighter, was missing from their home near Cedar Creek Lake in Henderson County, Texas. Six days later, a couple of fishermen, fishing on Cedar Creek Reservoir just after dark discovered an empty fishing boat drifting near the Redwood Beach Marina. They dragged it ashore and examined it, finding a fishing licence belonging to Jimmy Don. Also in the boat were a life jacket and some nitroglycerine pills.

The Coast Guard was contacted and they called Betty Lou to tell her they thought that the boat had finally been found. Betty Lou immediately drove over to the marina and identified it as her husband's.

It was too windy to start looking for Jimmy Don that night but the next morning an extensive search of the area, involving hundreds of people, began. For three weeks they looked for him but not a trace was found. It was surmised that he may have suffered a heart attack and fallen overboard. However, they were surprised that his spectacles were found in the bottom of the boat. As he wore them all the time, it might be imagined that they would have gone overboard with him.

When the search began to wind down, Betty Lou enquired whether it would be alright to collect the insurance and retirement benefits that Jimmy Don had accrued during his years working for the Dallas Fire Department. Disappointingly for her, though, she was informed that she would be unable to pick up the $100,000 life insurance and $1,200 a month pension until he had been missing long enough to be declared legally dead – seven years.

A year after he disappeared, the house in which she had lived with Jimmy Don and which she had been trying unsuccessfully to sell, burned down in a mysterious fire. When she tried to collect on the insurance policy, the insurance company refused to pay out because of the strange circumstances surrounding the fire.

In 1985, Rick Rose a curious investigator with the

Henderson County Sheriff's Department received information from Betty Lou's daughter-in-law that there might be some suspicious circumstances surrounding the death of Jimmy Don Beets. What he discovered was chilling. Betty Lou was a woman who, when she tired of a husband, or decided to collect on an insurance policy, had no compunction over resorting to murder.

Robbie Branson was questioned and confessed that his mother had told him she was planning to kill Jimmy Don. She suggested that he go out for a while as she did not want him around when she shot him. Robbie jumped on his motorbike, returning two hours later to find his stepfather dead of two gunshot wounds. She had shot him while he slept. He helped her carry the body out into the front yard where his mother buried it under a wishing well. The next day, he said, she placed some of her husband's medication in his fishing boat while he removed the propeller. He helped her get the boat out into the lake where they left it to be found.

Detective Rose took out a search warrant and turned Betty Lou's property upside-down, finding Jimmy Don's body. Under the garage, they also found the remains of another of Betty Lou's husbands, Doyle Wayne Barker. Two bullets were found in Jimmy Don's body and five in Barker's. All five were fired from a .38 calibre pistol. A .38 had been seized at the house during an earlier, unrelated incident. Betty Lou's daughter, Shirley Stenger then came forward to say that she had actually helped her mother to bury Barker's body in October 1981, after Betty Lou had shot and killed him.

Betty Lou was arrested on 8 June 1985.

They looked into her past and discovered that she had also shot her second husband, Bill Lane, in the side after they had separated. They had even remarried again for a while but it did not work out.

Her trial for the murder for remuneration and the promise of remuneration opened on 11 July 1985 in Henderson County and she entered a plea of not-guilty, claiming that her two children had committed the murders. In October, the jury returned a verdict of guilty and Betty Lou was sentenced to die by lethal injection, but only once the appeals process had been exhausted.

Much began to be made of Betty Lou's abuse through the years and the desperate poverty of her childhood. She was born into a poor tobacco share-cropping family in North Carolina in 1937 and the poverty was abject. The family – her parents and a brother three-years older than her – lived in a windowless shack without water or electricity. They later moved to Virginia where her parents found work in a cotton mill. Not long after, Betty Lou contracted measles which left her partially deaf which presented difficulties at school where she was diagnosed as having learning difficulties. Although she taught herself to lip-read, her deafness created huge problems for her.

She believes she was first raped when she was five. She married for the first time at the age of fifteen and remained married for eighteen years, during which time she gave birth to six children. When she was thirty-one, however, her husband left her very suddenly leaving her to try to bring up her children alone.

She was beaten and abused by most of her husbands and a coalition of death penalty opponents and battered women's advocates took up her cause. They maintained that her abuse was never introduced at her trial as a mitigating factor. They said that she was convicted before 'battered women's syndrome' began to be widely used by women as a defence in courtrooms and before states began commuting the sentences of victims of domestic violence, of which there have been more than one hundred instances since 1991. Betty Lou Beets, they claimed, was a victim of ineffective counsel.

But Betty Lou never showed any remorse nor confessed and the Texas Board of Paroles and

Pardons refused in 1991 to grant a reprieve or commute the sentence. Neither did she show enough evidence that domestic violence caused her to commit the crime. They still believed it was done for financial gain.

The last hope on 26 February 2000, was that Texas Governor George W. Bush would grant clemency, but it was not forthcoming. In a written statement, he said:

After careful review of the evidence of the case, I concur with the jury that Betty Lou Beets is guilty of this murder. I'm confident that the courts, both state and federal, have thoroughly reviewed all the issues raised by the defendant.

Betty Lou had no last meal and made no final statement to the world. She made no eye contact with the family of her victims as they led her into the execution chamber and strapped her to the gurney, but she smiled at members of her own family who were present. The smile remained on the face of the sixty-two-year-old grandmother as she slipped into unconsciousness.

DARLIE LYNN
ROUTIER

It was the early hours of 6 June 1996, in the upmarket neighbourhood of Dalrock Heights Addition near the town of Rowlett in Texas. Nights were normally quiet in this peaceful, law-abiding community but that night the dispatcher for the Rowlett Police Department was surprised by a 911 call at 2.31 a.m. At the other end was a hysterical woman. She shouted down the phone, 'Somebody broke in to our house…They just stabbed me and my children!…My little boys are dying! Oh my God, my babies are dying!' As the woman continued sobbing incoherently, the dispatcher traced the call to 5801 Eagle Avenue, a house owned by Darin and Darlie Routier. Having alerted the emergency services, the dispatcher calmed the woman sufficiently to get some details of what had happened. She had been in bed, she said, when someone came into the house and stabbed her two sons, six-year-old Devon and five-year-old Damon, before stabbing her. She fought the intruder who ran out of the house through the garage, tossing the knife away as he left.

At the house, Darlie's husband, Darin, who had been sleeping upstairs but had been woken by his wife's screams, came running down. In the entertainment room he found the boys soaked in blood and his wife, her nightdress stained red by her blood, screaming into a mobile phone. Running to Devon, he saw two huge wounds in his chest. The boy had no pulse and his eyes were wide open and empty of life. Turning his attention to Damon, he saw some blood coming through the back of his shorts. As he breathed, his lungs rattled.

Darin decided the best thing to do was to try to resuscitate Devon. He started to give him the kiss of life, but horrifically, as he did so, blood sprayed out back onto his face.

The first police officer arrived on the scene moments later and took charge, ordering Darlie to grab a towel and apply pressure to Damon's wounds, to try to staunch the flow of blood. Strangely, however, she did not follow his instructions, merely standing in the middle of the carnage, screaming that the killer might still be in the garage.

Paramedics and other police officers arrived and took over. The policemen left the medics to get on with their desperate work and followed the trail of blood through the house, through the kitchen and utility room to the garage that joined on to the house. There was no one there, but a screen on the side window of the garage had been cut down the middle. They searched the remainder of the house, finding a third child, six-month-old Drake, unharmed upstairs in his cot. But the intruder was gone. The kitchen, through which he had probably fled, was a mess, the floor was awash with blood and a butcher's knife, dripping with blood, lay on a work surface. Noting that some pricey jewellery and Darlie's purse lay there untouched, they deduced that robbery was unlikely to have been the intruder's motive.

Devon was dead by the time the medics arrived but Damon was still alive, although only just. He was stretchered out of the house for the journey to Baylor Medical Center, but died before the ambulance reached its destination.

As Darlie Routier was attended to, she told police officers that she had been asleep on the sofa when she felt a man on top of her. She awoke, screamed and started to try to fight him off. At that point he ran out of the room. When she looked round, however, she discovered that he had already knifed her sons. She described the killer as of medium height and dressed in black jeans, T-shirt and a baseball cap.

She was driven off for medical treatment, leaving officers to scour the house for clues. They were concerned, however. Something did not seem right about this night of carnage at 5801 Eagle Avenue.

For a start, the children had been killed by deep, thrusting stabs, but Darlie Routier's wounds to the neck and arm were more superficial – described by experts as 'hesitation wounds'. The slash on her throat, although close to a vital artery, had been made at a forty-five degree downward angle, which could suggest a self-inflicted wound. Then there was the floor of the kitchen which was covered in broken glass. Darlie had run into the kitchen, picked up the bloody knife and put it on the work surface, in the process destroying fingerprints that might have been on it. However, her feet showed no cuts from the glass. Another knife in the kitchen was found to show traces of the screen that had been slashed by the intruder to gain access to the garage; interestingly, the soil under that screen showed no trace of a footprint. Importantly, the sink in the kitchen had undoubtedly been washed out but traces of blood were discovered on the cupboard doors below. Investigators began to construct a scenario where Darlie killed her sons and then inflicted her own wounds over the sink before washing away the blood.

There were other things that made them uneasy: she never once asked how her sons were or even whether they were still alive and when she arrived at the hospital, she was wheeled into the same ward as them, but had absolutely no response to the sight of their bodies; spots of blood on her clothing suggested that she had been in close proximity to them when they were stabbed; there was no real sign of a struggle in the entertainment room and there was no blood trail away from the property.

Darlie Peck had been born in Pennsylvania in 1970 but moved to Lubbock, Texas, at the age of seven after her parents divorced and her mother remarried. She met and fell in love with Darin Routier when they were both teenagers and they married in August 1988, honeymooning in style in Jamaica. They would continue to live in style, style that they could not really afford.

Darin worked in the computer chip industry before launching his own business, testing circuit boards, from his home. Before long, the business had grown sufficiently for him to move into premises in an upmarket office building. By this time, too, Devon and Damon had been born, in 1989 and 1991, respectively.

Business was booming and they amassed enough

money to build a $130,000 Georgian-style small mansion in the desirable Dalrock Heights Addition and Darin drove off to work each morning in a gleaming new Jaguar. But, as fast as they were earning it, they were also spending it. Darlie had expensive habits, always wanting the biggest, the best and the gaudiest. When she had breast implants, they were size EE, the kind that topless models in men's magazines have done. Her clothes bills, meanwhile, were astronomical. They also bought a twenty-seven-foot cabin cruiser that they berthed at the expensive nearby Lake Ray Hubbard Marina.

As for the boys, Devon and Damon, they seemed more of an encumbrance to Darlie, interfering with her sumptuous lifestyle. They were often left unsupervised, even when very young, according to neighbours.

By 1995, they were spending more than Darin earned and their money problems started to get to them. They argued about it, but did nothing to stem the flow of cash. Meanwhile, the business started to lose money and creditors piled up. The Saturday before the deaths of the two boys, the bank had denied them a loan of $5,000.

As police pondered the reason for the boys' murders, Darlie staged a ghoulish event – a graveside posthumous seventh birthday birthday party for

Devon. Present were Darlie and Darin, baby Drake, Darlie's mother and her sixteen-year-old sister Dana, some friends and other family members and a camera crew from the local TV station. Darlie had contacted them to let them know about the party. The police were also covertly filming and taping the event.

As the pastor finished his eulogy as they circled the grave, Darlie pulled out a can of Silly String and started to spray its contents across the grave of her son, dead for just over a week. She was chewing gum, laughing and shouting, 'I love you, Devon and Damon!'

Four days later, she was arrested for the murder of her two children and her trial opened in Kerrville on 16 October 1996. Needless to say, it was sensational. The prosecution pushed for the death penalty although it seemed unlikely that would happen; the last woman to be executed had been during the Civil War, more than a hundred years previously.

They focused only on the death of Damon, reasoning that they could prosecute her for the murder of Devon if she was only given a life sentence or in the unlikely event of an acquittal.

The prosecution tore her apart with the substantial amount of evidence that was piled up against her, but her team responded by rebutting the assumption that she was unaffected emotionally by the deaths of her sons. Darin, called to testify, said she had been devastated. Darlie's testimony had been contradictory before and after her arrest but an expert was called to testify as to the psychological trauma from which she must have been suffering.

Fatally, however, Darlie was allowed to take the stand as the defence's final witness. The prosecution team destroyed her, asking why the sink had been cleaned up, why her dog failed to bark when the intruder entered the house and accused her, quite simply, as having lied throughout. She was left distraught and destroyed in front of the jury.

On 1 February 1997, the jury found her guilty of first-degree murder and three days later she was sentenced to death.

Thirteen years after Darlie Routier was sentenced, questions remain and many believe she deserves a retrial. A bloody fingerprint was found at the scene, for instance, that cannot be linked to Darlie, her sons, or anyone involved in the investigation. Witness statements are said to have been ignored; one claimed to have seen a man fitting Darlie's description of her attacker earlier that day, but did not tell police about it until six years after the murders. Photographs of bruises that Darlie had suffered on the night in question were never shown to the jury. Darin also said that the couple's financial difficulties had been exaggerated, that his business was actually owed $30,000 at the time. It had been said that Darlie had been suicidal prior to the night of 6 June, but Darin refuted these claims. He also said that she did not enquire about her sons on arriving at the hospital because she already knew they were dead. A doctor also pointed out that her neck wound missed her carotid sheath by just two millimetres, almost killing her.

Her defence team believe that DNA testing would help to get her a retrial but following a review of the evidence, in 2003, the State of Texas upheld her conviction. In September, 2008, the Texas Court of Criminal Appeals rejected the request for more DNA testing.

Meanwhile, Darlie remains on death row in a Texas prison, either a heartless murderer or an innocent victim of an overly-aggressive investigation.

FRANCES ELAINE NEWTON

Frances Elaine Newton was only the third woman to be executed by the State of Texas since 1982 and the first black woman executed there since the American Civil War. Those facts alone would make her remarkable, but her case is also made remarkable by the fact that there was absolutely no incontrovertible evidence against her and what evidence the prosecution did bring forward, was suspect.

She was executed for the shooting to death on 7 April 1988, of her twenty-three-year-old husband Adrian, her seven-year-old son, Alton and her twenty-one-month-old daughter, Farrah. It was alleged that she did it for money, having taken out insurance policies, worth $50,000 each on herself, her husband and both her children. They said that she forged her husband's signature on the insurance forms and hid from him the fact that she was setting money aside to pay the premiums. She was the beneficiary of the policies.

The marriage of Frances and Adrian Newton had been in difficulty for some time before that fatal day. Each was involved in an extra-marital relationship and to make matters worse Adrian was using drugs. A marijuana smoker, he had recently graduated to cocaine and was coming home late and was tetchy and difficult to talk to. Nonetheless, their relationship had weathered a number of storms and they had after all been together since they were kids.

In the version of events as told by Frances, that afternoon they decided to try to work things out. Adrian told her he had stopped using cocaine and marijuana and they smoothed out a few other issues. They finished their conversation and he sat down to watch television.

Wanting to see for herself that he was no longer using drugs, Frances sneaked into the room where he kept his stash in a cabinet. When she opened it, however, she was horrified to find not drugs, but a gun. She thought back to a whispered conversation between Adrian and his brother earlier that day. It seemed then that something was going on that Adrian did not want her to know about, that he might be in some kind of trouble. No matter what, she did not want there to be a gun in the house, especially as their two children were there.

She slipped the gun, a .25 calibre Raven Arms

pistol, into a duffle bag and when she left the apartment at around 6 p.m. to do some errands, she took the bag with her. Little did she know that she would never see Adrian, Farrah or Alton alive again.

When she had run her errands, at about 7 p.m., she decided to visit her cousin Sondra Nelms. The two spent some time talking before Frances invited Sondra back to her apartment. Turning round as she was backing out of the drive, she noticed the bag containing the gun on the car's rear seat. She braked and, with Sondra Nelms watching, got out, picked up the bag and took it to a burned-out house next door to Sondra's house, a property that was actually owned by her parents. There she hid the bag and returned to the car. All of this was confirmed by her companion.

At around 8 p.m. they pulled up outside the apartment. When they went in, everything initially seemed perfectly normal. Adrian was still sitting down with the television on but it looked as if he had fallen asleep. Frances walked round the couch, however, and screamed. He was covered in blood. She flew towards the children's bedroom and started to scream uncontrollably. The children were also lying still, covered in blood. Frances was hysterical. In the two hours she had been gone, her life had been wiped out.

Despite her confused state, Newton told police officers everything she knew. She even told them that she had removed the gun from the house earlier that evening and where she had hidden it. She told them that Adrian was a drug-user and explained that she knew that he owed some money to a drug-dealer. This vital fact was corroborated by Adrian's brother, Terrence, who even gave them the address of the dealer to whom he owed the money. For some reason, however, they failed to follow up the lead. Later, in court, when Newton's attorney asked Sheriff's Officer Frank Pratt whether to his knowledge the drug-dealer was interviewed by anyone in connection with the murders, Pratt replied, 'No.'

On 8 April, it was confirmed that the gun the police had retrieved from the duffle bag in the abandoned building was a match for the bullets used in the murders. The gun, it emerged at Frances Newton's trial, was loaned by its owner to Jeffrey Freelow five or six months before the killings. Freelow identified the gun and testified at Newton's trial that he kept it in a chest of drawers in his bedroom. Freelow, who had known Frances Newton since the pair had been at high school together, began a relationship with her a couple of months before that murders. He told the court that as Newton often did his laundry, she would have gone into that drawer and would, therefore have had access to the gun.

It took them two weeks to arrest Frances Newton, after she had cashed in the insurance policies on Adrian and Farrah. They charged her with the murder of twenty-one-month-old Farrah.

The primary evidence against her was, apart from the insurance, some traces of nitrate – gun residue – on the hem of her skirt. The nitrate, however, might arguably have come from fertiliser at her father's house that had been transferred from Farrah's hands onto the skirt.

Frances Newton insisted she was innocent from the beginning but despite the paucity of evidence, she was found guilty and sentenced to death on 24 October 1988. The appeals process began.

One issue that would not go away was the vexed and complicated matter of the gun. Harris County Sheriff, Sergeant J. J. Freeze told Newton at one point that police had in their possession two guns and Newton's father has said, under oath, that Freeze told him the same thing, adding that Frances would soon be released. The existence of a second gun was actually confirmed by Assistant District Attorney Roe Wilson at one point. She said another gun had been found in the apartment but it had not been fired. With that she tried to dispose of the second gun theory. Soon after, however, Wilson and her boss, District Attorney Chuck Rosenthal withdrew her statement, Wilson saying she had, as she put it, 'misspoken'. Rosenthal insisted there was only one gun.

There was also the matter of whether Frances Newton had been properly represented in court. Her court-appointed attorney Ron Mock had a record of incompetence and professional misconduct charges had been brought against him five times. It transpired that Mock had never actually investigated the case. If he had, perhaps he would have pursued the story of Adrian owing money to a drug-dealer, or would have made more of the second gun theory. Newton and her family pleaded with the judge to permit them to replace him. When the judge quizzed Mock, the lawyer admitted that he had neither talked to any prosecution witnesses nor subpoenaed any defence witnesses. The judge granted the motion to remove Mock but, strangely, did not grant a postponement or delay in the trial to allow Newton to find a new attorney. She was left with no alternative other than to continue with her existing attorney.

The case was raising too many doubts as time passed, but an execution date was set for 1 December 2004. Two hours before the moment when Frances Newton was due to die, however, Texas Governor

Rick Perry granted a one hundred-and-twenty-day reprieve to allow time to look at the forensics again.

On 24 August and 9 September 2005, stays of execution were turned down and on 12 September the Texas Board of Pardons and Paroles voted unanimously not to recommend that Newton's sentence be commuted to one of life imprisonment. Further appeals were raised that claimed that she was not connected to the murder weapon but they were all declined.

Forty-year-old Frances Newton was strapped to the gurney to receive her lethal injection on 14 September 2005, still insisting that she was innocent of the murders of her husband and two children. With her parents watching, when asked if she wanted to make any final comment she simply said, 'no'. She turned her head briefly to look at her family as the drugs began to course through her veins and seemed to be trying to say something to her parents but the drugs began to take effect and she coughed and gasped as her eyes closed.

Eight minutes later, at 6.17 p.m., she was pronounced dead.

LINDA CARTY

Harris County in Texas holds the unenviable record of having executed more convicted murderers than any state in the United States apart from Virginia. It contains the city of Houston which has 1.3 per cent of the population of the United States but carries out 10 per cent of the country's death sentences.

British citizen, Linda Carty was tried in Harris County for ordering the killing of a neighbour, for the astonishing reason that she allegedly wanted to steal her baby. Almost inevitably, she was sentenced to death and now sits in Mountain View Prison – the state of Texas's death row for women – watching the clock tick down to the time of her execution by lethal injection, as her appeals fall by the wayside.

It was not always like that for Linda Carty. She was born on the Caribbean island of St Kitts, then a British colony and lived there until she was twenty-three-years old. She worked as a primary school teacher, taught at a Sunday School and was the leader of a volunteer socialwork group. She is remembered as passionate and committed. Her family was acquainted with Kennedy Simmons, the St Kitts Prime Minister at the time, and she was an activist on behalf of his party, the People's Action Movement.

In 1982, Linda Carty emigrated with her family and her two-year-old daughter, Jovelle to the United States. She found a job as a pharmaceutical technician but by the end of the 1980s she had found a second, far more lucrative job. She became an informant for the Drug Enforcement Agency (DEA). At the time, she was dating a Jamaican who, unknown to her was a drug-dealer the DEA were after. She was approached by a Houston police officer who introduced her to Charlie Mathis, a DEA agent who worked in the recruitment and management of confidential informants, known as CIs. Carty was checked out and became part of his unit, with a codename and a new telephone number. Her job was to befriend suspected drug traffickers. It would sometimes involve buying drugs from them to make sure what they were telling her was correct and was dangerous work. The people she was after were usually Caribbean but they were also sometimes from Colombia, at the time the drug capital of South America.

Incredibly, none of this came out in court and it seems almost certain that if it had, she would never have received a death sentence. Charlie Mathis did give evidence at her trial, but for the prosecution. He testified that at the time of the murder with which Carty was sentenced, she was no longer on the DEA's books.

The facts of the case for which Linda Carty languishes on death row are simple. On 16 May 2001, three men burst into the apartment of twenty-five-year-old Joana Rodriguez in Houston, demanding drugs. They beat up a couple of men who were there – Rodriguez' partner Raymundo Cabrera and his cousin Rigoberto Cardenas – and Rodriguez and her three-day-old baby were abducted and thrown into the boot of a car. The baby was later found unharmed but Joana Rodriguez was found asphyxiated, in a second-hand car that had been rented by Linda Carty. She had been tied up and a plastic bag had been taped over her head.

It was never suggested that Linda Carty played an active role in the killing or had even been at Rodriguez' apartment but it was suggested that she had ordered that Rodriguez be killed so that she could kidnap her baby and pass her off as her own. Carty had suffered several miscarriages and believes that this theory originated from a woman who took her to hospital after one of them.

Her trial was a travesty. The three men who had

carried out the attack and the abductions turned State's Evidence and pleaded against Carty in exchange for immunity from the death sentence. It is suggested that the story of Carty wanting Joana Rodriguez' baby was fabricated by them on the orders of someone for whom Carty had caused trouble for during her time as a DEA informant. It was horrific revenge.

Her court-appointed attorney Jerry Guerinot was next to useless. He has succeeded in getting life for his clients instead of the death penalty only five times since 1983, while no fewer than twenty of the capital clients he has had have been sentenced to death. Linda Carty described him in an interview with a British newspaper as 'an undertaker for the state of Texas.'

Guerinot failed to present the good aspects of Linda Carty's life. Her time on St Kitts would have demonstrated to the jury the kind of person she is. He is reported to have applied to the court for funds to travel to St Kitts but neither he nor any of his staff made the trip. He took nothing to do with her British connections, did not contact the British consulate who knew nothing about Linda Carty until after she had been sentenced to death. He failed to talk to DEA agent Charlie Mathis to understand the extent to which he used Linda Carty as an undercover agent and he certainly did not use this important element of her defence properly. He never spoke to Carty's common-law husband, Jose Corona, but the prosecution did. They called him to testify that Carty had suffered three miscarriages, the third shortly before the murder. It made it seem that she had become desperate as the result of her last miscarriage. Incredibly, Guerinot failed to inform Corona that in Texas spousal privilege means that husbands and partners are not obliged to testify against their partner. Had he done that and Corona had not testified, the motive for the killing might have been rendered doubtful. Guerinot admits that it was a mistake. Unfortunately, however, he realised too late.

Carty claims that Guerinot would never talk to her, never took her calls and hung up when he heard it was her on the line. For his part, he claims that he could not get her to talk to him. He says that she is 'crazy' and has 'mental problems' and describes her as 'hedonistic and self-centred'. He has gone as far as to say that to get her to talk to him on one occasion he had to bribe her with a bar of chocolate. Carty laughs at what she describes as an outlandish assertion; she is, after all, severely allergic to chocolate.

Needless to say, she dispensed with the services

of Jerry Guerinot and her case was taken over on a pro bono basis by Baker Botts, the firm of former US Secretary of State, James Baker. They launched an appeal on the basis that the attorney appointed by the judge at Carty's trial, Guerinot, was ineffective, but the appeal failed.

Linda Carty has just about exhausted every stage of the appeals process. On 12 September, the Fifth Circuit Court of Appeals rejected her appeal which means only the United States Supreme Court and the Governor of Texas stand between her and the execution chamber. A date for her execution is likely to be set for some time in 2010.